Advance Praise for *The Art and Science of Self-Defense*

In *The Art and Science of Self-Defense: A Comprehensive Instructional Guide*, Master Joe Varady, a true Renaissance man, shares real stories, technical expertise, applicable techniques, detailed photos, and a dash of humor, all designed to helps readers confidently learn the art of self-defense. His instructional guide keeps learning simple yet fun while sharing a wealth of knowledge.

I taught my first seminar, "Common Sense Self-Defense," in 1984 at Prudential Insurance Company. There were over three hundred people who attended the class, and I realized how important the subject was for people who may be concerned about safety. I used the acronym PEACE to explain Principle, Education, Awareness, Creativity, and Evolution. Back then "Evolution" included looking at a map before driving to an unfamiliar destination. The acronym still works today but has changed from paper maps to electronic GPS navigation. The evolution of self-defense is similar. Master Joe has kept up with the latest "best practices" and presents them to you in this book in an easy-to-follow format.

Master Joe has stayed consistent with his two other books, *The Art and Science of Staff Fighting* and *The Art and Science of Stick Fighting* in how he educates and entertains his readers. He "edutains" as he delivers a professional, concise, and evolving body of knowledge that has something for everyone, from novice to advanced. His background as a schoolteacher, martial arts instructor, and graphic artist all complement the way he communicates and keeps the reader engaged with the subject matter. Master Joe is the real deal—he truly walks the talk!

Joe keeps it simple yet true. There are facts, stories, levels and parts, photos and drawings, and an easy-to-follow format.

"Vision without action is a dream soon forgotten" is my favorite quote and one I share as often as I can. It reminds me to put actions behind thoughts and words while staying proactive in getting things done. I am honored to be included in Master Joe Varady's latest effort to help others become knowledgeable and confident in the game of life!

> —**Master Kirk Farber,** 7th-degree Black Belt
> President and owner of The Working Warrior, Inc.
> Founder and Executive Director of FACE4Kids, a nonprofit organization

"Like his previous books, *The Art and Science of Stick Fighting* and *The Art and Science of Staff Fighting*, Joe Varady's latest work is extremely well-organized and provides a systematic instructional guide to self-defense. *The Art and Science of Self-Defense* tackles this multifaceted subject in a logical and practical manner, providing overriding principles of safety and self-defense as well as instructional activities and simple physical techniques. It is a terrific addition to any self-defense library. This is a guide that contains not only material to be studied but also activities and techniques to be practiced. This combination of study and practice will provide the reader the knowledge, skills, and confidence to hopefully avoid but also, if necessary, to better face potentially dangerous situations. I highly recommend this book to anyone wanting to increase their understanding of self-defense to be better prepared to live safely in our modern world."

> —**Alain Burrese,** fifth dan hapkido, former Army sniper, author of *Survive a Shooting*, 101 Safety Tips series, and *Tough Guy Wisdom* vols. 1–3

"'The Art and Science' series continues, and I am once again honored with an advance read of Master Joe Varady's latest work, *The Art and Science of Self-Defense*. In it, I am reminded of the importance of the most basic of skills, such as general awareness, avoidance, understanding effective strike points, and choosing the right technique. This work offers Master Joe's customary flavor of amusing anecdotes, reality-based scenarios, and well-crafted technical prose to what is a topic that has been written about endlessly. What is most intriguing about this particular work is how both a novice and an accomplished martial artist can read through the text and learn from this greatly accomplished master's perspective. *The Art and Science of Self-Defense* walks you through the legal aspects of defending yourself, awareness, and assessing and recognizing threats in addition to delving into defensive tactics at all levels. I particularly loved the references to old schoolyard games as creative training tools. Master Joe's *The Art and Science of Self-Defense* is extremely thorough and comprehensive, covering everything from the most obvious of techniques to the more advanced; from understanding the human body and how it reacts to utilizing what is around you and immediately available as a weapon; from throws, locks, and escapes to perfectly explained and illustrated training methodologies. This book does not disappoint and absolutely everyone who reads it will walk away with something they will greatly benefit from."

—**Michael Gallagher,** USA Taekwondo National Weapons Champion; owner/operator/instructor, Generations Taekwondo; executive board member for Universal Systems of Martial Arts; board member and trustee for the Pennsylvania Karate Hall of Fame; board member of the Philadelphia Historic Martial Arts Society Hall of Fame; 2015 inductee into the Philadelphia Historic Martial Arts Society Hall of Fame; 2018 inductee into the Pennsylvania Karate Hall of Fame; Pennsylvania state officer for the World Taekwondo Masters Union

"I have been involved in the martial arts for over forty-two years and have researched many books on self-defense to create my own classes and seminars. *The Art and Science of Self-Defense* is a great resource for both teachers and students as the organization of the material is logical and each chapter builds on basic principles in an easy-to-understand format of concepts, explanatory photos and illustrations, and personal stories and insights to support the ideas presented.

"It is perfect for beginners, seasoned martial artists, and instructors of self-defense. The techniques depicted are practical and effective and, more importantly, easy to train as reflexive responses. I appreciate the chapter 'Self-Defense and the Law,' as that is something that is so important to understand—how situations can develop that could become litigious, even if you are just trying to defend yourself.

"Master Joe is a wonderful teacher, and this book should be part of every dojo library."

—**Allyson Appen,** master-level *shichidan* (seventh-dan), Cuong Nhu martial arts

"I highly recommend *The Art and Science of Self-Defense* by Master Joe Varady. I found it to be very well written, well illustrated, and full of great tips, training methods, and advice for anyone wanting to learn the science of self-defense. You can apply all the techniques in real-life situations and even use this book as a teaching manual for other instructors or students. Well done, Joe, keep up the great work."

—**Grandmaster Ted Gambordella,** author of 140 books and 47 DVDs

"I read the instructional book *The Art and Science of Self-Defense* by Joe Varady and consider it a thorough, all-encompassing, and valuable manual for self-defense for both the untrained and the trained. In addition to covering basic and effective techniques, the book also offers words of encouragement, wisdom, and caution. I have over forty years of training and self-defense experience, and I believe this book distills a myriad of concepts into an easy-to-follow set of instructions. I would recommend this guide to those wishing to learn self-defense, combined with carrying out the physical drills recommended by the author."

—**Master Michael A. Ponzio,** *shichidan* (seventh dan),
Cuong Nhu martial arts, author of the *Ancestry* novels

"*The Art and Science of Self-Defense* is perhaps Varady's greatest achievement yet and should be required reading for anyone interested in self-defense. Varady's background as an educator glows as he deftly distills a lifetime of inquiry, evaluation, and application into a text that is both practical and just plain enjoyable to read. So much so that I found myself not only rereading the technical elements of instruction but rereading the anecdotal tales that are as entertaining as they are illustrative of the concepts they are intended to illuminate.

"Have you ever heard the phrase, 'People don't care how much you know until they know how much you care'? I've known Joe for over thirty years, and his sincerity and humility is never in question; his heart and voice ring true throughout. Through his adept use of humor and narrative (often autobiographical and perfectly embarrassing!), couched within deep research and data, we see clearly both Varady's expertise in the field as well as his uncanny ability to deliver to every reader what is most needed when engaging the complex topic of personal defense."

—**Michael Hornback, MEd,** fourth dan Cuong Nhu martial arts,
founder and owner of HERO Academy Martial Arts & Leadership

"What is self-defense? How can we defend ourselves from the various attacks we may encounter in the world? Are there easy-to-learn techniques that will allow us to protect ourselves? *The Art and Science of Self-Defense* answers these questions and many more.

"In the pages of this well-written guide, Master Varady shares his deep knowledge of the many concepts and techniques essential for self-defense and survival. *The Art and Science of Self-Defense* is perfect for anyone who would like to gain in-depth insight into self-defense and the encounters that may be faced in the real world. The techniques in the book are broken down into steps and have descriptions under the illustrations ensuring that anyone can follow along and learn the techniques. Master Varady provides various levels of topics and instruction that build an understanding of self-defense.

"Master Varady's passion for the martial arts has not only been shown throughout his martial arts career but also in the books he has written. I highly recommend *The Art of Science and Self-Defense* to all as well as the other books Master Joe Varady has written. I want to thank Master Varady for sharing his knowledge of self-defense and other topics, and for his continuous passion for the martial arts."

> —**Ramon Santiago Jr.,** Grandmaster, seventh dan, Universal Systems of
> Martial Arts (board member), 2015 inductee into the Philadelphia Historic
> Martial Arts Hall of Fame

"I have worked with Master Joe Varady in many of our Universal Systems of Martial Arts Organization (USMAO) seminars. Master Varady has always provided excellent technical explanations in very simple terms that students of different levels and instructors of various styles can understand and apply. This book demonstrates the same level of exceptional instruction. Joe has captured the essence of self-defense in this book with his extensive knowledge of the topic along with his personal experiences that serve as guidance to the nine graduated levels of awareness. This book is a must for anyone interested in learning self-defense or for any martial artist interested in furthering his or her knowledge of this topic. This book provides additional illumination for the endless path of learning in the martial arts.

"For Master Joe Varady's continuous inspiration and his great contribution to the arts, USMAO has promoted him to seventh degree black belt. Grandmaster Varady served as the president of Universal Systems of Martial Arts Organization (USMAO) from 2015 to 2017. The USMAO exists as a vehicle for growth by providing martial artists with a professional network for sharing knowledge with the objective of promoting quality martial arts in our region."

> —**Alan Shen L. Cheung,** Grandmaster, ninth dan Shorinji ryu karate-do,
> seventh dan Universal Kenpo and fifth dan American Kenpo,
> cofounder of Universal Systems of Martial Arts Organization (USMAO)

"There are many books written about self-defense, each with its unique way of implementing and executing theoretical concepts, techniques, and methodology. *The Art and Science of Self-Defense* takes a different approach, giving a fuller picture of what self-defense is and should be. Joe Varady has created a manual of information that would benefit martial arts practitioners, law enforcement, and self-defense instructors as well as individuals interested in learning how to avoid harm from potential aggression.

"*The Art and Science of Self-Defense* touches upon topics that include environmental and situational awareness, avoidance, picking vulnerable target areas, effective striking mechanisms, technique application, weapon usage, how to fight 'dirty,' and more. The material in each chapter is highly researched and presented in a well-illustrated and concise manner, helping the reader digest the information quickly. The high-quality photography and detailed graphics help bring to life the many ideas covered in this book. Joe Varady is great at making the learning process fun as well. Joe uses wit, cleverness, anecdotes, and philosophy to draw you in.

The Art and Science of Self-Defense is by far one of the best books on the subject. I have known Master Joe Varady for many years, and I have had the privileged to work with him on numerous occasions. Joe has a breadth of knowledge of combat arts and their actual applications. He is truly passionate and dedicated to learning, teaching, and sharing of his experience with everyone. He has written a book that belongs on the bookshelf of every martial artist enthusiast."

—**Tom Lugo,** founder of Integrated Kung Fu Academy; Sijo,
Zonghe Quanfa Gung Fu; president, Universal Systems of
Martial Arts Organization; advisory board member,
Philadelphia Historic Martial Arts Society

"I have trained in the martial arts for well on fifty years and have taught for a substantial portion of that time. I have known Joe Varady for well on thirty-five years, and I daresay most of his martial arts career. We have trained with, and learned from, the same teachers. I have taught him things and learned things from him. Many of those things are detailed here. Few are not. I have many books on the martial arts and self-defense and refer to them often. I have personally trained with many of the authors, adding true meaning to their words. I am sincerely grateful to have Joe amongst that group."

—**Joe Montague,** training since 1972, Yondan, Cuong Nhu martial arts;
Shodan, TenchiKai Aikido Shomokuroku, Shinto Muso Ryu Jodo

JOE VARADY

The Art and Science of Self-Defense

A COMPREHENSIVE INSTRUCTIONAL GUIDE

JOE VARADY

The Art and Science of Self-Defense
A COMPREHENSIVE INSTRUCTIONAL GUIDE

YMAA Publication Center
Wolfeboro, NH USA

YMAA Publication Center, Inc.
PO Box 480
Wolfeboro, NH 03894
800-669-8892 • www.ymaa.com • info@ymaa.com

ISBN 9781594398728 (print)
ISBN 9781594398735 (e-book)
ISBN 9781594398995 (hardcover)

Cover design by Axie Breen
Typesetting by Westchester Publishing Service
Photos by Andrea Hilborn
Edited by Doran Hunter
Illustrations by the author

Publisher's Cataloging in Publication

Names: Varady, Joe, author. | Quesenberry, Gary, writer of foreword.
Title: The art and science of self-defense : a comprehensive instructional guide / Joe Varady ; foreword by Gary Quesenberry.
Description: Wolfboro, NH USA : YMAA Publication Center, [2022] | "9 levels, basic to advanced"—Cover. | Includes bibliographical references and index.
Identifiers: ISBN: 9781594398995 (hardcover) | 9781594398728 (softcover) | 9781594398735 (ebook) | LCCN: 2022931493
Subjects: LCSH: Self-defense—Handbooks, manuals, etc. | Situational awareness—Safety measures. | Safety education—Handbooks, manuals, etc. | Self-protective behavior—Handbooks, manuals, etc. | Hand-to-hand fighting—Handbooks, manuals, etc. | Crime prevention—Psychological aspects—Handbooks, manuals, etc. | Martial arts—Handbooks, manuals, etc. | BISAC: SELF-HELP / Safety & Security / Personal Safety & Self-Defense. | SOCIAL SCIENCE / Violence in Society. | SPORTS & RECREATION / Martial Arts / General.
Classification: LCC: BF697.5.S45 V37 2022 | DDC: 155.9/1—dc23

The authors and publisher of the material are NOT RESPONSIBLE in any manner whatsoever for any injury which may occur through reading or following the instructions in this manual.

The activities physical or otherwise, described in this manual may be too strenuous or dangerous for some people, and the reader(s) should consult a physician before engaging in them.

Warning: While self-defense is legal, fighting is illegal. If you don't know the difference you'll go to jail because you aren't defending yourself. You are fighting—or worse. Readers are encouraged to be aware of all appropriate local and national laws relating to self-defense, reasonable force, and the use of weaponry, and act in accordance with all applicable laws at all times. Understand that while legal definitions and interpretations are generally uniform, there are small—but very important—differences from state to state and even city to city. To stay out of jail, you need to know these differences. Neither the authors nor the publisher assumes any responsibility for the use or misuse of information contained in this book.

Nothing in this document constitutes a legal opinion nor should any of its contents be treated as such. While the authors believe that everything herein is accurate, any questions regarding specific self-defense situations, legal liability, and/or interpretation of federal, state, or local laws should always be addressed by an attorney at law.

When it comes to martial arts, self-defense, and related topics, no text, no matter how well written, can substitute for professional, hands-on instruction. **These materials should be used for academic study only.**

Printed in Canada

Table of Contents

Foreword

by Gary Quesenberry

In 1995 after getting out of the Army, I decided to take a job in West Virginia working for the Federal Bureau of Prisons (BOP). It had only been a few years after returning home from Desert Storm, and I was still in good shape, lean, mean, and looking for something to keep me "in the fight." When I left for the Federal Law Enforcement Training Center in Glynco, Georgia, I had high expectations regarding the level of self-defense training I'd receive. After all, this would be a dangerous job, so I assumed we'd be learning some pretty high-speed fighting techniques. At the time, the BOP was focused on finding a self-defense system that could be learned quickly, give an advantage to smaller officers, and minimize the risk of injury to both staff and inmates. They landed on aikido joint locks and pressure point manipulation. This was all new to me at the time, so I practiced diligently and put forth maximum effort to be as proficient as possible with the techniques I was being taught. I naïvely assumed that this would be all I'd need to handle myself in a prison fight. Now imagine my surprise when I tried controlling an enraged inmate with a wristlock seven weeks later, only to find myself thrown violently against a block wall. "Oh shit! now what?" To save myself, I quickly scrapped the wrist locks and fell back on the brute-force, gross-motor-skill techniques I'd learned in the military.

Once the fight was over and the inmate was in cuffs, I came to an important realization. By focusing on one specific fighting style and trying to apply those techniques outside of a training environment, under far from controlled conditions, I had put myself in serious danger. What I learned that day was that real self-defense is an amalgamation of different fighting styles and that what works best for one person may not work as well for someone else. Maximizing your chances of success in a violent altercation requires exposure to a variety of fighting techniques as well as some real-world experience. Experience is what separates the good from the bad, the theoretical from the practical. Through experience, you learn what works best in the heat of battle and what things need to be discarded, leaving you with a system of self-defense that's stripped of all the impractical nonsense.

The book you now hold in your hand is unlike any other I've read. It's a self-defense guide that's grounded in the realities of street-level combat, one that eliminates the fluff and self-aggrandizing chatter that permeate a lot of books in this genre. Right off the bat, author Joe Varady demonstrates his credibility by acknowledging the stark distinctions between basic forms of practice, sparring, and practical self-defense. I particularly like how the book is broken down into nine separate self-defense levels that walk you through everything from situational awareness and avoidance to taking on multiple attackers. Each level is filled with practical explanations of how the techniques are performed and under what circumstances the methods are best applied. Each level is then closed out with a series of activities that you can complete to cement that section's learning points into your subconscious mind. This is all accompanied by "reality checks" that keep the teaching points grounded in their practical application and never let the book stray into the realm of theoretical fantasy.

Joe has done an incredible job of walking readers through the complex world of self-defense without prioritizing form over function. Everything you read in this book is practical, proven, and efficient. Throughout my career, I've read more self-defense books than I care to remember, but never have I had the privilege of reading one that's so thorough and well organized. If you care about your safety or the safety of your loved ones, you owe it to yourself to read this book. Then, when you've finished, pick up another copy for someone you care about. I can assure you they will be safer for reading it.

Gary Quesenberry

Federal Air Marshal (Ret.)

Author of:

Spotting Danger Before It Spots You: Build Situational Awareness to Stay Safe

Spotting Danger Before It Spots Your Kids: Teaching Situational Awareness to Keep Children Safe

Spotting Danger Before It Spots Your Teens: Teaching Situational Awareness to Keep Teenagers Safe

Preface

Ideally, we would all prefer to live in a safe and peaceful society. The unfortunate reality, however, is that we live in a world where violence can and does unexpectedly occur. The fear of becoming a victim of violent crime is one reason people begin training in the martial arts. As a martial arts instructor, I practice and teach a vast array of skills in my school. However, there are important differences between traditional exercises such as *kata* (solo forms), *bunkai* (partner applications to the solo forms), *kumite* (sparring), and practical, functional self-defense. It took me a long time to learn them. Self-defense needs to be proven effective in high-stress scenarios, especially against larger, stronger attackers. Failure could be life altering. Therefore, I take teaching self-defense as a very serious responsibility.

To keep up with the latest developments in my field, I am continuously reading books and watching videos on the martial arts, combat sports, and self-defense. I have distilled my decades of experience researching, teaching, and training down to the most effective essentials and present them to you in this book. It contains information not only on how to protect yourself, but perhaps more importantly, how to prevent becoming a victim of violence in the first place.

This is a workbook as much as it is a guide. Take the time to practice the activities presented in each level to train and develop your newly acquired skills. Then, continue to learn and grow by augmenting the knowledge presented here by reading books and watching videos about self-defense on your own. There is no substitute for hands-on learning, though. Enrolling in a martial art or combat sport, even for a brief period, can give you experience, help you build your physical skills, and provide you with regular opportunities to hone them.

Each journey begins with a single step. This book is a wonderful start. Enjoy the journey and make it your own.

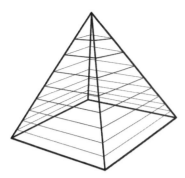

Introduction

Part 1: Combat Sports, Martial Arts, and Self-Defense

The first step toward preparing yourself for self-defense is understanding what self-defense is and what it isn't. Passive self-defense is the act of keeping yourself safe from harm, and the best way to achieve safety is to avoid situations in which nonconsensual violence is likely to occur. When such situations cannot be avoided, active self-defense requires that you have the knowledge and skills to stun an attacker and escape to safety.

For maximum effectiveness, your self-defense training needs to be specific and aimed toward helping you achieve the immediate goals of escaping to safety. It begins by being mindful of why and how you are training. While training in the martial arts or for competition in combat sports can aid you in a self-defense situation, it does not prepare you for certain aspects unique to self-defense.

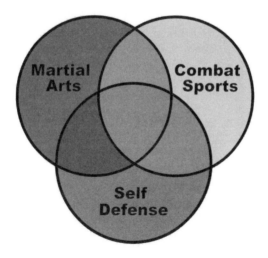

Before I go any further, I'd like to state that it is not my intention to denigrate the martial arts or combat sports. Each has its value, and I am personally heavily invested in, and have a great affinity for, both. I have literally dedicated my life to teaching and training in the martial arts, and my record shows that I obviously enjoy participating in combat sports. However, martial arts, combat sports, and self-defense are different realms, and, while interconnected, they are not entirely the same.

This book can serve to help bridge the gap. If you are already a student or instructor of the combat sports or martial arts, you will be pleased to find that you are already familiar with many, if not all, of the physical techniques presented here. The secret that you may not be as familiar with is how all these parts work together to best keep you safe in a reality-based self-defense scenario.

Combat Sports

Combat sports such as mixed martial arts (MMA), boxing, kickboxing, jujitsu, and eskrima are games of consensual violence in which participants test their abilities against comparably skilled fighters. Each sport is unique and focuses on its own specific skill set that is taught and learned systematically, practiced repeatedly over time, and then tested often by its participants in highly structured situations, contests, and mock fights. These structured tests occur within agreed-upon boundaries in both time and space and are regulated by a predetermined set of rules. Since the focus in these matches is winning by physically dominating your opponent, combat sports usually appeal most to the fittest and more athletically inclined among us. These people dedicate countless hours to developing and honing their athleticism and abilities. Learning, practicing, and using self-defense skills, on the other hand, is quite different. Self-defense skills have to be easily learned and implemented in a wide variety of circumstances by ordinary people with a minimal amount of training.

While the skills gained from training in combat sports can be used effectively in self-defense, combat sports also have the potential to ingrain mind-sets that might work against you on the street. Combat sports occur in a relatively safe, controlled environment and progress like a game of physical chess. If at any time you find yourself in a dangerous position, there are rules to ensure your safety, and you always have the option of stopping the action by tapping or bowing out. Self-defense is not a competition match. There are no referees and no rules, as well as no option to tap or bow out. Your goal is to avoid confrontation. If it is necessary to physically resist, you may have to employ methods that are unfair to your attacker, or, in other words, cheat. Combat sports, on the other hand, condition you to fight in a particular fashion and to abide by a certain set of rules. The reality is that you are going to fight the way you train. Therefore, for self-defense, you need to train the way you'll have to fight.

It is also important to note that, in any given self-defense encounter, the odds are low that you will be defending yourself against another fighter trained in your particular sport or art. Employing your arsenal of techniques in self-defense as you would in competition might be akin to using a hammer to smash a fly sitting on your television screen. Using the wrong tools at the wrong time could end up being regrettably costly. In self-defense, you need to be prepared to deal with a threat in a variety of ways, but you should also be ready and able to avoid or verbally de-escalate a bad situation.

Martial Arts

While many martial arts schools also claim to prepare their students for self-defense, this may only partially be true. The primary goal of most traditional martial arts styles has changed in the last century from self-protection to self-perfection. This shift is especially evident in those arts ending with the suffix -do. The suffix "-do" in words like judo, karate-do, and aikido indicate that these arts emphasize a path of personal development over *jitsu*, or raw fighting technique. This is not necessarily a bad thing. We live in an era where people train in the martial arts for a wide variety of reasons besides self-defense: to develop discipline, for calisthenic exercise, to build strength or relieve stress, and to develop coordination, among others.

Training in most martial arts will help you in self-defense because it helps you develop many attributes and abilities that can be great assets in a physical confrontation. The missing component is usually the pressure testing of techniques. The martial arts are only validated if they can produce reliable results demonstrating that the techniques can be successfully applied by a wide range of people in high-stress situations simulating, as closely as possible, the conditions under which actual self-defense would have to be used. Therefore, students need to regularly practice applying their skills against noncompliant attackers under progressively greater levels of resistance. Only then can students develop the neural pathways, or muscle memory, required to perform the same techniques successfully under stress. While there are some martial arts schools that do engage in regular pressure testing of their self-defense techniques, the unfortunate reality is that most do not.

Kata

Kata, and other solo patterns performed without a partner, are a traditional training method commonly used in many martial arts schools to teach a style's core techniques and their applications. Aficionados of kata often find enjoyment in the graceful, balanced movement and opportunity for self-expression. However, when aesthetic beauty becomes the primary focus of the exercise, solo forms become more akin to dance or gymnastics routines. When practiced for therapeutic exercise or as moving meditation with health benefits, kata becomes more like a martial yoga, losing much of its practical value. Others study and practice kata as a vehicle for historical or cultural research. There is nothing wrong with practicing kata for any of these reasons. Since life is usually peaceful, we can afford to make personal enjoyment and development an important part of our training. However, this does not mean that kata practice is the same as developing practical self-defense skills.

Choreographed *bunkai* (kata applications) can be difficult to execute effectively when your training partner deviates from his prearranged sequence of attacks. This is an obvious weakness as in reality attacks are unpredictable. Katas' self-defense value increases when moves can be applied more generally to a wider variety of attacks and are then practiced under progressively greater levels of resistance. You need to be pushed out of your comfort zone in order to develop resilience, timing, and proper body mechanics applicable to a reality-based self-defense situation.

This argument may best be illustrated by the classic feud between karate masters Choki Motobu and Gichin Funakoshi in the 1930s. Funakoshi was a schoolteacher, and, partially due to his cultural sophistication, was chosen as one of the first ambassadors of karate from Okinawa to Japan. In his dojo, Funakoshi emphasized solo kata as a primary training method. Choki Motobu, on the other hand, was a renowned karate fighter who defeated many challengers, including a famous Western boxer. Motobu also practiced kata but believed that the applications needed to be practiced against attackers who were actively resisting.

One day, Motobu showed up at Funakoshi's dojo unexpectedly. Not approving of what he saw there, Motobu challenged Funakoshi to an empty-handed duel. Motobu later claimed that he did not want to injure Funakoshi, so he used a wrist lock, *kote gaeshi*, to throw Funakoshi to the ground three times in rapid succession, and that there was nothing Funakoshi could have done to counter his technique. Having proven his point, Motobu left. Since Funakoshi never gave his side of the story, we can assume that Motobu's account is accurate.

Motobu commented, "He (Funakoshi) can only copy the master's elegance by performing the outer portion of what they taught him and uses that to mislead others into believing he is an expert when he is not. His demonstrations were simply implausible. This kind of person is a good-for-nothing scalawag. In fact, his tricky behavior and eloquent explanation easily deceive people. To the naïve person, Funakoshi's demonstration and explanation represents the real art! Nothing is more harmful to the world than a martial art that is not effective in actual self-defense" (*Ryukyu Kenpo Karate-jutsu Tatsujin Motobu Choki Seiden* by Nakata Mizuhiko, translated by Joe Swift).

It is interesting to note that several students of Funakoshi who founded their own styles in later years sought a more balanced approach to karate by integrating Motobu's practical fighting skills with Funakoshi's more elegant style.

For more on this topic, check out *Meditations on Violence: A Comparison of Martial Arts Training and Real World Violence* by Rory Miller.[1]

Self-Defense

The U.S. National Crime Victimization Survey (NCVS) shows that violent crime has been on the uptick in recent years. After declining 62 percent from 1994 to 2015, the number of violent-crime victims increased steadily from 2015 through 2018. In just one year, from 2017 to 2018, the number of violent incidents in the United States increased from 5.2 million to 6.0 million, while incidences of rape or sexual assault more than doubled. Hopefully, this trend is coming to an end, as statistics for 2019 (the latest available as of the writing of this

1. Rory Miller, *Meditations on Violence: A Comparison of Martial Arts Training and Real World Violence* (Wolfeboro, NH: YMAA Publication Center, 2008).

book) showed a slight decrease in the rate of violent crime from 2018, but levels are still higher than they were in 2017.

Self-defense is the use of reasonable force to protect yourself from bodily harm resulting from an attack by an aggressor. Self-defense is not fighting in terms of pitting your skills against another. Since proper perspective is critical to good decision-making, this distinction becomes a very important one to make. You engage in self-defense only when necessary to ensure your own personal safety or that of another. On the other hand, fighting indicates an aggressive mindset in which you intend to physically dominate another person, unlike self-defense that prioritizes avoiding physical encounters altogether. Since the goal in self-defense is your personal safety, you'll need to keep your cool and check your ego at the door.

Self-defense training is beneficial for people of all genders. Although you often see courses advertised as "women's self-defense," self-defense is *not* just for women. Men experience higher victimization rates than women for all types of violent crime, except for sexual assault. According to the NCVS, in 2017, 1.7 percent of women aged 15 or older indicated that they had fallen victim to a violent crime compared to 2.5 percent of men. According to the National Center for Transgender Equality, transgender people face far greater levels of physical and sexual violence. More than 25 percent of trans people have faced a bias-driven assault, and rates are even higher for trans women and trans people of color.

Learning self-defense can be surprisingly empowering. Additional benefits gained from training include an increased sense of calmness and self-confidence as a result of facing and overcoming your fears. This, in turn, can improve your life by giving you a more positive, non-defeatist attitude. This increased confidence alone can reduce your chances of becoming a victim.

Self-Defense Story: When You Least Expect It

My wife shook my shoulder gently. "I see strange lights coming from the kitchen," she whispered. I opened my eyes and glanced at the clock. Four o'clock in the morning. I rolled out of bed and, wearing only my underwear, headed to the door. "It's probably just Dave," I reassured her. We had a friend staying over, sleeping in our dojo, an outbuilding separate from the house. I had left the back door open just in case he needed to use the bathroom. *He probably just got thirsty and wanted a glass of water or something*, I thought to myself as I headed toward the kitchen.

The dim light coming through the door was unusual. At first, I thought it was the light of the open refrigerator, but then it moved and the room went dark. A few steps later I entered the kitchen and flicked on the light just as someone ducked through the door into the garage. *What does Dave need in the garage?* I wondered. I followed close behind. Entering the dark interior of the closed garage, I turned on the light and scanned the room. I immediately saw someone trying to hide behind the trashcans.

Now, you have to understand that not only were David and I best friends, we were also martial arts brothers. This meant doing things that normal people usually don't do, like playing

"Cato." Cato is a game named for Inspector Clouseau's sidekick, Cato, in the Pink Panther films. It is a running joke in the films that Cato is instructed to attack Clouseau unexpectedly to keep the inspector's vigilance and fighting skills up to par. Cato often takes these instructions to the point of ambushing Clouseau in his own house or at times when Clouseau obviously would prefer not to be disturbed. With this in mind, I figured that Dave had been in the kitchen, heard me coming, and was now playing Cato. So, I call out in a jovial tone, "Good try! I see you back there. Come on out!" You can imagine my surprise when the black-clad figure that stood up wasn't David.

"Who are you?" I barked.

"What can I say?" he replied sheepishly. I'm six foot two, and he was about my size. I didn't recognize him.

"You can start by telling me what you are doing in my house!" I snapped back. He held a backpack and a big black flashlight. I saw the Maglite as a potential threat, so I said, "Give me your flashlight!" I was shocked when he actually held it out to me. I didn't think that would work. I took it and felt a little better. "Get in the house!" I commanded. Is now a good time to remind you that I'm still in my underwear?

I herded the guy back into the kitchen and yelled to my wife, "Kathy, call the police!" Well, my guest didn't like the sound of that at all and started to panic. He edged toward the back door, begging me to just let him go. I let him move because I realized that the kitchen was full of things he could potentially grab and use as a weapon, such as the rack of big knives on the counter. I think he was toying with the idea of fighting his way out, but I had his Maglite and was keeping my distance. He took advantage of that and suddenly made his move, bolting straight for the door. I grabbed the back of his collar with my free hand, but the thin material of his shirt stretched then snapped out of my hand as he ran out into the darkness. Without hesitation, I gave chase.

After a short pursuit through some overgrowth behind my house, I caught up and tackled him. We rolled over and I came out on top, pinning his body with one knee. With one hand, I grabbed the front of his shirt and with the other I brandished his flashlight, holding it high as though I were going to hit him with it. "Stop fighting me, or I'll bash your skull in!" I warned. He called my bluff and struggled to free himself. I remember glancing at the heavy metal club in my hand before tossing it just out of reach. It lay in the grass a few feet away, the beam casting an eerie light on us as I poked a finger in his face and gave him a final warning, "I'm going to slap some stuff on you that ain't gonna feel too good!" Unfortunately for him, he still wasn't listening.

He pulled his knee up between us and, planting a foot on my belly, kicked me backward. But I saw it coming and was already moving to apply an ankle lock when he kicked. I pushed his foot under my arm, trapping it from underneath. As I landed, I wrapped my legs around his body and slapped my bare feet up on his chest, preventing him from sitting up. I then cranked the bony inner edge of my forearm against his Achilles tendon. It all happened without conscious effort and in the blink of an eye. That's when the screaming started.

"You're breaking my leg! You're breaking my leg!" he bellowed. I knew I wasn't. The lock was painful but would have no lasting effects. I would ease up on him when he went slack, but whenever he started trying to escape again, I cranked on him as a reminder to settle down. I held him that way until the police showed up a short time later. The officer walked over to us with his flashlight, shined it on us lying there in the high weeds and thorn bushes, then started laughing.

Is this a good time to remind you that I was still in my underwear? Add that to the fact that my long hair was not tied back, and I must have looked like some kind of professional wrestler laying there. After a few seconds he stifled it to a chuckle, reached out to my burglar, and offered him his hand. I was reluctant to relinquish my hold. "Are you sure you have him?" I asked.

"Don't worry, I don't think he's going anywhere," the officer smiled. I released my hold on his leg, untangled myself, scrambled to my feet, and then followed them back to the patrol car.

Post-encounter Analysis: It was a good outcome, but I was lucky. That whole encounter could have ended badly in so many ways. Let's look at where I went wrong. First, living in the country, I assumed it was safe to leave my door unlocked. I was obviously wrong. Second, as soon as I identified the threat, the safest course of action would have been to retreat into the house and lock the door. He might have opened the garage door and escaped, but I would not have been in any danger. Third, I attempted to detain him. Desperate people do desperate things. Luckily, he did not have a knife or gun. Well, actually, he did have a gun, but it was back in his car. It was a commemorative firearm that he had stolen earlier from my neighbor up the street, an ex-marine. Turns out that my house was not this burglar's only target. The guy had already broken into several homes in my neighborhood and had a trunk full of loot.

Anyway, back to what I did wrong. Fourth, after he ran out, I probably shouldn't have chased him. Practically, I had no idea if he was alone or had a lookout waiting outside. I could have easily run into an ambush. Oh yeah, is this a good time to remind you that I was still in my underwear? Legally, I had no idea if castle law (see below) applied once we left the residence and I became the aggressor. Luckily, I had the good sense not to hit him with his flashlight, or we may have both ended up in jail. Thanks to my training, I instinctually read the situation and chose a technique that was low on the force continuum yet adequate to the task. That is something I actually did *right*. Since my attacker walked away unscathed, I did not have to go to court or face any costly legal ramifications for assault. Quite to the contrary, I was surprised when the local police contacted me to tell me I would be receiving an "Outstanding Citizen Award." I was honored, but I was also under no illusions. I know I got lucky.

Varady 'outstanding citizen'

An Outstanding Citizen Award was presented to Joseph Varady this week for capturing and detaining the alleged burglar who entered his home on July 20, 2004, until the arresting officer, East Pikeland Sgt. Ken Dobson, arrived.

Part 2: Self-Defense and the Law

When claiming self-defense, you are admitting that you are guilty of what would normally be a violent criminal action and that you did so intentionally and knowingly. However, you are also stating that your actions were justified under the given circumstances.

School systems often institute a zero-tolerance policy where physical confrontations between students result in mandatory punishment for all parties involved. However, this same set of rules does not apply in the legal world. A basic understanding of the law will still help you make good decisions should you ever have to physically defend yourself.

While self-defense law differs from jurisdiction to jurisdiction, the procedural concept of self-defense is universal. Statutes commonly provide that the use of force against another person is justifiable only when you believe that such action is immediately necessary for protecting yourself from harm. Unfortunately, after the physical action of self-defense has concluded, the legal process of claiming self-defense often begins.

It is important to understand that a plea of self-defense is a justification defense. This will require that you adequately explain exactly *why* you felt threatened and *why* you had to engage in what would otherwise be an unlawful act. If you are physically attacked, the reason for retaliating with physical violence should be abundantly clear. However, in cases where you anticipate the attack and strike preemptively, you may have to justify your actions in a court of law. This means articulating exactly what led to your fear in a way that demonstrates it was legitimate.

In *Scaling Force: Dynamic Decision-Making Under Threat of Violence*, Rory Miller and Lawrence Kane present the I.M.O.P. principle for self-defense.[2] This principle states that self-defense is legally justified only if an assailant demonstrates four qualifying factors: that the attacker had the intent, means, and opportunity to hurt you, and that you had no means of preclusion, or avoiding the situation. Let's look at each of these in more detail.

Intent

First, you must have good reason to believe you are in danger. When someone expresses, verbally or otherwise, an overt desire or willingness to do you physical harm, they have shown intent. While verbal threats are most common, intent may also be expressed in the form of a physical gesture, such as a pointed finger and an angry glare. However, merely expressing the desire to do you harm does not justify the use of physical violence.

Means

Your assailant must also have the ability to inflict serious bodily harm upon you. Means describes the way the attacker intends to hurt you, either with his empty hands or with a weapon. Unfortunately, you often do not know if your assailant is armed until he brandishes his weapon.

Opportunity

The attacker must also have the opportunity to actually employ his means against you. If he is unarmed, he must have the ability to get very close to you. Weapons can increase an attacker's effective striking range.

2. Rory Miller and Lawrence A. Kane, *Scaling Force: Dynamic Decision-Making under Threat of Violence* (Wolfeboro, NH: YMAA Publication Center, 2012).

Preclusion

Preclusion is an action taken to prevent something from happening, and it can be a crucial factor when arguing self-defense. A prosecutor will ask questions such as, "Were there any steps you could have taken to de-escalate the situation? Did you have an opportunity to leave?" The legality of your actions may ultimately depend on where you live. In jurisdictions under "Duty to Retreat" laws, you must be able to explain why you had no safe alternatives other than to resort to using physical force. In other jurisdictions, which follow a "Stand Your Ground" doctrine, this may not be required.

Duty to Retreat

"Duty to Retreat" indicates that you have a responsibility to take all reasonable steps to avoid a conflict prior to employing physical force, even in a situation where you are unlawfully attacked or defending someone who is being unlawfully attacked. The intention of this type of law is to encourage citizens to avoid situations where self-defense may become required. However, it can be argued that, instead, it puts undue duress on the victim to prove that they acted in self-defense.

Stand Your Ground

Under "Stand Your Ground" laws, you have the right to defend yourself so long as you are lawfully present (i.e., you have no ground to stand if you are trespassing). Also called "Line in the Sand" law, this type of statute provides that you may use deadly force if you believe it to be necessary to defend yourself against great bodily harm, kidnapping, rape, and, in some cases, robbery. Under this type of law, the burden of proof lies with the prosecution to clearly demonstrate that you did *not* act in self-defense.

Castle Doctrine

Even "Duty to Retreat" jurisdictions generally follow the "Castle Doctrine," named for the concept that "a man's home is his castle." This means that the law considers deadly force to be a reasonable response to someone attempting to unlawfully enter your home, work, or occupied vehicle, or remove you from the same. Under the "Castle Doctrine," you would theoretically be protected from prosecution even if you were to seriously injure or kill an unarmed intruder. Since the law already states that the use of deadly force is reasonable under these circumstances, it would be difficult for the prosecution to prove your actions to be otherwise.

The Force Continuum

The force continuum describes the levels of force you can employ in a self-defense situation. These can vary greatly from a low-level response, such as giving a verbal warning, to a higher, potentially lethal level of force, such as a throat punch. The law states that the amount of force you employ in defending yourself has to remain commensurate with the amount force with which you are being threatened. Appropriate force is considered to mean reacting in a manner consistent with how any reasonable person would react in a similar situation. That is, proportional to the amount of force with which you are threatened.

The law allows you to calibrate your response to the disparity of force the attacker presents. Several factors can increase the disparity of force used against you, including the size of your attacker, the number of attackers, and the weapons involved. If you are a one-hundred-pound woman facing a two-hundred-pound man, that is a clear disparity in size and strength that would justify your use of greater force. If an unarmed attacker who is about your size or smaller is assaulting you, the situation probably does not warrant counterattacking with a deadly weapon. However, if that same attacker were armed with a knife, even if he were much smaller or not yet within striking range, a potentially lethal level of force might be warranted to defend yourself. Similarly, it is more difficult for you to defend yourself against multiple attackers, justifying the use of more aggressive and potentially lethal force.

So, how do you know how much force you need to employ in order to successfully defend yourself? This question works from the assumption that the techniques you employ have been mastered at a high level, and that, when deployed, these techniques will actually do the damage they are intended to do. However, physical altercations are chaotic situations with many unexpected variables that could prevent your technique from having the full desired effect. With this in mind, it may be a bad decision to underestimate the situation and respond with "minimal force." Once a violent assault is underway, you do not want to merely escalate the situation by further irritating an already aggressive attacker. You need to inflict enough pain or damage to instead discourage further aggression, thus ensuring your safety.

Legal Representation

What qualifies as a self-defense situation? Is an altercation at a concert a self-defense situation? What about a road rage incident? Or a kid who is being bullied in school? There are many cases of people who fought back and injured an aggressor, only to later find him or herself charged with assault. Just because *you* feel you were justified in using the amount of force you did is no guarantee that a judge and jury will see things the same way.

There is no such thing as a "legal" physical altercation. Should you ever find yourself charged with a violent offense, it's important to have a lawyer who knows and understands the self-defense laws where the incident took place. Since the right lawyer can mean the difference between a prison sentence and an acquittal, you will want to be represented by an aggressive and experienced attorney.

When you say you engaged in physical self-defense, you are acknowledging that you may have broken the law in assaulting another person. You can argue later, in court, that your actions were required to ensure your physical safety; however, the amount of force used will have substantial bearing on the legality of your actions. You can only justify as much force as is needed to prevent you from being harmed. The use of excessive force, force greater than the amount needed to ensure your protection, is assault and is against the law.

It is important to note that, even if you are exonerated in the criminal trial, civil suits could follow, at large expense of time, money, and emotional stress.

Responsibility to Educate Yourself

Since self-defense laws vary widely from jurisdiction to jurisdiction, you should find out what the laws are where you live, or in any places you may plan to travel to. A simple internet search should turn up that information. If you have any questions, contact local law enforcement for their opinion. Be aware that college and university campuses, key places where women often feel threatened, may constitute separate jurisdictions from local and state law enforcement. For example, mace isn't allowed on most campuses, and sexual assault is often investigated and prosecuted by campus police. This knowledge will help you make educated decisions as you analyze your options, allowing you to formulate effective yet legally appropriate responses to potential situations.

Part 3: The Art and Science of Self-Defense

Art: *A diverse range of human activities involving creative imagination to express technical proficiency, beauty, or emotional power.*

Science: *Systematic knowledge about the material world based on facts learned through experiments and observation.*

Self-defense: *Protection of one's person or interests, especially through the use of physical force, which is permitted in certain cases as a response to a violent crime.*

The world can be a very scary place, and nothing feels better than knowing that you can protect yourself in the case of a personal attack.

Unfortunately, there are people in the world who prey on other people. These predators look for easy prey, weak victims incapable of defending themselves. Therefore, it is important that you invest some time in your personal safety and learn self-defense techniques.

Complex and sophisticated combat systems take years to learn. Self-defense is most effective when it is based on instinctual movements that are easy to remember and utilize in highly stressful, real-life situations. If techniques are based on your body's natural reactions, almost anyone can learn practical and effective self-defense techniques that increase their likelihood of survival in a relatively short period of time.

Any act of self-defense will be unique depending on the specifics of the situation. Despite the high number of variables that could occur, there are some things that can be predicted with a good degree of accuracy. When you know a situation has a high likelihood of occurring, you can take steps toward preparing for it by learning effective strategies and tactics.

The science of self-defense provides you with both a solid core foundation and a flexible framework you can build upon according to the situation or your personal preference. Learning how to identify and play to your strengths is the *art* of self-defense.

The most reliable way to protect yourself from injury is to avoid any situation that may escalate into a violent physical confrontation. In order to do this, you must know how to identify signs of danger. Therefore, the first step in learning how to defend yourself is learning how to be aware of your surroundings. Situational awareness allows you to identify signs of danger and to take active measures to avoid potentially hazardous situations.

Should an encounter become physical, you'll need to know how to navigate the situation safely. Physical encounters occur at predictable ranges such as verbal, striking, or grappling, and each has its own skill set. Therefore, it helps to be a "jack-of-all-trades." This book will teach you how to build an arsenal of dependable techniques and tactics that will allow you to contend with a variety of situations. Since you should be trying to keep distance between you and a would-be attacker, you'll want some long-range striking techniques, such as a few simple yet effective kicks. You'll need a different set of techniques for medium-range fighting, such as elbows and knees. At close range, you'll need some skill in clinching, throwing, and grappling.

Some of you may be thinking, "Do I really need all this? I just want to know how to fight off a rapist or mugger." This may sound like a lot right now, but don't worry. We'll go through it all slowly, step-by-step. In the end, your newly acquired knowledge of the basic strategies and tactics to deal with an aggressor in a self-defense situation will allow you to operate effectively in all phases of the encounter.

**A jack-of-all-trades may be a master of none,
but that is oftentimes better than a master of one.**

System Overview

Good self-defense doesn't just happen. It requires mental and physical preparation, providing you with the tools needed to ensure your safety. *The Art and Science of Self-Defense: A Comprehensive Instructional Guide* provides you with a condensed system of distilled skills and techniques, each carefully selected for its reliability in a high-stress environment. In other words, they work!

Level 1: Awareness: An ounce of prevention is worth a *ton* of cure. Develop the skills needed to spot danger before it spots *you*.

Level 2: Avoidance and Anticipation: Recognizing a bad situation early allows you to prepare yourself for a potential confrontation, maximizing your odds of survival.

Level 3: Building an Arsenal: From your head to your toes, learn how to use your whole body as a weapon as well as *where* to hit for maximum effect.

Level 4: Action: The only way to survive an ambush is to fight your way out. Learn how to protect yourself and turn the tables on your attacker.

Level 5: Dirty Tricks: When the going gets tough, the tough fight dirty. These typically un-sportsman-like techniques could save your life.

Level 6: Takedowns: An attacker who is on the ground will have a difficult time hurting you. Learn the secrets of sweeping the feet out from under an aggressor.

Level 7: Groundwork: If your attacker has you on the ground, you must know how to escape and get back on your feet or hold down and neutralize your attacker.

Level 8: Weapons: Weapons are a two-way street. You not only need to know how to find and use improvised weapons yourself but also what to do against an armed assailant.

Level 9: Multiple Attackers: Wolves travel in packs. Learn the strategies and tactics needed to survive a multiple-attacker scenario and escape to safety.

If you fail to plan, then you plan to fail.
—Benjamin Franklin

Keys to Success

There are many things you can do to help develop your self-defense skills and make them fully functional and effective. Any holistic training program must include:

Practice

The key to mastering any new skill is dedicated *practice*. Create daily personal challenges for yourself covering different aspects of self-defense. Life can be busy, but you have to make time for training and stick with it. Your life may depend on it!

Hard Work

Unfortunately, real growth occurs outside of your comfort zone. Self-defense training can be uncomfortable, both physically and mentally. Yet, through hard work, you will discover and expand your mental and physical potential. Persevere, and you can develop absolute discipline over your mind, body, and spirit.

Stretching

Your body must be prepared for action. A proper warm-up not only minimizes your risk of injury during practice but also keeps your body in good working order for living your everyday life.

Stamina Training

Self-defense is physically demanding. The aerobic component of your program, such as jumping rope or jogging, will increase your ability to sustain peak performance for as long as possible.

Strength Training

You need to be able to strike fast and hard. Anaerobic components, such as weight training, are essential to strengthen your body so your techniques will be effective.

Formal Instruction

While *The Art and Science of Self-Defense* is based on the best available information, there is only so much you can learn from a book. It is beneficial to train with a competent instructor who can teach you in ways a book cannot.

Intensity

Success in any physical altercation requires intensity. Begin by adopting a look of determination, intention, and absolute seriousness. This will spark the right tone throughout your entire body. Focus your mind like sunlight through a magnifying glass, concentrating every fiber of your being on the task at hand. Visualize yourself completing your goal. When your mind is completely focused, your intensity will show physically through your body. Your moves will become quicker and stronger, reflecting your focused intent. Without spirit and intensity, your self-defense moves will be just that: rote movements that lack effectiveness.

Know this:
You are important.
Your life is worth fighting for.

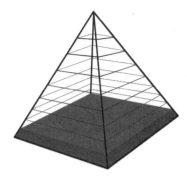

LEVEL 1
Awareness

The solution to violence in America is the acceptance of reality.
—Gavin De Becker, *The Gift of Fear: Survival Signals That Protect Us from Violence*

Awareness

Awareness is your ability to be cognizant of the environment and events going on around you. When people think of self-defense, they often picture reacting to a violent assault. However, the ultimate goal of self-defense is actually to protect you from harm *before* an assault by recognizing and *avoiding* dangerous situations altogether. Learning to recognize signs of danger gives you the ability to steer clear of situations that might put you at risk. To accomplish this crucial first step you must develop and employ awareness.

Awareness begins with a realistic acceptance of the threat of violence. The sad fact is that bad things happen to good people every day, often unexpectedly. Developing a self-defense mindset is all about habitually doing things that keep you in an advantageous position, allowing you to respond with maximum effectiveness should an emergency arise.

Part 1: Situational Awareness

Situational awareness is paramount for maintaining your personal safety and security. After all, you can't avoid a situation you are unaware of. The foundation of situational awareness is learning how to use your complete set of observational skills to scan the elements in any given environment. Develop and hone your senses of sight, sound, smell, touch, taste, and the passing of time.

Graduated Levels of Awareness

You will naturally go through a range of different levels of awareness throughout your day based on the type of activity in which you are engaged. These levels can be represented with different colors to better visualize these otherwise intangible states of consciousness.

The lowest level of awareness is represented by the color white. This is a state in which you are basically ignorant of the majority of what is going on around you. This would be

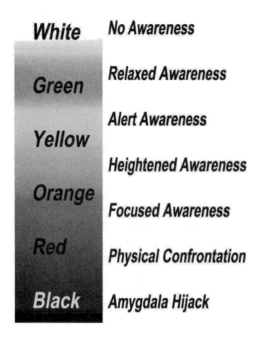

White — No Awareness

Green — Relaxed Awareness

Yellow — Alert Awareness

Heightened Awareness

Orange — Focused Awareness

Red — Physical Confrontation

Black — Amygdala Hijack

anytime that you are relatively unaware, such as when you are sleeping, tanning on a beach while listening to music with headphones, or watching a movie with the volume up and your eyes locked on a screen. While you may be taking in a great deal of information, it is very limited in its scope and has a low degree of relevance in regard to your current state of situational awareness and relative safety.

Green, representing a state of relaxed awareness, occurs when you feel safe and are able to let your guard down. This is the state you are in when you are secure at home or work, focused on everyday tasks and activities. It is natural to be distracted to some degree by your life, family, or job. This state is normal and healthy, and the natural feeling of safety that accompanies it allows your mind to de-stress and your body to heal.

Yellow represents a state of alert awareness. You are alert for signs of danger, unconsciously scanning and assessing both your external environment as well as gauging your internal radar systems. The situation around you registers as normal, so you feel comfortable and at ease. This is the lowest state you should be in when you are not in a secure location such as your home.

Shifting into a state of heightened awareness is represented by a shift toward orange. This level of response is appropriate to any changes in your environment that increase your exposure to potential threats or dangers, such as traveling through a less safe area or being approached by a suspicious person.

When a possible threat has been identified, requiring a state of intense, focused awareness, the scale turns deep orange. Even though you are still working to maintain 360 degrees of awareness, your powers of perception are being directed most at the threat in an effort to determine intention and anticipate what will come next.

As the threat level increases, the orange turns to red, representing an escalation of events that lead you to confirm that the threat is indeed real. With luck, this will occur early enough that you are still able to avoid the situation, either by physically leaving the scene or through passive tactics such as verbal de-escalation or submission. We'll get into that more in Level 2.

Deep red represents the phase where an encounter has turned physical. The time for talking or capitulating has passed. Your immediate goal becomes survival either through escape or physical domination of your assailant.

Although you may be fighting for your life, you still need to retain a degree of calmness to avoid slipping into the black. Black represents an amygdala hijack. An amygdala hijack is an overwhelming emotional response in which the stress essentially shuts down your brain, effectively taking you out of the fight.

A simple example of the graduated levels of awareness might look something like this:

Sleeping	White
Relaxing at home	Green
Out for a jog	Yellow
See a suspicious jogger	Orange
Suspicious jogger follows	Deep Orange
Suspicious jogger attacks	Red

You don't have to pass through each level sequentially. If a stranger invades your personal bubble, the space around you in which you feel safe, it is best to assume that he has bad intentions and shift directly into a state of focused attention, ready for a physical confrontation (red).

While it may seem desirable to maintain a sustained high level of awareness throughout your entire waking day, this is not a very realistic approach. The unfortunate reality is that your brain only has a limited amount of processing power available to you. This limits your ability to pay attention in any given moment, and when you divide your attention across multiple objects or tasks, your awareness further degrades. Since there is such an incredible amount of data around you all the time, maintaining a constant level of high alert is impractical and unhealthy. Sustained high levels of stress can have harmful effects on your body. It is more realistic to remain at ease, maintaining a relaxed level of awareness, while running a tactical triage program in the background to determine what potential threats may require further attention. We'll discuss this further in Level 2.

Self-Defense Story: Boy Uses Sword to Defend Home

When I was a kid, I got home from school one day and, as usual, there were no cars in the driveway. My parents owned a jewelry business, and they would often not get home until after the store closed at eight o'clock. I had the house to myself, so I went inside and took a nap. Because it was winter, by the time I woke up a short time later, it was already dark outside. I went to the kitchen to get something to eat and then went to the living room to watch some TV.

So, there I was, about twelve years old, eating my dinner and watching television, when I suddenly heard a low cough. I froze mid-bite. It came from my parent's bedroom down the hall. For almost a minute I sat there with the spoon in my mouth, not moving a muscle as I strained my ears over the sound of the TV. I had almost convinced myself that it was all just my imagination when I suddenly heard it again, the undeniable sound of a man stifling a cough. Being the owner of a jewelry store, my mother owned a lot of expensive jewelry, so we always set an alarm when we were not at home. However, the alarm had been off since I came in over two hours before. It was all very clear. Someone had slipped in while I was sleeping and was in the process of robbing us when I woke up, trapping him in my parents' bedroom. That would explain why their bedroom door, which was usually open when no one was home, was now closed.

I had yet to study any sort of martial arts, but I had recently purchased a cheap replica Civil War cavalry sword at a flea market. It was pointy, but it wasn't sharp. I set down my bowl of food and slipped quietly into my room, emerging a few seconds later. I stood at the end of the hallway with the sword in one hand and nervously flipped the light switch with the other. The hallway lit up, and I quickly moved my free hand to awkwardly reinforce the one holding the sword (a cavalry sword is a single-handed weapon). I assumed a wide stance and braced myself for what was about to happen next. Then I yelled, "I hear you back there! Come on out!"

It was a small house, so the hallway was short. My parent's room was the last door on the left, only about ten feet away. At first, nothing happened. Then I suddenly heard someone move. Everything shifted into slow motion and my vision narrowed. I heard clear, heavy footsteps cross my parents' room and then the doorknob started turning. The door opened and a man with disheveled hair emerged into the hallway. I wouldn't say that he was angry, but he was definitely *not* happy. He glared at me.

"What the hell do you think you're doing?" my dad asked.

I lowered the sword and breathed a very deep sigh of relief. "I thought you were at work," I replied sheepishly.

"I came home early because I wasn't feeling well. You were sleeping, so I didn't wake you up." Then it dawned on him what was happening. "So . . . you woke up and thought I was a burglar?" A smile spread across his face, "And what were you planning on doing with *that*, tough guy?" he asked, pointing to the unsheathed sword at my side. My face flushed. I guess I hadn't really thought that far ahead. "I can't wait to tell your mom about this when she gets home," my dad chuckled as he turned away, shaking his head. "Next time," he added over his shoulder, "you'd be better off calling the cops." Then he closed the door and went back to bed.

Post-encounter Analysis: Having identified a potential threat, rather than doing the smart thing and fleeing the scene or calling for assistance, I thought it was a good idea to arm myself and then . . . do what? Make a citizen's arrest at sword point? As courageous as that might have been, I was just a kid with a dull sword and no training. What if it had been someone with a gun? Even if the assailant had been unarmed, chances are I would have been easily overwhelmed and possibly killed. I knew my mom's jewelry was insured. I had absolutely no reason to stay in that house. It was a classic case of overestimating yourself and underestimating your attacker. There was also the false sense of power I got from having the sword. In retrospect, it is a good thing it was all that I had. I hate to think of what might have happened if I had had access to a handgun. My dad was right: if I thought there was a burglar in the house, I should have called the cops.

Since we just discussed graduated levels of awareness, this is what mine looked like during the different phases of this encounter:

Napping after school	White
Eating dinner/watching TV	Green
Heard a strange noise	Yellow
Confirmed the threat	Orange
Doorknob turning	Red
My underwear	Brown

Spatial Awareness

Picture someone you know who commands the space they occupy, someone who moves with a confident grace. One characteristic of these people is a heightened sense of spatial awareness. Moving effectively involves the unconscious mental mapping of the location and distance of objects in your environment and how your relationship with those objects changes as you move through space. Spatial awareness is what allows you to navigate through your surroundings without bumping into things and falling down. You can increase your spatial awareness by playing movement games like tag, negotiating an obstacle course, or urban running like parkour. The ability to move over, under, and around objects requires a significant amount of spatial awareness.

Visualization exercises are another way to develop spatial awareness. Close your eyes and picture the room you are in right now. What size and shape is it? Where are the exits? What objects are in this space? Be aware that almost anything, from a large table to a small pen, can be used to your advantage, or disadvantage, during a self-defense encounter. Spatial awareness is an important part of developing a self-defense mindset and, like most skills, you'll get better at it with practice.

Since your primary source of information for spatial awareness is vision, you will logically want to maximize your field of view at all times.

Field of View

While it would be optimal to possess 360-degree awareness, the placement of your eyes in the front of your head means that you have to turn your head in order to look around. Be aware that you always have a blind spot directly behind you in relation to your eyes; it moves when you turn your head. When you are focusing your awareness on a threat in front of you,

you are probably unaware of what is going on behind you, leaving you susceptible to an ambush from the rear. Minimize the risk of being caught off guard by maximizing your field of view. This is accomplished by habitually turning your head from side to side, a technique commonly referred to as "keeping your head on a swivel."

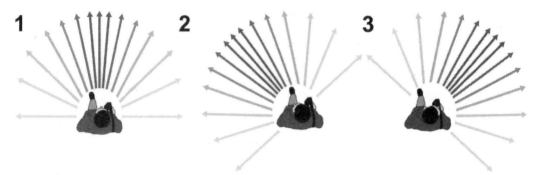

Optimizing Your Field of View: 1) Optimally, you should walk with your hands free, head up, shoulders back. 2) For a greater field of view, keep your head on a swivel, periodically looking left 3) and looking right to minimize any blind spots.

Self-Defense Story: The Oldest Trick in the Book

When I was in middle school, I was waiting for the bus after school one day when I suddenly became the target of three other kids my age. To this day, I have no idea why they targeted me. Maybe it was just for fun. Anyway, they circled me and pushed me around between them, not really hitting me but engaging in bullying behaviors intended to humiliate and intimidate me. I was surprised, intimidated, and didn't know what to do. I remember meekly protesting while trying to escape. By this time, a bunch of other kids had gathered around to see what all the commotion was about. After a minute or so, one of the bullies drew my attention to the front while another got down on all fours behind me. Once in position, the kid in front gave me a big shove that sent me sprawling backward. I hit the pavement hard, but not as hard as the crowd laughed. The oldest trick in the book, performed flawlessly. I got back to my feet just in time for a much bigger high school boy to take pity on me and step in. He must have seen that I was completely out of my league and overwhelmed by the situation. He told the kids who were bullying me to back off before turning to me and telling me to run. I told him I wasn't going to run away. Then he yelled right in my face, "*Run!*"

I ran.

Post-Encounter Analysis: Those three kids caught me completely by surprise. Obviously, they chose the perfect target. I was alone, unaware, and untrained. I had absolutely no idea they were setting me up for that fall. I'm just lucky that 1) they didn't seem to really want to hurt me, 2) I didn't crack my head open when I fell backward, and 3) someone with enough power chose to intervene on my behalf. If I had kept my wits about me, I should have turned my head to keep my other assailants in view. Then that kid could never have gotten on all fours behind me. If only I had kept my head on a swivel and used my peripheral vision, things might have gone differently.

Peripheral Vision

Lower the odds of being caught off guard by learning to use your peripheral vision. Too often people focus only on what is directly in front of them. This is because central vision, also known as foveal or tunnel vision, is incredibly sharp and focused, a result of a concentration of ultra-sensitive rods and cones in the center of the retina. As you move your attention away from the center of your vision, you'll notice that objects begin to appear less and less distinct. However, the visual signals from your peripherals can travel from your eye to your brain up to 25 percent faster than information picked up in your central vision, allowing you to literally react faster.

Increasing your field of view is sometimes just a matter of awareness. Peripheral vision is slightly different for everybody. To test your peripheral vision, look directly ahead as you spread your arms wide to see how far you can see to either side. You can develop your peripheral vision the next time you are having a conversation with someone. Focus on the person directly in front of you, but also see past them, observing your surroundings by looking out of the corners of your eyes.

Another way to expand your field of view is to use mirrors, windows, and other reflective surfaces to see around and even behind you. While this is not a skill you would employ all the time, it can be useful if you think there might be a threat.

By combining the techniques of keeping your head on a swivel, maximizing peripheral vision, and incorporating reflective surfaces to maximize your field of view, you'll be able to see almost everything around you.

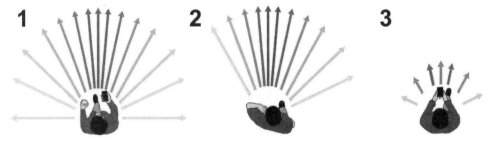

1) If you have to talk on the phone, use the speaker option and hold it low in front of you so you can keep your head up and look around while you talk. 2) When holding a phone up to your ear, you block the field of view on that side of your head. This blind spot creates the perfect avenue for an ambush. 3) When you walk looking down at your phone, texting or checking in on social media, your attention is on the screen, not looking forward or around you. This limits your field of view to the area directly around you.

Seeing Around Corners

If you are caught unaware by an ambushing predator, there is little you can do to avoid an attack. Therefore, to avoid ambushes, don't cut corners too closely. If you walk too closely to a wall, you can't see what's around a corner ahead of you until you are right on top of it. Rather than walk close to the wall as you approach a corner, keep some space between you and the wall. This gives you a view of what is around the corner while putting additional distance between you and any possible threat, giving you more time to respond.

When cautiously searching around a corner, take small steps, leaning slightly with your upper body so you can spot an assailant before he spots you. This is called "pie-ing the corner" because each time you take a step forward you can see a new section around the edge of the wall, like slices of a pie.

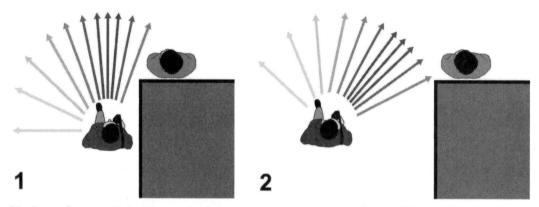

Pie-ing a Corner: 1) Avoid an ambush by not cutting corners too closely. 2) Instead, increase your field of view by maintaining some distance from the wall.

Hearing

There are sounds that can tell you as much as sights: a furtive step, the sliding of a weapon out of a sheath, or the movement of a concealed assailant are obvious threat indicators, but so is the sound of a dog barking, or a cat meowing. In the woods, the birds announce what's going on for hundreds of yards around them just by their alarms and regular call patterns. Of course, you have to know the wildlife in your area. And you'll have to remove at least one of your ear buds. Just as with your eyes, you must keep your ears focused and free from distraction.

Your Sixth Sense

Have you ever known who was calling before you even picked up the phone? Similarly, after a self-defense encounter, it is not uncommon to hear victims make comments such as, "I had a feeling something was wrong." In addition to the conventional senses of sight, hearing, smell, taste, and feeling, you also possess a sixth, less understood sense that somehow picks up on unconscious clues that can warn you of danger.

I know what some of you are thinking: "Come on, ESP?" In *The Reality of ESP: A Physicist's Proof of Psychic Abilities*, Russell Targ, who worked for the CIA, presents experimental data on the existence of extrasensory perception (ESP), including telepathy, clairvoyance, and precognition. Based on decades of data, he believes it would be empirically illogical to deny the existence of some kind of human ability, commonly known as ESP, that allows for the perception of events that are generally blocked from our ordinary perception.

We now know that the CIA spent millions of dollars on their remote viewing programs. Visit the official CIA website to read Russell Targ's declassified 1971 paper entitled "Learning Clairvoyance and Precognition with an Extra Sensory Perception Teaching Machine" (https://www.cia.gov/readingroom/docs/CIA-RDP96-00787R000700010001-5.pdf). In it, he unequivocally states, "We conclude from this work that it is possible to teach and enhance ESP phenomena through techniques of feedback and reward in much the same way as visceral and glandular functions are brought under volitional control."

Although I believe that the evidence supports the reality of ESP, I recognize that not all readers will share this conclusion, opting instead to attribute abilities associated with ESP to subtle capabilities of the brain and sensory apparatus. Regardless of the specific processes involved, you would be wise to always trust your instincts. Listen to the subtle clues your body gives you. Do not approach what you suddenly and inexplicably perceive to be a dangerous situation. And don't try to use logic to justify or reason away your feeling by chalking it up to paranoia. Instead, "trust your gut" and alter your game plan.

Part 2: Variable Assessment

Be aware of the many variables that can either place you in danger or keep you safe. Variables are the things in your environment that change, such as your location, attire, the time, weather conditions, and much more. Your control over a given situation depends on how many of these variables you are able to influence. To understand the importance of variable assessment, examine the following two equations:

1) Observation + Action Plan = Predictable Outcome
Versus
2) Observation + Action Plan + Unknown Variables = Unpredictable Outcome

There are many variables that can change the equation. Some are important for self-defense while others are not. What are you carrying? What type of footwear do you have on? Are you alone or with family? Are there other people around? What buildings are nearby? What can you control, and what is out of your control? The number of relevant variables can be overwhelming. Maintaining an effective level of situational awareness requires gathering useful data while not burning yourself out. Since it is impractical to attempt to control every variable, you should instead learn which are the most critical to your safety and give them special attention.

Becoming a Hard Target

Be aware of the fact that crime happens. While it is unrealistic, paranoid, and unhealthy to live your life on constant high alert 24/7, there are certain things you can easily do to reduce your chances of being targeted for victimization.

Deterrence is more about perceived ability than actual ability. An ambush predator chooses his prey by looking for a vulnerable target. Therefore, you want to present yourself as someone who is strong, confident, and in control. Increase your awareness by removing ear buds so you can hear the noises around you. Put away social media and look up from your phone. Even if you don't feel confident, fake it till you make it and project confidence. Maintain a good posture by keeping your chin up, shoulders back, and chest out. Breathe deep and keep calm. Own your space and walk with a confident purpose. This can be aided by knowing where you are and where you are going ahead of time. Maintain a full field of view at all times by keeping your head up and on a swivel, periodically glancing behind you. Maintain distance from potential threats and enforce your personal boundaries. Don't shy away from making eye contact. Exhibiting a confident mindset, air, and attitude can minimize your odds of being victimized.

Reality Check!

All of this information is being presented to you so you can make educated, informed decisions regarding your personal safety and the safety of your loved ones. Unfortunately, however, every self-defense encounter is different. There exists no single best response, no sure-fire way to guarantee self-protection. You have to read your situation and act in what you believe to be your best interests at the time. There are plenty of uncertainties and "what if's" that can and will occur. No matter how well trained you may be, the unfortunate reality is that no one can be prepared for everything. That said, it is advisable to focus your attention on preparing as best you can for those scenarios you are most likely to encounter in your everyday life.

Preparation

Your physical and mental preparation are variables within your control. Since self-defense can be physically demanding, you'll want to maintain a certain level of physical fitness, taking care of your body through proper nutrition and exercise. Not only does fitness give you coordination, strength, speed, and stamina, it also has the added benefit of increasing the oxygen supply to your brain, resulting in better mental acuity.

Developing a self-defense mindset is all about habitually doing things that put you in an advantageous position should a threat arise. Make a conscious decision to pull yourself away from your cellphone and focus on the here and now. Be in the present moment. Avoid dumbing down your senses through technology, intoxication, or simple complacency due to familiarity. When you enter a new space, make it a habit to take a second to look around. Check left and right, just like crossing a street, identifying possible exits and potential threats.

As with anything in life, practice makes perfect and success fosters self-confidence. After receiving proper self-defense training, you should have both the skills and confidence to safely travel nearly anywhere.

Prevention

There are many preventive measures you can take to avoid becoming a victim of violent crime. They cover a wide range of actions, some of which, such as locking your doors or walking confidently, apply generally to many aspects of daily life. Others, such as sitting with your back to the wall or covering your drink, are specific to certain situations. Most are common sense, like as telling your friends and family where you are going and when you are going to be back or carrying a personal protection device (and knowing how to use it!). Use the buddy system, as predators will often avoid the unpredictability of assaulting two or more people, passing over even easy-looking targets to assault someone who is alone instead.

Personal Protection Devices

You should be aware that there are many devices designed exclusively for self-defense. They range from lethal firearms to nonlethal devices such as pepper spray, stun guns, and personal alarms. There are defense tools disguised as everyday items. Pens are popular because of the plausible deniability that it is not a weapon. These are usually designed for easy carrying, concealment, and deployment. Always research the legality of carrying any personal protection device, keeping in mind that laws can vary from jurisdiction to jurisdiction.

Firearms

A gun is undoubtedly an effective weapon. Just brandishing it can deter an aggressor from escalating a situation. A handgun gives you the ability to minimize your contact with an assailant, decreasing your potential for injury. However, there are also drawbacks to carrying a handgun. First, you need a license to carry one, and some places restrict them altogether. Brandishing a weapon is against the law, and firing a handgun in self-defense is always considered lethal force, even if you only fired a warning shot. The resulting inflexibility regarding your ability to scale the amount of force you employ to meet the situation makes a handgun a weapon of last resort.

Possessing a handgun can also pose an unintentional threat to innocent people around you. Young people are particularly susceptible to accidental shootings due to certain behavioral characteristics associated with adolescence, such as impulsivity, delusions of invincibility, and curiosity about firearms.

Air Guns

There are similar but less lethal options to carrying a firearm. There are pistols, powered by compressed air similar to a paintball gun, that shoot both kinetic projectiles that inflict blunt force trauma and chemical irritant projectiles capable of disabling a threat at a distance. In the United States, these can be purchased with no waiting period, no special permits, and no background checks.

Stun Guns

Stun guns and Tasers deliver a strong but nonlethal shock of high-voltage electricity to your attacker's nervous system, effectively rendering him immobile. Stun guns must make direct contact with the assailant to work. They are typically less expensive and less regulated than a Taser, which resembles a gun and shoots out electric probes capable of penetrating light clothing. These are attached to the hand piece with wires, giving the Taser an effective range of about fifteen feet. Once the probes make contact with a target, the device delivers a powerful electric shock that affects the target's muscles. Many people find Tasers easier to use than stun guns because of their similarity to a firearm, allowing you to stay a safe distance from your attacker. However, you only get one chance with a Taser whereas with a stun gun you can just try again if you miss the first time. While in the United States, Tasers are not considered firearms and are often legal to carry, in other countries, such as Canada, civilian use of Tasers is prohibited.

Chemical Irritants

Pepper spray contains an inflammatory compound derived from chili peppers called capsaicin. When capsaicin comes into contact with a person's eyes, it causes burning, pain, and involuntary tearing. A study of military recruits exposed to pepper spray as part of training rated their eye discomfort between a 9.6 and 9.7 out of 10. Pepper gel is dispensed as a thick, sticky substance that can travel 20 percent farther than typical pepper spray and is much more difficult to remove. Keep in mind that chemical irritants can misfire, so take the time to learn how to carry and deploy these products safely. Be advised that pepper spray is often not allowed on college campuses.

Personal Alarms

Most predators prefer to avoid situations that might attract attention. A loud whistle you can blow is inexpensive and extremely effective. Electronic personal alarms emit a piercing, high decibel sound, while some are capable of placing an automated emergency call reporting your exact GPS location. Personal alarm devices come in many varieties such as key chains, pendants, bracelets, or wristwatches. Many of them have advanced features that can be synced up with a smartphone.

Palm Sticks

A palm stick, also called a *yawara* or *kubotan*, can be any object about the shape and size of a pen. Some are constructed exclusively for self-defense, with pointed ends that protrude from either end of your fist. Some have pins that extend between your knuckles, but these can sometimes work against you, hurting your own fingers when you hit something.

Tactical Whips

Unless you happen to be Indiana Jones, a bullwhip is probably not a very practical self-defense weapon. However, a tactical whip is another story. These short whips hurt . . . *a lot.* While a seemingly obvious personal defense tool, they are often advertised as for "dog defense only" or as a car emergency tool, with a special hardened steel handle that can be used to break a car window. Some models clip around your waist and can be worn as a belt.

Flashlights

Security guards and police often carry large flashlights that can also be used as improvised striking weapons. Small, handheld flashlights are great multi-purpose tools as well. They not only provide you with helpful illumination but can also be used like a palm stick, augmenting the strength of your blows by concentrating your power into a small impact area. Some even come with a stun gun feature. Tactical flashlights are legal to carry anywhere, making them good defensive tools in jurisdictions with strict laws against carrying weapons.

This introductory list is by no means exhaustive; it did not include canes, walking sticks, collapsible batons, car keys, pens, or a host of other improvised weapons. While all of these personal protection devices can act as power multipliers, zero times anything is still zero. The amount of protection a self-defense tool can provide in a crisis depends largely on your level of training. We will discuss more about weapons and their use in Level 8.

Attire

Be aware that what you are wearing can have a big effect on what you are capable of doing. Think about how your clothing be either an advantage or a disadvantage during a self-defense encounter. Take your footwear for example. It is hard to run in flip-flops or high heels. If you need to escape and evade an assailant, will your shoes allow you to run, jump, or climb? What about your clothing? Tight pants or a tight skirt can restrict your leg movement, making it hard to run or fight. On the other hand, clothing can be an asset. Are you wearing sturdy shoes or boots that can focus the energy of your kicks? While a leather jacket is not going to stop a strong stabbing attack with a knife, it might protect you from a slicing attack. A belt with a metal buckle can make an effective improvised weapon, so long as your pants don't fall down!

Environment

Your environment is a crucial variable, so you'll want to pay attention to it. Where are you? What time is it? Are you indoors or outdoors? What are the conditions? Is it dark or well lit? Is the area cluttered or open? What type of traction do you have? Is it slippery, wet, or muddy? Is there snow or wet leaves? You will want to maintain a high level of vigilance when navigating through these and other potentially hazardous environments.

Public spaces such as streets and parking lots are potentially dangerous areas that require extra situational awareness. Approximately half of all violent crimes are street crimes. Use caution or avoid moving through spaces that offer a degree of privacy such as parking garages, stairwells, and elevators. Since there is safety in numbers, when you are in an area known for violence, it is best to stay with a crowd even if you do not know them. In bars and restaurants, sit with your back to the wall and your eyes on the door. Identify your exits. Look for concealment and cover in case assailants were to block your egress.

If you find yourself harassed by the occupants of a car, abruptly turn and walk in the opposite direction. The driver will have to turn around or back up to follow you. Is there a way to alert help, such as notifying a security guard or pulling a fire alarm? Criminals don't want anyone to witness their crimes. If there is a security camera, point it out to the threat in hopes of de-escalating the situation.

Home Defense

Since you probably spend a good portion of your time in your home, it is worth taking the time to properly secure it. Keep the entrances well lit. Deter intruders by installing a home security system or automatic lights with motion detectors. Make sure all your windows and doors can be locked securely, particularly sliding glass doors. Then, make it a habit to use the locks, even when you are at home, especially at night. If a door looks breached or open, you should immediately shift into high alert. If you have not yet entered your home, don't go in. If you are already inside, consider leaving.

Install a door viewer and look before opening your door to anyone. Never admit that you are home alone. Don't let a stranger inside your home to use the phone. Instead, make the call for him. If a service person should arrive unexpectedly, check his identification and leave him locked outside while you call his employer for verification before letting him in. If you live in an apartment, use extra caution going to the laundry room or parking garage by yourself, especially at night.

Charge your phone in your bedroom so you have it handy should you need it suddenly in the middle of the night. After my grandfather passed away, my grandmother used to keep a cap gun by her bed. If anyone ever broke in, she planned on yelling, "I have a gun, and I'm ready to use it!" and then start popping off caps. I can't tell you if her plan would have worked. Thankfully, she never had to test it.

Run through different scenarios of what you and your family should do in the case of any emergency, not just a human threat. Walk through each room of your home surveying and analyzing what you can do and use against an assailant, as well as what an assailant could do and use against *you*. Are there blind corners that you, or they, could use? What are expedient weapons? What are your avenues of escape? How would you deal with X in room Y? Train yourself to anticipate what you could use to mitigate an attack or leverage to your advantage should your home ever be invaded.

Parking Lot Safety

Parking lots require an extra degree of situational awareness. Here are some guidelines that will help you maneuver from the parking lot to the store and back again in a safe manner.

First, you are far less likely to get attacked at 11 am than you are at 11 pm. Simply planning ahead so you're not doing chores after sundown can significantly lower the chances of something going wrong. If you do have to go at night, try not to go alone. When you first pull into the parking lot, assess the general situation inside the store. Look in the windows. Does everything seem normal, with people coming out slowly and calmly?

Use caution when parking. Predators use concealment such as walls, bushes, or vehicles to get as close as possible to their prey without being detected. A predator will only break cover when his prey is vulnerable and not paying attention. Therefore, park under a light, preferably in a middle row close to the entrance. Park facing outwards, in a spot that allows for a quick and easy exit. While convenient, parking near the cart return gives a predator an excuse to be walking toward you under the guise of returning or getting a cart. Park next to short cars that you can see inside, avoiding vans and trucks. Be wary of vehicles with heavily tinted windows. Use extra caution in underground and enclosed parking garages. Don't leave valuables in your car, especially in full view. Instead, tuck them under the seat or, better yet, lock them in your trunk. Always lock your doors.

Use extra caution when exiting the store, as a predator may have identified you as a potential target and be lying in wait. Carjackers and muggers often target people when their attention is elsewhere. Because of this, you need to have a strategy to mitigate your vulnerability in these situations. Avoid having to search for your keys on your way to your car. Have them in your hand before leaving the building. Carry your purse close to you, not dangling. Don't walk too close to the rows of parked cars as someone could be hiding in ambush. Instead, walk down the center of the lane, keeping alert for potential threats. Keep your eyes open for anyone who stands out, bearing in mind that people do not normally loiter in parking lots unless they are hunting.

Be aware of what is around and under your car. If you notice anything odd, such as a flat tire or something placed under your car or even on your windshield, it may be a trap. Go back inside and ask or call for assistance. Look in your windows to check the back seats and floor. If your car seems clear, unload quickly, keeping your head up and on a swivel. As soon as you get in, lock your doors and go. Don't spend time sitting in your car fidgeting with things or swiping on your phone.

Defensive Driving

The automotive equivalent to empty-hand self-defense is defensive driving. Whenever you are behind the wheel of a car you must stay vigilant and maintain a 360-degree awareness. Regularly check your side and rearview mirrors. When you stop in traffic, keep a little space between you and the car in front of you, staying far enough back that you can see where their tires touch the road. This ensures that you can get around them quickly if you should need to.

Stay informed about where you are and where you are going. Know where your destination is and how to get there just in case your cell phone were to die. Download Google Maps for offline use in case you lose reception. Keep your car well maintained and in good working condition, with the gas tank at least half full. Get in the habit of driving with the doors locked and never pick up hitchhikers. Don't pull over for anyone unless you are sure it is a policeman, and even then, pull off somewhere safe and preferably well lit.

If you find yourself the target of an aggressive driver, attempt to defuse the situation by changing directions and driving somewhere he would not wish to follow, such as a police station. If you have a cell phone, hold it up, showing your bully that you are calling for help and recording their actions. Whatever you do, keep your cool, act smart, and don't get cornered.

If you are being followed, don't drive home. Call the police if you have a cell phone. If not, drive to the nearest police or fire station. Alternately, you can drive to a gas station or other business where there are many people. Don't leave your car unless you are certain you can get inside the building safely. Stay locked in your car and honk the horn to attract attention. If possible, obtain the license plate number and description of the car and driver following you. Using your phone to take pictures or record their actions may deter a potential assailant.

If you have a flat tire, drive on it slowly until you reach a safe place to pull over. If you have engine trouble, turn on your hazard lights, pull off somewhere safe, and raise the hood. Then get back inside your vehicle, lock the doors, and call for help. If someone stops to offer assistance, roll the window down just enough to speak with them. If you don't have a phone, ask them to place a cell phone call to a relative, friend, garage, or the police for you. If they do not have a cell phone, request that they stop at the first available phone to call for help. Do *not* get out of your car, and never accept a ride in a stranger's car. Men should use caution, and women should never stop to aid a stranger with a flat tire or broken-down car when driving alone. Instead, use your cell phone to report the stalled vehicle to the police.

Lastly, if you should ever be targeted for mugging or assault while fueling your car, remember that the pump nozzle is capable of spraying gasoline a considerable distance and can be an efficient deterrent against attack.

Travel Safety

Be aware that travelling away from home presents a whole new set of risks. Avoid travelling alone. Get to know your destination before you arrive by researching traveler reviews. Stay in the safest neighborhoods, away from places with high incidences of crime.

Don't draw attention to yourself. People who look like they're from out of town often become targets of crime. Try to blend in by wearing inconspicuous clothing that won't attract attention. Be discreet when checking your map and be careful about who you approach for directions. Avoid alcohol or drugs that can hinder your judgment. Stay vigilant when taking pictures or posting to social media. Avoid carrying extra money or valuables, as well as withdrawing cash from an ATM. To deter pickpockets, think in advance about where to securely carry your valuables.

Make copies of your important documents such as your passport, driver's license, and other forms of identification. Send a copy of your itinerary to your main contact, and then check in regularly with them so they know if your plans change. Regardless of how far away you are going or for how long, always keep someone you trust in the loop.

Hotels

Due to their high traffic rate, hotels are potential danger zones. Precautions begin as you pull into the parking lot (see "Parking Lot Safety" earlier in this section) and continue as you check in at the front desk. Don't announce if you are travelling alone when checking in. Keep an eye out as you approach and unlock your hotel door. Assailants sometimes hide across the hall and come in behind you as soon as you open your hotel room door. Once safely inside your room, conduct a quick search. Look under the bed, behind curtains, in the shower, and closet. Lock both the door and the second security device. If your hotel room door has no second security device, it's not safe. A portable door alarm can add an additional layer of security. These small devices can be used to monitor a door or window. If someone attempts to get inside, they trigger a high decibel alarm. Keep your key, shoes, and ID near the door in case you have to leave quickly.

Don't let any strangers into your room, even if they say they work for the hotel. If an attendant shows up unexpectedly, call the front desk to check whether they were ordered by hotel staff to come to your room. When you are away, put your valuables in the safe (if one is provided). Give the impression that your room is still occupied by keeping the blinds closed and posting the "Do Not Disturb" sign on your door.

Part 3: Recognizing a Threat

While the foundation of self-defense is awareness, merely knowing what is around you is just the beginning. In order to identify signs of danger, you must also have the ability to correctly interpret observational data in a timely manner. In other words, you have to stay sharp and think quickly. When dealing with people, this often requires an understanding of human body language and behavior.

Reading a Room

Reading a room means using your intuition to analyze the people in a particular setting to assess their general mood, allowing you to act accordingly. Developing this intuition begins with an analysis of the available data, so let's begin with statistics. Chances are you can ignore people who do not statistically pose a threat, such as women with children or the elderly. Instead, scan for suspicious characters. If someone triggers your interest, make a quick initial examination of the person's attire. Is it appropriate given the time and place? For example, a winter jacket on a warm day should raise a red flag because baggy clothes could be used to conceal a weapon. Likewise, evaluate the person's behavior. Does this person seem to have a logical reason for being where they are? Is he acting suspiciously? Acting erratically? Is the person looking at you? Approaching unprovoked? Trust your instincts and respond accordingly.

Kinesics

Reading body language can help you to identify potential threats early so you can react accordingly. Kinesics is the interpretation of body language and gestures, allowing you to predict a person's behavior based on subtle clues. Begin by examining their facial expression. Does the person seem happy, sad, nervous, or angry? What is his tone like, subdued or boisterous? How about his proximity? Is this person maintaining distance or invading your personal space or someone else's? If you feel nervous or uncomfortable, stay away.

Since the signs are often very subtle, the moment you perceive that you might be in danger, you need to act. Rather than stick around looking for further evidence to substantiate your suspicions, the correct response would be to immediately start distancing yourself from the threat or preparing to defend yourself.

If you happened to be in the jungles of India and caught a glimpse of something orange with black stripes moving through the underbrush, would you stick around just because you are not *sure* it is a tiger? Better safe than sorry.

Alertness in Passing

Predators often use ruses to get close to their intended targets. Passing by you gives a potential assailant an opportunity to "size you up." If you keep your eyes straight ahead, you will not be alert to possible threat indicators. Looking straight ahead can also leave you vulnerable to an ambush from behind.

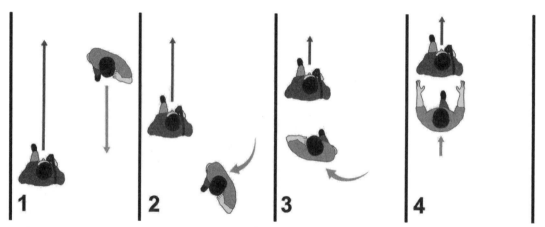

Unaware Passing: 1) The predator identifies you as unaware, making you a target. 2) He waits until he is past your line of sight, then turns in behind you. 3) The assailant follows you, careful to stay in your blind spot. 4) He will likely keep his distance, stalking you until he senses the perfect time to strike.

Therefore, it is best to look at someone who passes you. If he looks back, make eye contact. Do not feel intimidated. This action alone can deter a would-be assailant, since you have demonstrated that you are aware, alert, and confident. Furthermore, you have seen the person's face and could potentially identify him.

If someone happens to trigger your internal alarms, glance back to make sure that the person has not turned around to follow you. Your unconscious mind may have caught onto something you have yet to consciously process. If you think you may have identified a potential threat, do not hesitate. Trust your instincts, formulate a plan, and act.

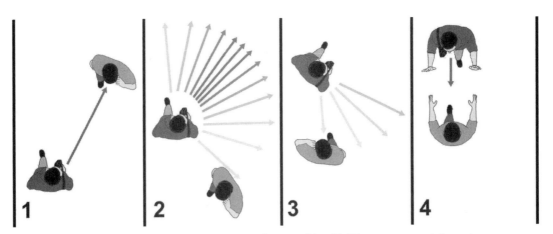

Aware Passing: 1) When you pass someone, glance at him. 2) If he seems suspicious, turn your head to keep him in your peripheral vision. 3) If you see him turn to follow you, turn to meet him. 4) This puts you in a better position to confront a threat.

Are You Being Followed?

Predators will often stalk their prey, waiting for an opportune moment to pounce. If you suspect you are being followed, your awareness level should shift from yellow to orange. Conduct a quick test by suddenly changing directions. This may mean turning a corner or crossing a street. If there are people around, abruptly turn around as though you had just forgotten something and walk directly past the person you suspect is following you, taking the opportunity to turn the tables on him and make a threat assessment. If the suspect turns around and starts walking behind you again, it is safe to assume that he is stalking you. Your awareness level should be turning red.

If you feel you're being followed, walk into a store or knock on a house door. If this is not an option, take the initiative by turning around and confronting your stalker. Ask bluntly, "Are you following me?" If he says no, follow up with, "You are making me feel very uncomfortable. Stay back!" Be loud, indignant, and exude confidence. Since predators prefer easy victims, by challenging him directly you can actually discourage an attack. At this point, any normal person should back off. If the person continues to follow or close the distance between you, assume they have bad intentions and act accordingly.

Threat Indicators

Awareness means keeping an eye out for threat indicators, subtle warning signs that telegraph a possible attack. It is best if you can pick up on these clues early so you can take evasive action. If you perceive multiple threat indicators, then you have enough information to move into a highly focused state of awareness.

Criminals do not want to be identified, so be on the alert for anyone trying to conceal his identity. This could include hiding his face by tucking his chin while hunching his shoulders forward, keeping his eyes down, and avoiding eye contact. Other red flags are wearing sunglasses, especially indoors or at night, pulling a hat down low, or having a hoodie up, especially indoors.

Is the person acting suspiciously? Is he pretending to talk on the phone, or trying to look busy? Is the person scanning left to right as though they were waiting for someone? He could be checking to make sure the area is free of witnesses or authorities before he attacks.

Drunkenness should be considered a threat indicator. Intoxicated people are unpredictable and prone to sudden outbursts of belligerent and irrational behavior. Impaired judgment, whether through alcohol or some other drug, could make an aggressor a greater threat than if he were sober. If so, the use of greater force may be required and justified.

Anxiety can cause signs of nervousness. Does the person seem uncomfortable? Look for tell-tale behaviors such as profuse sweating, shaky hands, or excessive fidgeting. Does the person have balled-up fists? Is he clenching and unclenching his hands, rocking, or shifting his weight onto the balls of his feet? A would-be assailant may express his intentions before acting on them. Is he making overt, veiled, or insinuated threats?

Does he have a "thousand-yard stare": chin dipped, looking through the eyebrows with an aloof gaze, checked out yet intent? If you don't like how someone is looking at you or your children, pay attention to that! You may have unconsciously clued in on subtle threat indicators.

Common Ploys

A smart assailant will use a ploy to get close to you or control you. By familiarizing yourself with ploys commonly used by predators, you can learn how to defend against them effectively. The following examples include suggestions on how to best respond to each approach, but these are not the only responses you could employ. It is important to act on your own perceptions and good judgment.

"Excuse me, but do you know what time it is?"

Simple requests such as for directions or the time give a potential attacker an opportunity to assess you while he closes the distance between you. Stay on your guard and enforce your personal space. An assertive response can deter the situation from escalating. "No, I'm sorry, go ask someone else."

"Aw, come on, you can't help me out?"

The guilt trip is used to make you feel badly for asserting yourself, questioning, or being distrustful. The attacker will play on your sympathy and concern for others by bringing attention to his hurt feelings or bad predicament. Remember that you are not responsible for managing anyone's feelings or problems other than your own. Don't put yourself in jeopardy. It may seem calloused, but just walk away.

"Who taught you how to drive, you stupid jerk?!"

Insults and negative comments are employed as a means of clouding your judgment by eliciting an emotional response. This is a test to see if you are submissive and easily intimidated. Either ignore any name calling all together, or call the person out on his behavior by saying, "Where I come from, that is considered rude!" Ignore any further responses.

"I have never seen anyone as beautiful as you!"

Flattery is a ploy that is commonly used on women. Compliments are nice, but any unsolicited and repetitive comments about your looks, clothes, or talents from strangers or acquaintances should arouse precautionary awareness. Don't be smitten by flattery.

Direct Confrontation

Sometimes the best way to avoid becoming a victim is to show strength through direct confrontation. By confronting someone who you suspect may be targeting you or your family, you show you are aware of the threat they pose and refuse to be a victim. Of course, the idea is to make you safer, not to put yourself at risk. Only approach someone in a safe location, preferably with other people around. Ask a direct question, such as, "What are you doing here?" or make a clear statement like, "Stop staring at me. You are making me very uncomfortable." Make eye contact to show that he has been noticed, that you are not afraid, and that you can identify him. If he persists, seek assistance. Look for a shopkeeper, bartender, security guard, or bouncer, and let them know, "I need your help. That man over there is bothering me."

Level-1 Activities

Situational awareness can take years to develop completely and considerable discipline to maintain properly. Training is the most critical element to acquiring new skills. Reading and watching videos is important for acquiring new information, but you must actually try things out in order to see what works for you. Become proactive, get hands on, and train. The following activities will help you to develop the skills you need.

Toothpicks and Straws

This is a simple exercise that can rapidly improve your peripheral vision. All you will need is a straw and two toothpicks. First, use a marker to draw a line around the middle of the straw. Then, have a friend hold the straw horizontally one to two feet in front of you and focus your central vision on the line. With a toothpick in each hand, try to place the tips of the toothpicks into each end of the straw, all the while keeping your central vision focused on the line. Perform this exercise daily until you can consistently place the toothpicks into the straw.

Meditation

Meditation is a practice where you focus your mind on a particular object, thought, or activity to develop your attention and awareness. Through meditation, you can achieve a mentally clear and emotionally calm state of mind. Although there are many different types of meditation practice, the core concept is not as esoteric as it is often made out to be. Simply sit and concentrate on your breathing. With practice, your internal dialogue gradually ceases, and you will be able to focus for longer and longer periods of time without becoming distracted. Start by setting a timer for one minute, and then just sit, breathe, and listen. As your abilities improve, gradually increase the duration of your sessions.

Kim's Game

This game is derived from a 1901 Rudyard Kipling novel, *Kim*, in which the main character plays this game as part of his training to be a spy. It is an excellent tool for learning situational awareness and developing your memory. The Kim Game develops your capacity to observe and remember details by staring at a group of objects for a short period of time, then covering the objects or turning away before writing down as many of the objects as you can remember.

I Spy

This classic guessing game is wonderful for developing your observational skills. One player, the spy, chooses an object within sight and announces to the other players, "I spy with my little eye . . ." The phrase then ends with a clue such as "something blue," "something alive," or "something made of glass." Players then take turns guessing until someone gets the right answer. The winner gets to be the next "spy."

People Watching

Train your brain to observe people. Learn to collect as much detail as possible in a short amount of time, noting distinguishing characteristics that cannot be changed, such as race, height, build, eye color, tattoos, or pitch of voice. Hair color and length, including facial hair, can be changed, but not easily, so they are worth noting. Clothing, on the other hand, can be changed easily and provides the least amount of useful information to describe a perpetrator. When it comes to attire, observe those things that are least likely to change by working from the bottom up, noting his shoes, pants, shirt, and hat in that order.

Draw out details as you try to figure out who the person is and what they are doing while also trying to predict what are they are going to do next. Try not to stare for too long, though, or someone might accidentally mistake *you* for a predator! Instead, take this opportunity to also practice looking out of the corners of your eyes.

Did You See That?

Have a friend quiz you about your surroundings. Begin by looking around, examining your surroundings closely. Then, close your eyes and have someone ask you questions such as: "What color shirt am I wearing?" "How many people are in the room?" "Point to the nearest exit." "What could you use as an improvised weapon?"

This is a good game to play when traveling in the car or on walking on foot. You don't even have to close your eyes. Simply ask random questions like, "What did that sign say?" or "Was that guy wearing sunglasses?" This type of questioning should begin to automatically increase your level of awareness.

Recommended Reading

The Gift of Fear: Survival Signals That Protect Us from Violence is a self-help book written by Gavin de Becker (Dell Publishing 1997). In it, De Becker demonstrates how, in almost every case of violence, there were warning signs that were not noticed but in retrospect were quite easy to recognize. Even when we don't overtly recognize these warning signs, we can unconsciously sense them. This book teaches you how to trust your intuition to avoid violent situations.

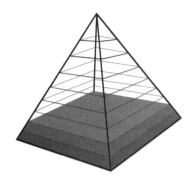

Avoidance, De-escalation, and Anticipation

To be prepared against surprise is to be trained. To be prepared for surprise is to be educated.
—James P. Carse

Avoidance, De-escalation, and Anticipation

Once you have identified a specific threat, proceed with an abundance of caution. Ensuring your safety should become your primary objective. This means leaving the situation as quickly as possible. If evasion is not a viable option, then attempt to de-escalate the situation before things become physical. Even though you are still trying to resolve the situation peacefully, the threat of attack is still a very real danger. Prepare yourself by learning to recognize the behavioral clues that precede a violent assault. These warning signs can give you the ability to anticipate an imminent attack, enhancing your odds of successfully defending yourself.

The stress and anxiety produced in a self-defense situation can be extreme. In order to control the situation, you are going to have to first keep control of yourself. Preparing for an encounter mentally, physically, and spiritually (the latter in the sense of cultivating your "fighting spirit"), will help you keep your cool when tensions run high. However, it is also important that you understand your body's possible involuntary physiological reactions to a high-stress situation. It is a little more complex than simply fight or flight. Depending on the circumstances, you may react by freezing, fleeing, submitting, posturing, or fighting. The first four can be grouped under avoidance and de-escalation, while the last reaction, fighting, is preceded by anticipation.

Part 1: Avoidance

In a best-case scenario, being aware of your surroundings and keeping alert for signs of danger will provide you with the opportunity to perceive a dangerous situation early and avoid it altogether. Avoidance is a type of passive self-defense in which you are hoping to evade the threat or de-escalate the situation. Either is preferable to a physical confrontation that has the potential to result in you or someone you care about getting hurt. The strategies to avoid a physical confrontation include flight, submission, and posturing. Before you can engage in any of these, however, you first have to avoid freezing up.

Freezing

Stress is your body's natural mental and physical reaction to real or perceived threats. Self-defense occurs under the extreme stress and anxiety of being suddenly attacked by a hostile, violent, and quick-moving attacker, statistically in low-light conditions. This may cause you to freeze, not unlike the proverbial deer in the headlights.

Freezing is an instinctual response to danger that frequently occurs in nature. The hope is that the threat will overlook you and move on. When you freeze, hormones are being dumped into your body, resulting in a temporary loss of your higher cognitive processes. If this should occur, you must first recognize the freeze then act to break it as quickly as possible. Take a deep breath and then actively engage your mind by asking yourself what you are going to do. Consciously make the decision to move, then will yourself to do so. You may need to tell yourself what to do. "I need to verbally de-escalate this situation," or, "In three seconds I am going to drop my bag of groceries and run for that open store. Three, two, one, GO!"

The main causes of freezing are intimidation and fear. These affect the autonomic nervous system, which will then naturally engage your sympathetic system. Understanding this process and the triggers that cause it can help us to beat the freeze.

Intimidation

Intimidation, also called cowing, is intentional behavior intended to cause you to fear for your safety. This includes ridiculing, insulting, making verbal threats, yelling, hostile physical posturing, and brandishing a weapon. Insults and inappropriate comments can be used to attack your self-confidence, weakening your resolve to mount a defense. Learn to recognize when you are emotionally off balance or being kept in a disadvantageous position.

The keys to countering intimidation are courage and self-confidence. Use body language to your advantage. Assuming a strong posture communicates to an aggressor that you won't be pushed around. Ironically, even if you don't feel especially confident, the act of standing tall and making eye contact can physiologically generate the feelings of confidence you are trying to portray.

> When you are weak, appear strong. When you are strong, appear weak.
> —Sun Tzu

Controlling Fear

Fear is a natural, innate response to potentially hazardous situations that evolved to help keep you safe. However, fear is also a predator's primary weapon. You can't let fear dominate your life. Either you control your fear, or it controls you. Learning to control your fear begins by learning to recognize your body's reaction to fear.

Understand that fear does not actually exist. Fear is a mental construct centered on a worse-case scenario. This is expressed in the acronym "False Evidence Appears Real." It is your body and mind's reaction to external stimuli. When you encounter something threatening, you experience an adrenaline dump. This makes you move faster, but you also lose some of your fine motor control. Fear can also have a numbing effect, temporarily inhibiting the sensation of pain.

Fear can turn into doubt. Controlling your fear is a matter of coming to terms with the reality of your situation. Of course, this is easier said than done. Inoculate yourself to the type of fear and stress induced by a potentially violent confrontation by participating in competitions such as martial arts tournaments. You can also practice with a trusted partner, taking turns roleplaying through intimidating situations.

Another way to train for confidence is by visualizing encounters. Begin by picturing yourself somewhere. Where are you? Picture the situation in great detail, as though you were actually there. Now picture an attacker entering the scene. What does he look like? Smell like? How is he threatening you? Allow your heart rate to rise as your body engages its fear response. Then, turn your fear into anger by deciding that you will not be a victim. Choose instead to be aggressive and turn on your attacker. Picture exactly how you would defend yourself. Imagine getting hit but fighting on to victory.

The Autonomic Nervous System

To control your fear, it helps to understand the physiological effects your body involuntarily undergoes and why you experience them. Your bodily functions are regulated by your autonomic nervous system. It acts largely unconsciously and is the primary mechanism in control of your fight-or-flight response.

Your autonomic nervous system consists of two parts: the sympathetic nervous system and the parasympathetic nervous system. Your parasympathetic system is engaged during your normal, resting state. However, when you are frightened, your sympathetic system instantly activates. Nonessential systems such as mucous production in your nose, throat, and bowels, shut down while other systems go into overdrive. Your pupils enlarge to let as much light into your eye as possible. Your heart rate increases, airways expand, breathing quickens, blood sugar spikes, blood pressure rises, and your muscles tighten up, all in preparation for a physically demanding, possibly life-threatening encounter.

As much as you might like to, this is why you can't stay in high alert all the time. Situational awareness requires an expenditure of physical and mental energy. Constant stress experienced over a prolonged length of time can have a negative impact on your body. Consistently increased heart rate, high blood pressure, and elevated levels of stress hormones can result in long-term cardiac issues.

The Autonomic Nervous System

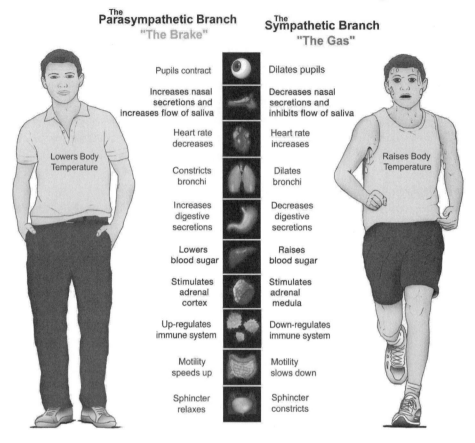

The
Parasympathetic Branch
"The Brake"

The
Sympathetic Branch
"The Gas"

Parasympathetic		Sympathetic
Pupils contract		Dilates pupils
Increases nasal secretions and increases flow of saliva		Decreases nasal secretions and inhibits flow of saliva
Heart rate decreases		Heart rate increases
Constricts bronchi		Dilates bronchi
Increases digestive secretions		Decreases digestive secretions
Lowers blood sugar		Raises blood sugar
Stimulates adrenal cortex		Stimulates adrenal medula
Up-regulates immune system		Down-regulates immune system
Motility speeds up		Motility slows down
Sphincter relaxes		Sphincter constricts

Lowers Body Temperature

Raises Body Temperature

Flight

No harm can come to you if you distance yourself from the perceived threat. Your body instinctually knows this and will do everything it can to persuade you to flee. Flight can take on several forms, from casually leaving a situation to uncontrollably running away as fast as you can. If you sense danger, immediately act on your intuition. Look for threat indicators to assess your current risk level and help you determine when to walk away and when to run.

Running

You probably recognize some version of this classic quote by Sir John Mennes in 1641: "For he that fights and runs away, may live to fight another day."

I can personally think of at least three times running has saved me from having to fight. I told you about one of them earlier in the self-defense story about the three bullies who targeted me after school one day. While it worked for me in that case, running can also be risky. That story could have ended much differently if those bullies had chosen to give chase and caught me where there was no one to step in and save me.

It is logical to assume that a larger, stronger attacker would probably also be faster than you. Do you possess the cardiovascular fitness required to realistically outrun your attacker(s)? How do you know? Do you run regularly? Can you run well in what you are wearing, particularly your footwear? Are you carrying a backpack or purse that will hold you back? Where are you planning on running to? Uneven ground can cause you to trip and fall. Clothing and bags may catch on fences or branches. These are important variables to take into consideration before giving in to the urge to flee.

If you decide that running *is* your best option, make sure to keep your wits about you as you run. Don't turn your back on your attacker until you are out of his grabbing range. As you run, swivel your head from side to side to watch for obstacles, especially moving vehicles in parking lots or on roadways. Stay in the open as much as possible to avoid being trapped. Along the way, scan for items that might be useful to create a barrier or obstacle between you and your pursuer. If you run through a gate or door, quickly close it behind you. Shove a shopping cart into his path or knock a trashcan down as you go by. Anything that will take you less time to accomplish than it will take your pursuer to overcome is worth doing. Look to acquire power multipliers that can give you an advantage over your attacker, such as fishing a key out of your pocket or picking up an empty bottle that could be used as an improvised weapon.

If your attacker turns out to be faster than you thought, or for some other reason you sense that your choice to run is not working, alter your strategy from passive resistance to active resistance. Suddenly turn and confront your attacker. Be sure to include your best battle cry (more on this in Level 3). Hopefully, your abrupt change of tactics from timid to brazen will catch him by surprise, allowing you to get in a shot. You don't even need to hurt him. All you need to do is get him to momentarily throw up his defenses. Then you can take advantage of the momentary change in dynamics to quickly turn and resume running.

It is always best to err on the side of caution by underestimating yourself and overestimating your attacker.

> ### And why am I alive when everyone else around me has turned to meat? It's because of my list of rules. Rule number one for surviving Zombieland: Cardio.
> ### —Columbus

Hiding: Concealment and Cover

Sometimes, running is not the best way to evade an adversary. Concealment is the act of hiding from a threat. You can quickly conceal yourself by slipping into a shadow, hiding in a closet, or ducking under a car. The word "concealment" is also used to describe the physical object that you are using to hide yourself. When searching for a place to hide, scan for objects you can get behind, under, inside, or on top of; find anyplace that obscures your attacker's line of sight.

If a gun is involved, you don't just want concealment, you want *cover*. Cover is concealment that can deflect, slow down, or even stop a bullet. Of course, the effectiveness of any particular piece of cover will vary according to the size of the weapon and the proximity of the shooter. A bookcase full of books is remarkably bulletproof lengthwise but less effective widthwise since the stacks of paper are much thinner. A car, masonry wall, or corner of a building can all offer good cover. When indoors, look for heavy wooden furniture or a thick mattress. Interior walls, while good for concealment, often cannot stop a bullet unless it happens to hit a wooden stud.

As you move throughout your day, practice looking for places and objects that offer concealment or cover. Which ones would protect you from a bullet? Once you identify a potential hiding place, think about how you would best get to it. The best way is usually to get low and sprint directly there. While running in a zigzag pattern might make you a harder target, this tactic also leaves you out in the open longer and increases your odds of tripping and falling.

Self-Defense Story: A Stroll Down Danger Lane

One night in 1994, about the time my wife, Kathy, and I started our martial arts school, we had decided to go for a midnight walk. We were talking and looking for shooting stars as we strolled along a quiet road on the edge of town that ran by a large scrap yard. We stepped off the road as a car came up behind us. It passed by us slowly. Too slowly. The windows were down, and I noticed at least four guys inside eyeballing us. Their car had just passed us, and I was already on high alert when the driver momentarily hit the brakes. I knew those brake lights were bad news. Suddenly, the taillights went off again and the car accelerated, only to take the first available turn just up the street. As soon as the car was out of sight, I grabbed my wife and started running. She protested at first until I exclaimed, "They're going around the block!" I remember her looking at me for just the briefest of moments, and then it was all I could do to keep up with her.

We were both in good shape and managed a fair distance before jumping off the road and concealing ourselves behind a discarded concrete highway barrier sitting in some high weeds. We timed it just right, too, because just seconds later we saw headlights coming down the road. It was the same car, and they were creeping along, obviously looking for us. They circled back once or twice, but they were concentrating their efforts on the area where they had originally seen us, and we had run just far enough down the road that we were avoiding their searches. After what felt like a lifetime but was probably only a few minutes, they gave up and drove off. We waited until we were reasonably sure they weren't circling around again before we hustled back the way we had come, keeping our eyes peeled every step of the way. Luckily, we made it home without further incident, but I shudder to think about what might have happened if we had not immediately reacted the way we did.

Post-encounter Analysis: My wife and I were in the wrong place at the wrong time, a deserted road in the middle of the night, when we were unfortunate enough to run into the wrong people. I imagine that the conversation in the car after they passed us went something like, "Hey man, did you see that? Stop the car!" to which someone else said, "No, no, go around the block, and we'll come up behind them." Whatever it was, we got lucky when the driver hit the brakes for a second, telegraphing their intentions. Otherwise, we may have been caught out in the open on their return run. Practicing the first three tenets of self-defense, *Awareness-Alertness-Avoidance*, may have saved our lives.

Part 2: De-escalation

Verbal De-escalation

Conflict occurs when two people disagree. Heated disagreement can lead to frustration. Untreated frustration turns into anger, which can lead to violent physical aggression. However, if you understand the principles of nonviolent conflict resolution, there is a chance that you might be able to verbally de-escalate the situation.

To the extent possible, it's a good idea to communicate verbally with a threatening aggressor. With men, it's often about ego. The first step is to apologize for the perceived slight. It doesn't matter if you were actually responsible or not. Don't let *your* ego get in the way. This will set the tone that you have no malicious intent and are presenting no challenge. Use humor to defuse the situation using remarks such as, "That's a really nice shirt. You wouldn't want to get my blood all over it." This statement helps the threat save face by complimenting the threat's shirt while recognizing his perceived physical superiority. You might provide him with favorable options such as, "Look, you can punch me in the face and get us kicked out of here, or I can buy you a beer. Personally, I prefer you choose the beer."

If things continue to escalate, change tack. Give him a clear verbal warning. Avoid using "fighting words" or unnecessary provocation. Instead, use calm yet firm verbal commands to lower the emotional level and prevent a physical altercation. Telling the aggressor to "calm down" usually has the opposite effect. Instead, say to your aggressor, "Stand back and lower your voice before someone calls the police. We can work this out like rational adults. If you touch me, I will call the police myself." If he calls your bluff, double-down and call 911 to request police assistance. Your call can also serve to create an audio record of events as they occur.

While your voice can be your most powerful weapon, for men, an audience can be counterproductive to peaceful conflict resolution. If possible, try to move to a quieter area without a large crowd. A change of environment can help to defuse a potentially explosive situation, but don't say, "Let's take it outside." Those are fighting words, and you do not want to threaten or antagonize an already irritated aggressor. Instead, show that you do not want to escalate the conflict. People respond favorably to hearing their name, so try to learn the person's name early on and use it often as you engage him in conversation. Keep in mind that this person is still potentially hostile, so respect his personal space and do not block his exit. As you talk, try to identify triggers in order to avoid them. Set your ego aside and don't take anything he says personally. Ignore challenging questions and focus on the thoughts behind the feelings instead. "Can I ask your name? Thanks. I understand you are angry right now, Bob. Heck, I'd be angry, too. I'm just hoping you can see that I am not your enemy."

Avoid overreacting by maintaining an even tone. Remain empathetic and nonjudgmental. Paraphrasing, repeating his own words back to him, and responding with open-ended questions help ensure that the person you are attempting to talk down is aware that you are actively listening and understand his frustrations. "I'm so sorry I backed into you, Bob. I can't believe I did something so stupid. Look, Bob, I understand why you are mad. If someone hit my new car, I'd be furious, too. I just didn't see it there. It was stupid of me, but it was an accident. You've made mistakes before, haven't you, Bob?" It is difficult for someone to stay angry toward you when you are agreeing with them. Ask a clarifying question where the other person must answer, "Yes."

A combination of these tactics will provide you with the greatest chance of resolving the conflict in the safest and most productive way possible. Throughout the process, maintain a constant state of alertness for attack indicators such as a sudden change in tone or body language, fidgeting, clenching teeth, a change in eye contact, or assuming an aggressive posture such as puffing out his chest. If the aggressor conceals one or both hands behind his back, in his pocket, or otherwise out of sight, assume that he is armed and preparing to attack. Immediately take whatever precautions are necessary to defend yourself (we'll get into exactly what this means in Part 3).

Submission

It takes two to tango. Capitulation and compliance are passive alternatives to active resistance. Simply refuse to engage an antagonist by declaring, "You win. I'm not going to fight you." Give him the "man points" he's looking for. If a mugger wants your wallet, give it to him. Valuables can be replaced, but your health and life cannot. If you needlessly resist and end up getting seriously injured, you may wish later that you had just given the assailant what he wanted. Even though your ego may have taken a hit, at least you would be able to move on with your life, having lived to fight another day.

Keep in mind that situations are fluid and change quickly, so remain flexible. You may initially choose to submit to an assailant, but if the situation worsens, such as your attacker trying to force you into a car or take you to a secondary location, it is advisable to change your strategy and resist. The sudden change in tack may take your attacker by surprise, giving you a temporary advantage.

Surviving a Mugging

If you are in an area that puts you at high risk for this type of crime, consider carrying a fake wallet with just a few dollars in it. Toss your wallet or purse toward the attacker, throwing it low and aiming for an area to the side or even behind him. As soon as he turns to retrieve it, run in the other direction. He now has to decide which he wants more, your money or you.

Posturing

Posturing (different than posture) is a dominance display with no serious threat behind it. By making verbal threats and purposely giving off other attack indicators, you attempt to convince your attacker to back down. The most common method of posturing is to look intimidating. Make the threat believe that you are an even more serious threat. Stand tall, look tough, be loud, and make threats, even though you don't actually intend on backing them up. Another tactic to deter an attack is to act mentally unstable. Even predators avoid particularly unpredictable individuals.

Posturing is a risky strategy. If the threat calls your bluff and attacks, you not only have to defend yourself, but by challenging your attacker, you may have aggravated him further and possibly even justified his use of force against *you* in self-defense.

A less aggressive form of posturing, just acting confident and in-charge even though you don't necessarily feel it, may be more effective. However, every self-defense situation is different. You must use your judgment, working off the best information you have at the time to choose a strategy and employ appropriate tactics to safely resolve the situation. Things happen fast and unexpectedly, so you'll have to stay observant and think on your feet.

Self-Defense Story: A Meeting with Mr. Road Rage

It was 2001, and I was a fifth-grade teacher in the town where I live. After school one day, I had to drive to a faculty meeting at the high school, so believe me when I say I was *not* in a hurry. I was in a quiet suburban neighborhood about two blocks from my destination when the minivan in front of me slowed down and pulled off to the left without signaling. Thinking he was pulling over on the left side of the road, I kept going straight, passing him on the right, only to have him suddenly cut back into my lane, almost hitting my driver's side door. He was jug handling into his driveway on the right-hand side but managed to hit his brakes before hitting me. He yelled and laid on his horn, I smiled and waved sorry in return, then kept going.

By the end of the block, he was back, his minivan now two inches from my back bumper. Ahead of me, the high school kids were just letting out, so I pulled over in front of the school, hoping that the presence of so many witnesses would keep the situation in check. I watched his door open in my side mirror, so I got out to meet him, closing my car door behind me. I met him in a defensive stance with my hands open and palms out. I could tell by his belligerent tone and flushed face that he was obviously very angry. I innocently asked him what the problem was, and he started screaming about me cutting him off. I told him I was sorry and that I thought he was pulling off to the left. He yelled some more, and I explained as calmly as I could that, if I had seen a turn signal, I never would have tried to pass him. By now, a group of high school kids had begun to gather around to see what all the commotion was about, and I guess it made the guy start to think twice, because he turned and went back to his car.

That should have been the end of it, but one of the kids knew me and yelled out, "Hey, Mr. V!" I turned to see one of my former fifth graders, now in high school, who then asked, "What was all that about?" I replied, "Nothing. Just some jerk." Well, the jerk had not quite gotten back to his minivan, and he heard me, a careless spark on a keg of dynamite. He hops back out of his blue minivan and yells, "JERK?!" causing me to turn back in his direction just in time to see him launching himself into a full boar charge straight at me.

I don't know if what happened next was technique or pure luck. I had no time to evade. He slammed into me, shoving me backward with both hands as hard as he could, but rather than bracing against his charge and probably being bowled over, I just sort of went with it. I landed on my feet five or six feet away, then used the remaining momentum from his push to start back peddling. In another few steps, I had moved to the passenger side of my car, placing the vehicle between us.

I credit my next strategy with the fact that I dealt with kids all day. Never taking my eyes off my attacker as he followed me around the car, I pointed my index finger at him and said in my best teacher voice, "YOU are in so much trouble!" I kept moving backward, maintaining distance as I said, "You laid hands on me. That's assault. I'm calling the cops!" By now I was at the rear of his vehicle. Still keeping distance between us, I announced that I was writing down his license plate number. I then pretended to pull a pen out of my pocket and write down his plate number on my hand. He got in his car and drove away.

I skipped my faculty meeting and called the police, who went to his house and gave the man a citation, which he fought. We went to court, where Mr. Road Rage went into another screaming fit, only this time in front of a policeman and district magistrate. In the end, the judge ruled in my favor and declared that the man had to pay the citation, which the man flatly refused to do, so the judge offered him another option. He told the man that he did not have to pay the $300 fine, provided he successfully completed an anger management class. This made the man absolutely livid, and he stormed out of the little courtroom, slamming the door behind him. I was stunned and then surprised when the judge hung his head in his hands and started laughing. The officer present saw the quizzical look on my face and explained that they were already quite well acquainted with Mr. Road Rage.

Post-encounter Analysis: My first mistake was passing on the right, which is technically illegal. I should have waited until I was absolutely sure of the other driver's intentions. Second, I should not have gotten out of my car. After I pulled over and he left his vehicle, there was nothing stopping me from just driving away. However, I think I responded correctly in pulling off in a location where there were a lot of witnesses present rather than continuing to the more deserted back parking lot. My initial attempt at verbal de-escalation went as intended, and the man was returning to his car when I made my third mistake, which was insulting him while he was still within earshot. Oops. Whether by luck or design, I weathered his initial attack unscathed and then avoided further physical contact while continuing to verbally de-escalate the situation This time, however, I used a different tack, flipping the script from being subservient and apologetic to being indignant and authoritative. Switching to a nonaggressive form of posturing, I clearly stated the logical consequences of his actions, and that proved enough to discourage him from any further aggression against me. I am sure the group of high school kids gathered around watching helped him make the right decision.

Part 3: Anticipation

Dealing with an Approach

If you find someone suspicious approaching you, take a deep breath and stay calm. If there is time, quickly scan your surroundings for additional threats and avenues of escape. Then conduct a quick threat assessment. Begin by looking at his hands. Can you see them? Are they empty, behind his back, or perhaps in his pockets? Is he holding anything? Bulges in clothing, usually at the ankle or waistband, can indicate that he may be carrying a concealed weapon.

How you conduct yourself when you are approached will send unconscious psychological messages to an aggressor. How you stand or hold yourself can have a definite effect on whether the confrontation escalates or de-escalates. Predators choose soft targets as victims of crime. Do not let him think he has the upper hand. You want to present a positive image of yourself, one that exudes confidence. Stand with your head up and shoulders back, taking up as much space as you can. Don't be a passive victim. Look up, making eye contact when appropriate but still being sure to keep your head on a swivel to maximize your field of view. Move with authority, demonstrating that you are aware, capable, and willing to do what must be done. Remember, it's more about *perceived* ability than *actual* ability. Give the perception that you are a hard target.

The Neutral Guard

The best stance is one that maximizes your strengths while minimizing your weaknesses. The neutral guard is a nonconfrontational stance that has good defensive as well as offensive capabilities. It provides you with a strong, mobile foundation that allows you to stand your ground firmly while also giving you the ability to move quickly in any direction.

Keep your feet about one shoulder width apart, with the toes of your rear foot roughly in line with the heel of your front foot. Your weight should be evenly distributed between your front leg and back leg. Keep the heel of your back foot raised slightly off the ground. Being on

The Neutral Guard: This nonconfrontational stance offers a good balance of defensive and offensive capabilities.

the ball of your rear foot gives you more mobility. The heel of your front foot can touch the ground, but try to keep your weight toward the front of your foot. Keep your knees bent slightly, making your hips feel settled and heavy.

Your shoulders and arms should be relaxed, with your elbows down and held close to your body. Keep your hands up and chin dipped. When you are able to maintain distance just outside of striking range, remain relatively square to your attacker, with your shoulders turned only slightly. While your hand positions will change throughout the encounter according to your offen-

sive and defensive needs, in the neutral, pre-fight scenario, your open hands should be held palms facing out, a little more than a foot in front of you at cheek level. This offers you good protection while appearing nonaggressive. Appearing defensive is important because it may prevent an escalation of tensions. Additionally, we live in an age of litigation. If there are any witnesses, they

Keep your gaze general, centered on your attacker's throat. This will allow you to see subtle body movements that telegraph when he is about to attack.

will likely perceive you as the defender, which can help you if the case should ever go to court.

Keep your cool and do not overreact. Mentally, physically, and spiritually prepare yourself for the encounter. Anticipate the aggressor's next move by observing and quickly evaluating his intentions. Be ready to respond without hesitation.

Avoid staring into your attacker's eyes as this can be seen as a challenge. He can also use his eyes to manipulate and mislead you. Instead, keep your gaze general, centered on your attacker's throat where his neck meets his body. This will allow you to see subtle body movements that telegraph an attack. Keep alert for any shoulder motion that might indicate he is cocking back an arm to strike you.

Positioning

Proper preparation in the moments leading up to a violent confrontation can be crucial to your survival. Begin in the neutral guard with your hands up, creating a barrier similar to a roll cage in a car or a shark cage in the ocean. As the threat attempts to get close to you, use your hands to maintain distance and protect your space. At the same time, try not to stand directly in front of him. This is his kill zone, where all his weapons are directed. Instead, move to keep yourself angled slightly off to one side of his centerline, limiting his attack choices. Against a right-handed attacker, it is usually best to assume a left lead, allowing you to check his dominant hand. Turning your body slightly also angles your vulnerable center slightly away from his dominant hand, limiting his targets as well as his attacks.

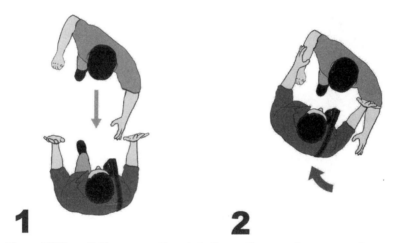

Move Offline: 1) If you stay directly in front of an attacker, you are in his kill zone. 2) Instead, as he closes distance, move off his line of attack, angling toward his dominant side to check his hands.

Preattack Indicators

Most attack situations are preceded by various warnings. Some may be overt, such as yelling, "I'm going to kill you!" Others are far subtler, like glancing side to side. However, all threat indicators are signs telegraphing a possible attack. Sometimes these signs can be difficult to pick up, so you will have to stay calm and observant. It is obviously best if you can pick up on these clues early, giving you more time to defuse or escape the situation, but even late in the game, these warning signals can give you the ability to predict if and when an assailant is about to attack you.

While a single indicator is certainly a warning sign, a series of indicators should be taken very seriously. Exhibiting these characteristics does not necessarily mean that a person intends to be violent. However, the more threat indicators you perceive, the greater the risk of a physical attack.

If you perceive multiple threat indicators, you have enough information to move into a highly focused state of awareness (red on the scale of awareness introduced in Level 1). An especially alarming series of threat indicators may justify the need for you to strike preemptively.

Body Language

An aggressors' body language can clue you in to his mental state. Dropping his hands and puffing up the chest to look larger are parts of an aggressive dominance display. This display may include removing clothing, such as ripping off the shirt, all in an attempt to maximize his intimidation factor.

Unfortunately, an assailant's behavior can vary from one extreme to another. Threat indicators such as yelling, throwing things, and throwing a general tantrum are obvious signs of dangerous levels of anger and frustration. Excessive fidgeting, clenching and unclenching his hands, rocking, or shifting his weight onto the balls of his feet are all unconscious displays of excitement or nervousness that may indicate an impending loss of self-control. On the other hand, a cool calmness may be an indicator that you are dealing with an experienced predator.

Hands

A perpetrator will often move to optimize his position just before launching an attack. Look for a clenched fist combined with a drawing back of his punching arm. This may or may not be accompanied by a step back or angling of the body in an attempt to maximize the power to his punch. If he puts away his cell phone, he is freeing his hands in order to attack or, worse, he may be transitioning to a weapon. Improvised weapons come in all shapes and forms, so pay attention to any items he may be carrying or have within reach.

While holding the hands behind the back may not appear to be an aggressive posture, it is often a dangerous preattack indicator. In this position, the attacker is already loaded up for a big haymaker. He also has access to his waistband, which is a common place to conceal a weapon. At the same time, his nonaggressive stance manipulates you into momentarily but unconsciously lowering your guard.

Accessing the Belt Line

People often carry weapons, such as knives and guns, tucked into their beltline, usually in the back. If you see him reaching behind his back or otherwise accessing his beltline, immediately move away to evade (in other words, run) or move in to check his arms. If you move in, grab his wrists to control his arms and deny him access to whatever he may be carrying. Remember, when you only have ahold of one arm, he can still attack or draw a weapon with his free hand. Instead of wrestling for position, unexpectedly change tactics and tiger claw his eyes (see Level 3).

Eyes

While the attacker is posturing, focus your gaze on his throat, using your peripheral vision to keep track of his hands. Then, use the edge of your central vision to take note of where he is looking.

If the threat steps back and looks around, he may be checking for witnesses. If he suddenly looks down and starts to turn away, he may be trying to get you to unconsciously drop your guard so he can catch you with a sucker punch.

Target glancing is a subtle telegraph that can be difficult to pick up on but is worth watching as it is a serious indicator that an attack is on its way. When an attacker is posturing, try to take note of where he is looking. Watch for his eyes to keep darting to his target. Glancing back and forth from your eyes to your chin is a sure sign that he is mentally preparing to punch you there.

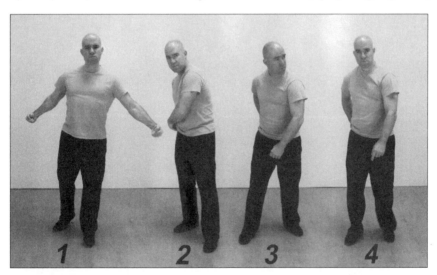

Preattack Indicators: 1) An aggressor is posturing by spreading his arms to make himself look as large and intimidating as possible. 2) He reaches for his beltline to access a potential weapon. 3) He looks around to check for potential witnesses. 4) He focuses on you with one hand held behind his back. While any one of these may be a serious cause for concern, when all these factors are taken into consideration, they indicate a serious and imminent threat.

Reality Check!

The stress resulting from the chaos and confusion of a self-defense encounter can cloud your judgment at a time when you cannot afford to make a poor decision. This is why it is important to put some thought into how you should best respond in certain situations before-hand. By contemplating various situations at your leisure, you'll be better prepared should you ever find yourself in similar circumstances.

What would you do if, while walking, someone blocked your path and demanded your valuables? Would you give them up? Run? Fight back? What if you were with a loved one, perhaps a child? How would your decision change if he were armed with a knife? What if he had a gun? What if he was not working alone?

Perhaps you have already decided that you would readily give up your valuables to an armed assailant. What if he and a buddy demanded you go down an alley? What if he ordered you into a vehicle? What if he told you to get into the trunk? What if your attacker wanted to tie you up? Would you comply? Where are your personal boundaries, the lines that you decide you ultimately *will not* cross?

After careful consideration, you might decide that you would rather take your chances getting stabbed or shot than allow yourself to be taken to a secondary location where he will have an even greater degree of control and privacy to enact his nefarious plans. Your deciding factor may be based on the answer to following question: are the consequences of your refusal to cooperate with your assailant(s) better or worse than the consequences you may face if you were to comply?

Level-2 Activities

Run

Running is a great activity to develop your stamina and cardiovascular fitness. Running on a trail develops your mental awareness as well. Being on an uneven, unpredictable surface makes you more conscious of every step you take, improving both your peripheral vision and coordination. In this way, trail running simultaneously improves your physical fitness and mental acuity.

Play Games

Unfortunately, many of us think we are too old to play games. Games are not only fun, they can be great ways to train! When you enjoy an activity, you will be more apt to engage in it and for longer periods of time. Luckily, there are several games that can effectively enhance your situational awareness. Although often regarded as "children's games," keep an open mind. They remain some of the best ways to enhance your avoidance skills. These games should be played both inside and outside, in a wide variety of conditions.

Tag

In the classic version of the game of tag, one (or sometimes more) players chase other players around a designated environment in an attempt to touch them with a hand. Traditionally, when a person is tagged, the tagger announces, "Tag, you're it!" and the two players switch roles. The classic version is only the tip of the iceberg. Make up variations to keep the game interesting and to work different skills. For example, you can develop your weapons skills by giving a child a short length of pool noodle and then challenging them to hit you with it. Don't worry, once you get hit, you can switch roles. I'll bet you still tire out before they do!

Hide-and-Seek

Hide-and-seek is a popular game in which players have a short time to conceal themselves in a given environment before being sought out by one or more other players. The seeker hides their eyes and counts to a predetermined number, at which time he or she yells, "Ready or not, here I come!" The game then begins. This is another great game to play with kids. A few rounds of hide-and-seek is one of the best ways I can think of to teach how to quickly identify and properly utilize cover and concealment.

Manhunt

In this variation of hide-and-seek, the seeker has to not only find the players but also tag them before they can reach a safety zone called "base." The players all run and hide before being sought out by whoever is "it." When a player is found, he or she has an opportunity to run for the safety of the base. If the player gets tagged before touching base, that player is removed from play while players who successfully make it to base without being caught are the winners. As with tag, feel free to experiment with different variations on this simple theme.

Contemplate "What if" Scenarios

I have this weird habit of sizing up attackers in elevators. I have been doing this for as long as I can remember. Once those doors close, and we're standing there in that awkward silence waiting to be whisked to our destination, I can't help but think, "What would I do if this guy, or these guys, attacked me?" I then play out various scenarios in my head until the doors open when I suddenly shift back to reality and go on my way.

Visualization is a powerful training tool that takes nothing but time. It can be done nearly anywhere, at nearly any time. "What if" scenarios are mental exercises where you speculate about how you might handle a given situation. For example, what if some type of emergency were to suddenly occur? I'll leave the specifics up to you. Where are the closest exits? How would you escape if that exit were blocked? What would you do if such and such person approached you? What weapons do you have at your disposal? Visualizing the details in your mind will help you get the most out of this exercise.

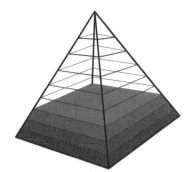

LEVEL 3
Building an Arsenal

Knowing is not enough; we must apply. Willing is not enough;
we must do.
—Bruce Lee

Part 1: Targeting

When you attack, you might only get one shot, so you'll need to make it count. This means not only knowing how to hit but precisely *where* to hit your attacker for maximum effect. The human body has several critical systems that are vulnerable to attack.

Since extreme stress causes a loss of fine motor control, you should target large vulnerable areas that affect specific, critical body systems. These include the visual system (eyes), circulatory system (neck), respiratory system (solar plexus), nervous system (face, groin, spine), and locomotor system (legs and feet).

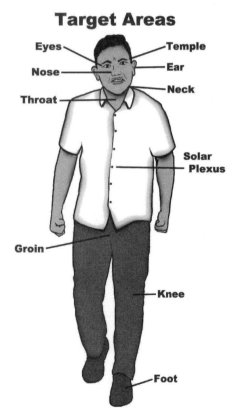

Target Areas

Eyes — Temple
Nose — Ear
Throat — Neck
Solar Plexus
Groin
Knee
Foot

Eyes

By far the most important sensory organs are the eyes. In fact, the average person perceives up to 80 percent of all external input by means of their sight.

The eyes also happen to be especially vulnerable targets. They are very sensitive to contact of any sort and susceptible to attack from virtually any angle. Striking the eyes with sufficient force will result in the attacker turning away as he covers his face with his hands. In addition to a great deal of pain, trauma

to the eye can cause involuntary tearing, effectively blinding your attacker temporarily.

Head

The head contains the brain and primary sensory organs, making it a prime target for self-defense. Besides the eyes, the human face is literally covered with sensitive tissue. Striking the nose can cause pain, bleeding, and tearing of the eyes resulting in temporary blindness. The bottom of the septum, located just below the nose, is very sensitive to upward pressure, and can be used to tilt the head back with just one finger. Striking the jaw or temple can render your attacker unconscious but requires that you strike with sufficient force from the correct angle. The cheeks, lips, and nose are vulnerable to hooking and ripping from the inside, while the ears can be slapped, twisted, and pulled.

Self-Defense Story: The Karate Kid

It was 1994. My girlfriend, Kathy (later my wife) and I were at a karate tournament in Richmond, Virginia. It was almost time for me to fight, so I went to the men's locker room to suit up. Suddenly, a student from another school burst in holding his face with his head tipped back. He hurried to the sink and started grabbing paper towels. I asked, "What happened to you?" At the sound of my voice, he looked sideways out of the corner of his eye, noticing me for the first time. We knew each other, and he rolled his eyes at me as he responded dejectedly, "Your girlfriend broke my nose."

Post-encounter Analysis: While not a real-life self-defense situation, this is an example of combat between a man and a much smaller woman. Since there were not very many competitors that day, the tournament coordinators combined divisions. My wife and this other gentleman were both brown belts, advanced rank students, so they were grouped together. Even though she was smaller, with one well-timed and well-placed punch to the face, she was victorious. Actually, she was disqualified for excessive contact, a breach of the tournament rules, but I think you get the idea.

It's not the size of the dog in the fight, it's the size of the fight in the dog.
—Mark Twain

Neck

The neck is vulnerable to strikes from almost any angle. In the front of the neck, the windpipe, or trachea, is exposed. Blunt force trauma to the trachea is a direct attack on the body's respiratory system that can result in difficulty breathing and possible death by asphyxiation.

Pressure to the side of the neck affects the circulatory system. When the blood vessels are squeezed shut, a special pressure receptor called the carotid sinus registers the increased blood pressure in the vessel. This triggers a reflex called a vagal response that causes an abrupt drop in blood pressure and a sudden reduction in heart rate. The resulting reduced blood flow to the brain causes lightheadedness, stunning or even knocking out your attacker.

Solar Plexus

The celiac plexus is a complex system of radiating nerves located deep within the body. Often referred to as the solar plexus, this spot is located just below the sternum; however, it lies too deep within the body to be vulnerable. A strike to this area actually attacks the diaphragm, a thin band of muscle that controls your breathing, contracting to inhale and relaxing to exhale. A forceful blow to the abdomen can cause the diaphragm to spasm, temporarily paralyzing it and making it difficult for your attacker to breathe.

Groin

The male genitalia are very sensitive. Striking the testicles can temporarily debilitate even the largest attacker. Common responses include increased heart rate, sweating, and a sudden rise in body temperature. The abdominal region shares pain receptors with the groin that can make the person involuntarily grab his stomach, bend over, or drop to the ground in the fetal position. This rush of severe pain and endorphin release can cause inner ear swelling, resulting in dizziness. The combination of abdominal pain, nausea, and dizziness can lead to vomiting. In extreme cases, part of the brain called the cervical sympathetic ganglia may activate, resulting in involuntary crying.

That said, men are notoriously good at instinctually guarding this vulnerable target. And, even if you *do* manage to score a solid shot to the groin, it can take several *long* seconds for the full effects to set in.

Spine

There are five sections of the spinal cord: cervical, thoracic, lumbar, sacrum, and coccyx. Each section of the spine protects different groups of nerves that control the body. The types of spinal cord injury depend on the section of the spine that is injured. Injuries located higher up on the spine are usually more severe. The top seven vertebrae make up the cervical spine. Cervical

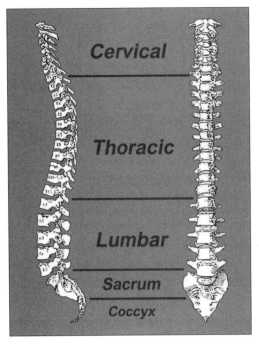

Parts of the spine.

injuries can result in full paralysis or even death. The next twelve vertebrae make up the thoracic spine. A sharp blow to the middle of the back, targeting the thoracic spinal cord, will cause pain to radiate into the arms, legs, and around the rib cage. It can also cause temporary leg weakness. From the lumbar down to the coccyx the spine becomes larger and not as vulnerable to attack.

Legs and Feet

The knees, shins, ankles, and feet are all vulnerable to attack. The knee is one of the most commonly injured body parts. A direct blow to the knee can cause an acute injury, often accompanied by an audible pop and intense pain that makes walking or weight bearing very difficult. The shin can be kicked or scraped with the edge of your foot. The ankle and foot are susceptible to blunt force trauma when attacked with a stomp.

Self-Defense Story: Stamping Out Predators

My cousin, Jenna, was in sixth grade when I decided to test her self-defense skills. I snuck up behind her at a holiday gathering and grabbed her in a bear hug, pinning her arms tightly against her body. I challenged her, "What are you going to do now?" I didn't even see her lift her right leg, but I sure felt it when her heel crashed down squarely onto the arch of my right foot. Not only was I caught by surprise, but it *hurt*! I immediately released her, asking, "Where did you learn that?"

"Gym class," she responded. "Some karate guy came in and taught us self-defense." I was impressed. Good job, karate guy!

Post-encounter Analysis: While I'm not sure that Jenna's foot stomp would have been enough to completely thwart a committed assault, it was certainly a *step* in the right direction.

Part 2: Offensive Techniques

Knowing where to hit is only part of the equation. You also need to know the right technique to attack a vulnerable target effectively. While the right technique is the one that works, there are certain techniques that work better than others. Those presented here have been chosen for their practicality and effectiveness. Of the plethora of techniques developed in the martial arts, these are the easiest to employ effectively with very little training. They make up the root movements from which you will create effective self-defense combinations.

Tiger Claw

The tiger claw is a versatile technique. The tips of your fingers can be used to poke, rake, or grab, while the palm of your hand can inflict blunt force trauma. Both work well, and it isn't an either-or situation. Go for the eyes and, if they miss, follow through with the palm strike. It is also a good set-up for grabbing and twisting an attacker's hair or ears, or fish hooking his nose or cheek (see Level 5). A tiger claw to the eyes can help to push an attacker away from or off of you. Use an inverted tiger claw to attack and grab the groin. Strike from wherever your hand happens to be in order to avoid telegraphing your strike.

A quick tiger claw to the eyes is a highly practical and effective technique.

The tiger claw to the eyes has a particularly high percentage of effectiveness. Five fingers multiplied by two eyes gives you ten opportunities for success with each strike. The tiger claw can be more effective than a punch because it poses less chance of injury to you while requiring minimal force to yield maximum results against your attacker. It can temporarily blind any attacker regardless of size or strength, making this the perfect technique for self-defense.

Self-Defense Story: The Baby Tiger

One year, I attended my martial art style's annual training camp with my family. My six-year-old daughter, Kayla, befriended another little girl her age, Naya. Naya's parents were also martial arts instructors whom I had known for years, and the girls spent the whole weekend playing together. I felt Naya knew me pretty well, so, on a whim, I decided to test her self-defense skills. I was just playing when I grabbed her around the waist and picked her up in front of me, asking loudly, "What would you do?!"

Without hesitation, Naya raised her right hand and scratched me straight down my face from forehead to chin. I dropped her like a hot potato, and she scampered off to continue playing. I, on the other hand, had to spend the rest of the weekend with scratch marks down my face. Naya's parents, John and Lucy, had taught her well.

Post-encounter Analysis: If you play with fire, don't be surprised when you get burned. Seriously, though, a six-year-old got the best of me. When I tell you these techniques are effective, it is because I know through personal experience. I paid for this knowledge with pain, which, I must admit, is an admirable teacher.

Palm Heel Strike

Palm heel strikes are effective because your arms are built to push things as well as absorb the impact of a fall with the palms of your hands. To execute a palm strike, pull your fingers back and drive the heel of your palm into the target. Force is generated by a sharp rotation of your hips that helps to drive your hand into the target, allowing you to get your body weight behind the strike.

Palm strikes are especially effective against the nose, mouth, or groin. High palm heel strikes should be thrown with your hand held vertically and your fingers pointing up, while low palm strikes are best executed with your fingers pointing downward.

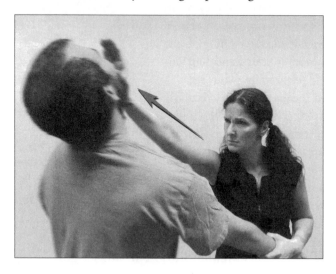

Making a Fist

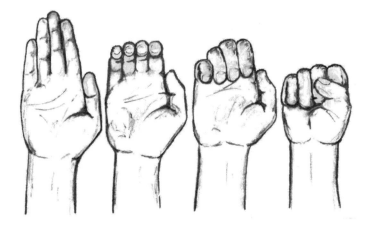

It is difficult to punch hard if you don't know how to make a proper fist. Beginning with your little finger, bend each digit in succession, pressing the tips firmly into the palm as close to their bases as possible. Your thumb is then folded tightly over your index and middle fingers. Keep your wrist straight so that the top of your forearm and the back of your hand form a straight line, which intersects the front of your fist at a 90-degree angle. The feeling should be one of a solid mass with no empty space within, your wrist becoming solid and immovable as well.

Punch

Striking with the clenched fist is one of the most common forms of attack. The striking surface consists of the biggest two knuckles, an area known as the fore fist.

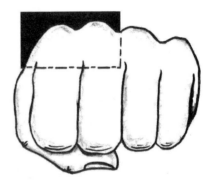

Punching can be risky because, if you hit incorrectly, you can break your hand. The harder you hit and the less you know about punching, the more likely this becomes.

Hammer Fist

The hammer fist is the underside of your clenched fist.

Swing your arm as though your clenched fist were the head of a hammer, striking in the same way you might pound your fist on a table or wall.

Unlike a punch with the fore fist, the hammer fist delivers a strong strike while presenting very little risk of injury to you.

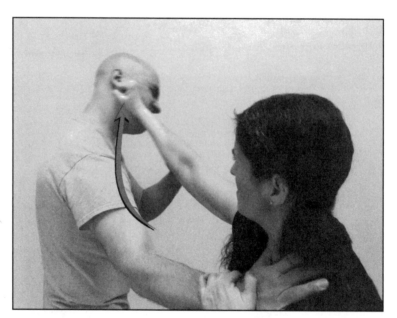

A hammer fist to the jaw. Note how the defender has secured the attacker's hand. This not only helps control him but can add power to your strike as well.

Chop

The karate chop is a powerful strike delivered with the edge of the hand, a position known as the knife hand. The most common target for this strike is the neck. To form a knife hand, extend your fingers and hold them firmly together, tucking your thumb tightly against the side of your hand. Keep your wrist straight so the back of your hand and top of your forearm form a straight line. A line of tension should run up 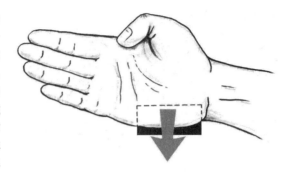 the outer edge of your arm and along the little-finger side of your hand. Swing your knife hand in a shallow arc toward the target, striking with the lower, outer edge of the heel of your hand.

The chop is not merely an arm technique; it's a whole-body technique. In addition to the chopping action of your striking arm, you generate force for the strike through a sharp rotation of your hips. A last-second rotation of the hand can add considerable force to the technique and is crucial for a focused, snappy chop. Keep your chopping arm bent slightly to add power to your strike and avoid hyperextending your elbow. You can chop with your hand held palm down, from the inside outward, or palm up, originating outside of and heading toward your centerline.

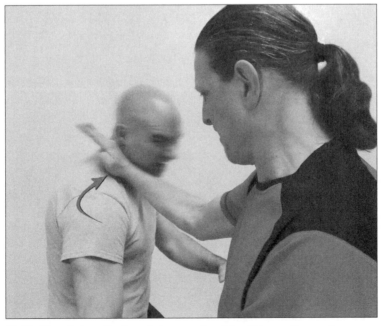

Knife Hand: A well-placed chop to the side of the neck can stun or even knock out an attacker.

Spear Hand

The spear hand is formed in much the same way as the knife hand, but the striking surface is different. The spear hand is a finger thrust made with a stabbing motion into the target.

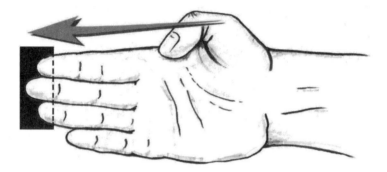

Your fingers must be held tightly together with your thumb bent and held firmly against your hand. Your fingers should be tensed and slightly bent. This ensures that, under pressure, your fingers will curl inward toward your palm rather than painfully bending backward. The spear hand is most effective when aimed at soft targets on your attacker's body such as his eyes or throat.

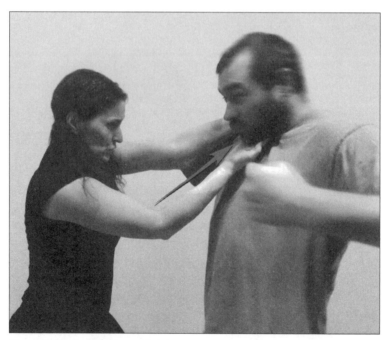

Spear Hand: A strike to the throat with the tips of the fingers. Note how the defender has grabbed her attacker's neck with her other hand, pulling him into her strike.

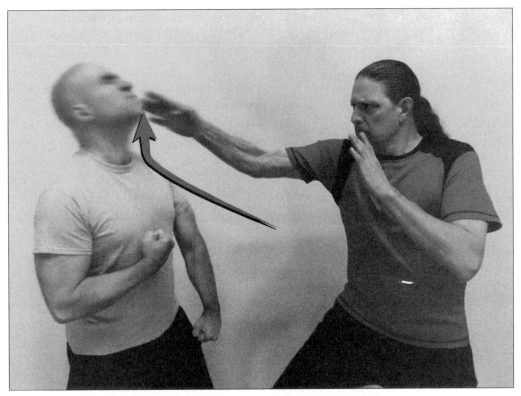

Finger Flick: A quick strike to the eyes can temporarily blind an attacker.

Finger Flick

You can also flick your fingers into an attacker's eye. The motion is not unlike that of snapping a dishtowel. Begin by driving the back of your wrist forward, leading your relaxed hand toward your target. When your wrist comes to within six to eight inches from the target, pull your arm back, causing your fingers to snap forward with a whipping motion, striking with the backs of your fingers, particularly the tips.

Elbow Strikes

Your elbows are some of your most powerful weapons, capable of delivering devastating blows to your attacker. Not all elbow strikes impact the target with the point of the elbow. Some strike with the outer edge of your forearm or back of your upper arm but are still classified as elbow strikes.

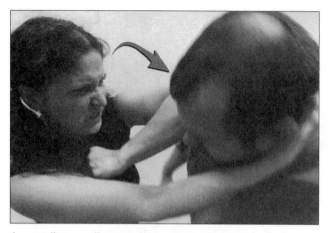

A roundhouse elbow strike to the head. Note how the defender is bracing his head with her other hand, holding it still to increase the power of her strike.

Roundhouse Elbow Strike

The roundhouse elbow strike is a close-range technique. It is extremely powerful and makes an effective finishing technique. To execute a roundhouse elbow strike, bend your arm and swing your elbow in an arc toward the target, striking with the bony ridge on the lower outer edge of your forearm. A roundhouse elbow strike makes a good set-up for an inner chop.

Back Roundhouse Elbow

The back roundhouse elbow strike is the reverse motion of the front roundhouse. The striking surface is the back of your elbow, the same surface used when you rest your elbows on a table. The back roundhouse elbow strike is an effective defense against someone who is close behind you.

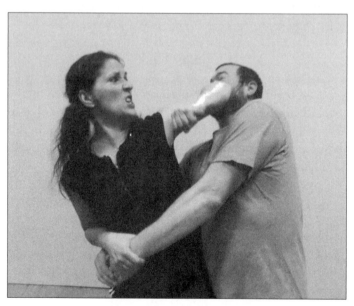

Back Roundhouse Elbow Strike: This attacker got more than he bargained for. Note how the defender grasps the attacker's wrist to keep him from moving with the hit, therefore adding power to her strike.

Downward Elbow Strike

The downward elbow strike is used to finish a doubled-over attacker. Begin the motion by raising your hand high above your head, then quickly drive your elbow down into the target. As you do, slide one foot sideways. Wide feet allow you to get your body weight behind your strike. Use the point of your elbow to target the attacker's spine between his shoulder blades.

A Downward Elbow Strike: Target the thoracic spine. Note how the defender has jumped in the air to add power to her strike.

Self-Defense Story: A Busted Lip

One day, at the very beginning of a martial arts practice, we were warming up with some very light sparring. I was working with my student, Pavlo, and managed to turn him enough to slip behind him and take his back. As I did, he spun and unintentionally caught me in the mouth with his elbow. I immediately let him go and put my hand to my mouth. It came back bloody. I bent over and thick drops of dark red blood started splattering on the mat. My tooth had punched a hole nearly all the way through my lip. I ended up going to the emergency room where I got three stitches outside my mouth and two more inside my lip.

Post-encounter Analysis: While this wasn't an actual self-defense situation, it clearly demonstrates the effectiveness of the technique. Pavlo wasn't even trying to hit me with his elbow. It was an accident. Yet, if it had been real and he had taken the opportunity to run away or turn and continue striking me, there was little I could have done about it.

Knee Strike

The knee strike is used when fighting in close to attack your attacker's thigh, groin, solar plexus, or head. Raise your leg swiftly and strongly, thrusting your fully bent knee up and forward into the target. At the same time, bring your hands down sharply to pull your attacker into the strike. Use the spring of your supporting leg and hip to add power to the technique.

A knee strike to the head can hit harder than any punch. Note how the defender is pulling her attacker's head down and into the strike.

Front Kick

The front kick is a powerful, natural motion that can be used to attack a variety of targets. To execute a front kick, shift your body's center of gravity directly over your supporting foot while raising your kicking knee into a ready position on a line between your hip and your intended target. Flow smoothly through this position, straightening your leg with a strong snapping motion. Thrust your hips forward slightly to add range and power to your kick.

Keep your ankle straight and fully extended. You can strike with the ball of your foot by pulling your toes back as far as possible toward your shin. You can also strike with the top of your foot, hitting with the instep and shin. To do this, point your toes and strike your attacker's groin from underneath. Both work equally well.

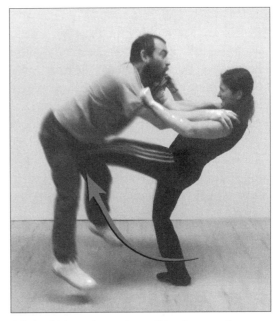

A front kick to the groin, striking from underneath with the shin and instep.

Roundhouse Kick

A roundhouse kick is performed like a front kick, only turned on its side. It is used to strike targets on a horizontal angle. It can be used to attack the knees, groin, or abdomen. Begin by turning the toes of your supporting foot outward as you lift your kicking leg to your side. Bend your knee and pull the heel of your kicking foot close to your buttock. Aim your kicking knee at your target and snap your lower leg out. As you do, pivot on the ball of your supporting foot until your heel points at your target and turn your hip into the kick. Like the front kick, you can point your toes and strike with your shin or instep, or strike with the ball of the foot.

Roundhouse Kick: A kick to the solar plexus can knock the wind out of your attacker.

Stamping Kick

Stamping kicks are typically used to attack your attacker's knees and disable his locomotor system. To chamber for a stamping kick, raise your knee high into a ready position with your foot fully flexed, ankle bent with your toes pulled back toward your shin. The kick can be performed at any angle: to the front, sides, or behind you. While you can strike with your heel, turning your foot and striking with the outer edge of your foot provides you with a broader striking surface, making it easier to strike the knee, shin, or instep of your attacker. As with all kicks, keep your supporting leg bent slightly to maintain your balance and absorb the shock of the impact with your target. After striking the target, you should either withdraw your knee quickly or continue through your target, either blowing out his knee or scraping your foot down his shin to stomp powerfully on his foot. The stamping kick is an excellent self-defense technique because it is an effective attack that can be performed even in restrictive street clothes and shoes.

Side Stamping Kick: A strike to the knee can end an assault as quickly as it began. Again, note how the defender is pulling her assailant into her attack.

Voice

Since most assailants do not want to draw unwanted attention to their crime, your best weapon throughout the entire encounter may be your voice. As soon as you realize you are being assaulted, you should start yelling loudly to alert others. Use phrases such as "Let me *go! Leave me alone! Someone help me! Call the police! Use your camera, film his face!" You can even yell, "I've hit my panic button! The police are on their way!" It does not matter if you really have a personal emergency device or not (although carrying one is highly recommended), as sometimes the threat alone will be enough to make the attacker retreat.

Battle Cry

Warriors in nearly every country around the globe use a battle cry to strike fear into the hearts of their enemies. In the Japanese martial arts, this loud shout is called a *kiai*. It is neither a word nor a scream but something more akin to a roar. A proper kiai originates from your diaphragm and forces the air from your lungs and through your larynx.

Your battle cry is an effective tool for self-defense, serving to startle and intimidate your attacker, momentarily turning the tables and putting him on the defensive. A loud yell also aids in mustering your strength and bolstering your confidence.

Researchers at Iowa State University studied the effects of the kiai and found that yelling actually does make you stron-

One of my students, a karate black belt, uses karate black belt uses a kiai to maximize her focus and power when breaking a set of wooden boards.

ger. When subjects made a short shout before squeezing a dynamometer (a device used to measure grip strength), they showed a temporary increase in strength over trials when they did not employ a kiai.[1]

Now, *that's* worth shouting about!

1. Mark Adam Tscampl, "The Use of Ki to 'Psych Up' and Increase Strength" (master's thesis, Iowa State University, 2009), https://lib.dr.iastate.edu/cgi/viewcontent.cgi?article=1664&context=etd.

Part 3: Defensive Techniques

An attacker is not just going to stand there and let you hit him. He's going to try to dominate both the situation and *you*. Therefore, no arsenal would be complete without some defensive techniques to help you counter your attacker's attacks long enough to land some of your own and escape. Defensive techniques can be divided into two main groups: escapes from grabs and countering strikes.

Escaping from a Grab

An attacker who is trying to dominate you will often grab your wrists in order to control your arms. Understanding how to get out of a stronger grip is a matter of understanding the structure of the grabbing hand. The weakest part of his grasp is the gap between his thumb and forefinger. Therefore, to escape a grab, you'll need to slip out through this opening.

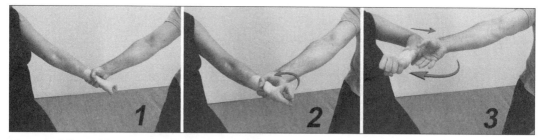

Turn and Snap: 1) An assailant has grabbed your wrist. 2) Rotate your arm so that the narrowest profile of your wrist lines up with the gap between the attacker's thumb and forefinger. 3) Then drive your elbow toward his elbow to snap your wrist out of his grasp.

Over/Under-Pop: 1) An assailant grasps your wrist. 2) Slip your hand either over or under the attacker's wrist and then push against his arm sharply with your palm to lever out of his grasp.

Clap and Turn

Two hands are better than one! Clasp your hands together and twist your whole body away to lever your arm out of his grasp. He'll have a difficult time resisting the force generated by your legs and body.

Clap and Turn: 1) An attacker grabs you with both hands. 2) Bring your free hand to your trapped one then clasp your hands firmly. 3) Slide your rear foot back. 4) Twist your body sharply and use your hips to rip your wrist from his grasp.

Windmill

This move allows you to get the momentum of your whole body behind the release.

Windmill: 1) An assailant grabs your neck. 2) Lift your arm, extending your shoulder as high as possible. 3) Twist your body, clearing his arms with your extended arm. 4) Keep your arm up as you escape his grasp and run away.

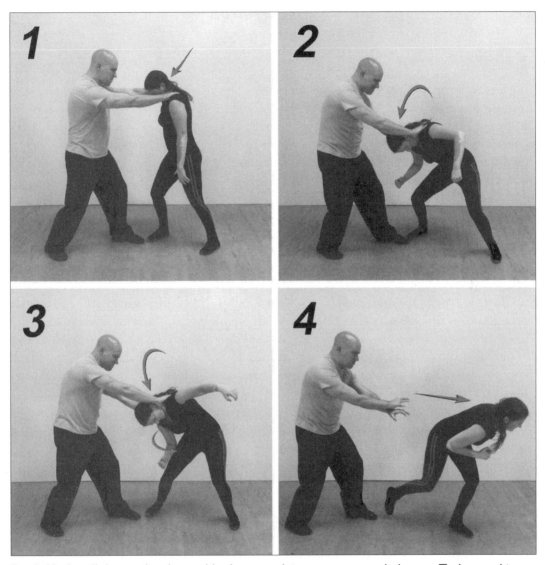

Duck Under: 1) An assailant has grabbed your neck in an attempt to choke you. Tuck your chin to your chest and shrug your shoulders to your ears. 2) Step back and duck your head directly between his hands. 3) As soon as your head is under the level of his arms, twist your body to slip your neck out of his grasp. 4) Turn and run, but keep an eye over your shoulder to watch for pursuit and act accordingly.

Countering Strikes

When some people get frustrated and upset, they get to the point where they start to hit things. If you are the focus of their frustration, expect that they may attempt to hit *you*. Striking attacks such as punches and slaps can be very unsettling, even when they do not do significant damage. Therefore, strive to stay calm and keep your head in the game. Your primary goal should be to minimize taking damage by countering his strikes. The first step to countering strikes, however, is understanding the strengths and weaknesses of the neutral guard and how to use it. Once we've done that, we can explore the three different ways to counter a strike: evading, parrying, and blocking.

Revisiting the Neutral Guard

The neutral guard should be considered your stance prior to an altercation becoming physical. The neutral guard position, introduced in Level 2, has several functions, both defensive and offensive in nature.

As mentioned previously, defensively, your hands in the neutral guard create a cage that protects your flanks. Since your attacker's hands are his primary weapons, you need to control them. Maintain your distance, staying just outside of the attacker's effective striking range. Stand fairly square, taking care not to be turned at close range, which not only deactivates your rear hand but also exposes your back to a grappler. Offensively, your hands are held away from your body, placing them halfway to their targets if you decide you need to launch an attack.

How you approach any self-defense situation will depend on your mindset. Keeping an open mind means staying calm and focused, not getting preoccupied or distracted. Use your awareness skills to read your attacker and anticipate his intentions. Keep an eye out for the threat indicators and subtle telegraphs that precede an attack, such as cocking an arm.

You only have two arms, making it impossible for you to defend your entire body at any given time. The neutral guard places your arms so that they cover your vulnerable flanks, protecting you from the dreaded haymaker (a wild hook punch). At the same time, it exposes your center to attack. This psychologically controls the attacker's decision-making process. The idea is to simplify the situation, making it more predictable by limiting the variables, particularly the ways he can attack. Since your hand position covers your sides, your attacker does not have a clear line of attack for a wide hook punch. Therefore, he is more likely to launch an attack up the center, between your hands.

Choice reaction time is the amount of time it takes you to decide from a given set of options. The fewer options you have, the less time it should take you to decide on an effective course of action. By cutting down on your attacker's attack options, you also minimize your choice response time by limiting the number of attacks for which you need to be on the lookout and prepared.

In the neutral guard, your arms and hands are in a good position for both defense and offense. Defensively, they are in a good position to check your attacker's arms and hands to defend against his attacks. Offensively, your open hands, although they appear benign, are already halfway to their targets.

Evasion

Evading a strike altogether prevents you from taking any damage, physically or psychologically, while still maintaining all four limbs for defense or attack. You can evade a strike by backing up, leaning out of range, or ducking. While avoidance may be the best choice, it can also be the hardest to pull off successfully.

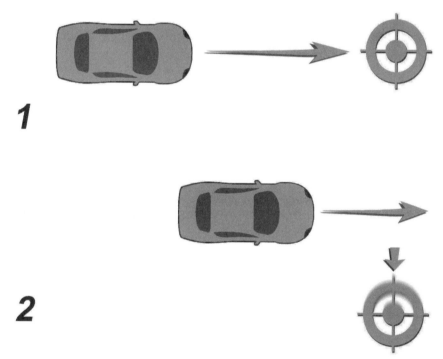

Evasion: This illustration uses a car to demonstrate the idea of evasion. 1) The gray car is on course to hit its intended target. 2) At the last second, the target moves, and the car is unable to correct in time to hit it.

Fade back: 1) An aggressor chambers to punch you in the head.
2) When he does, lean back, out of the range of his punch.

Duck: 1) The threat telegraphs a hook punch targeting your head.
2) Bend your knees to drop straight down, avoiding his punch.

Parrying

Parrying is the second-best option when it comes to countering strikes because it requires the use of one hand. Parrying involves redirecting the attacker's attack away from its intended target, preventing you from getting struck, but allows it to keep moving along an altered trajectory. It is superior to blocking because a successful parry stands a good chance of throwing your attacker off balance or breaking his rhythm, allowing you an opportunity to counterattack. Successful parrying requires anticipation and good timing.

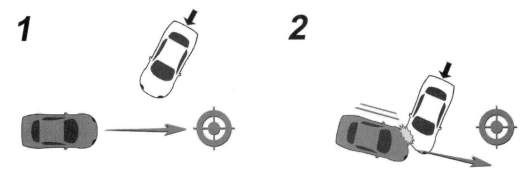

Parrying: 1) The gray car is on a collision course with the target. 2) When the cars hit, both cars continue to move, but the gray car's trajectory has been redirected slightly, so it will no longer hit its intended target.

Outside Parry

With your flanks protected, you can focus the majority of your attention on detecting and countering any linear attacks directed up your centerline. Defend against these by parrying them with the palm of your open hand, redirecting them with short, sharp slapping motions.

Using the same-side hand, contact your attacker's punch on the outside of his arm with the palm of your hand, pushing it across your centerline. Take care not to let your parry move beyond the line of your other hand. After parrying, snap your hand back to the neutral guard position.

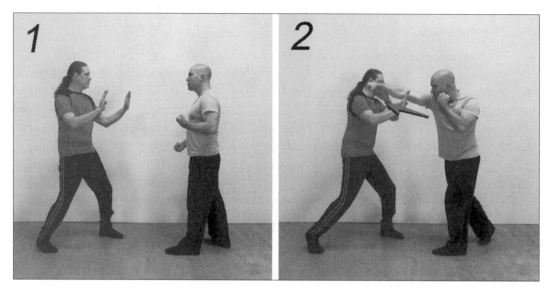

Parrying a Jab: I) Your attacker fires a shot right up the middle, between your hands. 2) Use the same-side hand to parry the punch across your center.

You can use an outside parry to gain control of the attacker's attacking limb. As you push his arm off the line of attack, use your free hand to grab his wrist. This momentarily turns his center away from you, allowing you to counterattack.

Blocking

The simplest and often least desirable method of countering a strike is blocking. Blocking requires the use of at least one limb, and, even when performed properly, you are still likely to sustain at least *some* damage from the strike. That is because, when blocking, you are using a part of your body to stop the attacker's energy by absorbing the force of the blow, bringing the attacker's attack to a sudden and abrupt halt. Blocking requires that you create a strong structure capable of withstanding the attack. This is accomplished through proper body positioning and aided by body conditioning exercises.

When blocking, don't confuse defense with passivity. Act decisively and with confidence. By moving into the attack, you can turn a defensive movement into a decisive technique. Defend and attack with your whole body. Begin every move with your hips, employing maximum force to deter further attack.

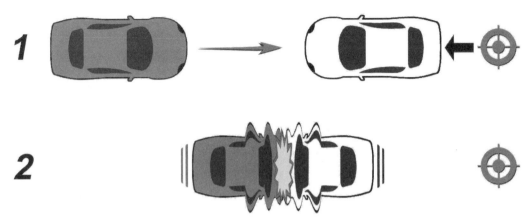

Blocking: This car crash illustrates the concept behind blocking. 1) The gray car is on a collision course with its target, but the white car moves to intercept it. 2) The cars meet head on, and their energy cancels each other out, preventing the gray car from reaching its target.

Inside Block

The inside block is an efficient defensive action that requires very little energy to execute. It is similar in appearance to karate's famous knife hand block and is very effective against wide, arcing attacks, such as a face slap or a hook punch. Hold your arms in neutral guard, which allows you to defend against arcing hook punches without major repositioning. The haymaker is an especially dangerous attack because it approaches from outside of your field of vision, making it difficult to see coming and difficult to block if your hands are not already in position.

When an assailant attacks you with a wide swing, usually referred to as a hook punch or haymaker, use your same-side hand to block his arm's path toward its target. Your hand should not move very much from the neutral guard position. Keep your palm facing out and contact the inside of the attacker's arm with the bony ridge on the outer edge of your forearm. Take care not to make a big motion or over block by straightening your elbow as this can leave you open and vulnerable. All that is required is a small pulse to stop your attacker's punch dead in its tracks. Having blocked your attacker's punch, you are not only in range, but you are also in a dominant inside position. This puts you in the perfect position to launch a counterattack. Take advantage of the opportunity and quickly respond with an attack of your own. Your counter should be so fast that it lands while your attacker's punch is still in contact with your blocking arm.

Blocking a Hook Punch: 1) The attacker squares off, and you assume the neutral guard. 2) As he throws a hook punch aimed at your head, block his punch with the same-side arm.

Low Inside Block

The inside block can also be performed low to defend your abdomen against kicks, knees, and uppercuts. As in the high version, block with the same-side arm, only now you are dropping it down and across the attacker's leg or arm, blocking with the boney ridge on the outer edge of your forearm. In the martial arts, this motion is often referred to as a low block.

Low Inside Block: 1) Drop your forearm across your attacker's thigh to block a knee strike. 2) You can also use the low block to defend against an uppercut.

Even though evasion is preferable to parrying or blocking, there will be times when you will, and should, employ a parry or block to counter a strike, so practice them all. My purpose in ranking them was only to deepen your understanding by pointing out the distinctions among the three.

Reality Check!

Here's the bad news: if things get physical there is a good chance that you are going to get hit. It's probably going to hurt. The shock, surprise, and pain will throw you off your game. The good news is that the damage is probably not as bad as it seems. You are not made of glass. Muscle and bone can be very resilient. Don't let damage, actual or perceived, stop you from thinking and acting effectively to ensure your safety.

Full Defensive Cover

The full cover is a temporary solution useful for warding off a vicious barrage of punches. Protect your chin by tucking it to your chest and raising your shoulders to your ears, like a turtle pulling its head into its shell. Cup your open hands over your head, just above your ears, keeping your elbows close together in front of you. Bend over slightly to protect your midsection.

It is important to recognize that the full defensive cover is only a temporary position allowing you to survive through the defensive reaction phase long enough to understand that you are under attack. You must then force yourself into the recovery stage by switching from defensive mode to counterattack mode. Explode out of the freeze and either run or retake the initiative by exploding into your own offensive barrage of strikes.

Level-3 Activities

Physical Fitness

Since a violent assault is a physical confrontation, your physical fitness level will play an important role in determining your success or failure in a self-defense situation. Muscular strength in your legs helps you to stand strong, kick hard, and run fast, while a strong core and arms will lend power to your strikes. The most common method for developing muscular strength is through a weight-training regime.

Likewise, a high level of cardiovascular fitness may be required. This is your body's ability to deliver oxygen to the working muscles to keep them from burning out so you can stay in the fight and survive it. Regular participation in aerobic activities such as jogging, cycling, swimming, hiking, soccer, basketball, or tennis will help you improve your cardiovascular fitness.

Hitting Things

Striking does not come naturally. If your techniques are going to be effective, you need to practice hitting things. Take the time to train and develop your striking ability. Practice your techniques against commercial products such as focus mitts or a heavy bag. You can also use an improvised striking target, such as a large pillow or seat cushion. Hitting things will eventually condition your fingers, hands, and wrists. In the beginning you will want to protect your hands with a pair of light, padded bag gloves. Practice to the point where effective, accurate striking becomes automatic. Perform each technique a minimum of ten times on each side. Start hitting softly, increasing the speed and force of your strikes as you become more comfortable and confident in your abilities. Take care not to injure yourself. Gradually build your skills over several sessions.

Building Combinations

Once you feel comfortable throwing single techniques in isolation, begin putting several together into logical, effective sequences. Shadow box by punching the air or hit a heavy bag or other target.

Training with a Partner

You also want to practice aiming your techniques at vulnerable targets on a living person. When practicing, remember to respect your partner. Make it understood that you are trying to practice your techniques in a controlled manner and not performing full-force applications as you would in a true self-defense situation. Ask your partner to attack you slowly, with only a fraction of their full speed and power. If this is still too fast, ask your partner to please slow down or go softer until you can perform the technique successfully. Execute your techniques strongly, but for your partner's sake, pull them just short of striking their intended targets. Thank your partner before and after the exercise to express your gratitude for their trust, time, and energy.

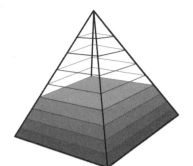

LEVEL 4
Action!

Don't hit at all if it is honorably possible to avoid hitting;
but never hit softly.
—Theodore Roosevelt

The Four Rs of Self-Defense

Despite your best efforts, you have been unable to avoid or verbally de-escalate the situation. An aggressor has demonstrated clear intent to cause you harm. He has the means and the opportunity. Now is the time for action.

The next steps you take next need to be aimed at quickly ending a physical altercation. Your decisions and actions should be based on good information and sound judgment. The Four R's of Self-Defense encapsulate the wisdom that should guide your actions in a fight. They are:

1. Right Time
2. Right Place
3. Right Technique
4. Right Perspective/Run

Part 1: Right Time

Knowing the right time to strike is critical. You basically have three options: hitting before the attacker attacks, striking at the same time that your attacker attacks, or counterattacking after the attacker has already attacked you.

Preemptive Attack

By its very name, self-defense should be defensive. This is often interpreted to mean that that one should never strike first in self-defense. While this sounds good in theory, in reality it is impractical and unwise to wait until you are potentially taking damage before you can engage in active, physical resistance. Legally, you are permitted to engage an attacker once

Preemptive Attack: An aggressor has shown enough threat indicators that you firmly believe an attack is inevitable and your life is in danger, justifying you to strike first.

you have perceived enough threat indicators to justify your actions as necessary to protect you from physical harm.

Attacking before the attacker launches his attack gives you the element of surprise, throwing him off balance mentally and psychologically as well as physically. Since action beats reaction, the initiator will almost always have an advantage. If that person is you, you will have shock and surprise on your side. You may even cause your attacker to momentarily freeze.

Strike First. Strike Hard. No Mercy.
—Motto of Cobra Kai Karate

Do unto others before they do unto you.
—Terry Pratchett

Simultaneous Attack

If you are quick, you can counterattack at the same moment your attacker moves to strike you. Attacking at the same time as your attacker requires that you remain aware of his actions. This means closely monitoring and correctly interpreting the threat indicators that allow you to anticipate and mentally prepare for his attack. When it comes, your actions have to provide you with adequate defense against his attack while simultaneously allowing you to effectively counterattack him.

That sounds like a lot to accomplish in the heat of the moment. However, it need not be as hard as it seems. Thinking simply is the key. Your advantage lies in knowing what moves will give you the most bang for your buck and reliably deliver results. The key is to consistently train hard to develop and hone your self-defense skills, mentally as well as physically.

Grabbing attacks offer the easiest opportunity for simultaneous attack. Your attacker has grabbed you with one or both hands, presumably to restrain or control you. This strategy is his weakness. If he does not gain immediate and complete control of you, it gets him close and opens him up for an effective and unexpected counterattack.

Simultaneous Attack: 1) An aggressor has grabbed your shirt, bringing him in range and opening him up for a front snap kick to the groin. 2) Parrying a punch allows you to defend while simultaneously attacking your attacker's eyes.

Counterattack

A violent attack is basically an ambush. An assailant has caught you by surprise and attacked, leaving you no choice but to protect yourself. The best way out of an ambush it to fight your way out of the attacker's kill zone. This requires that you counter your attacker's initial attack before launching an attack of your own. Then, a rapid, efficient, and effective return of aggression is probably your best chance for success.

Counterattacking: 1) Cover up to block an attacker's punch. 2) Then drop his sensory grid with an unexpected strike to his eyes.

Part 2: Right Place

The term "right place" has two meanings. The first addresses targeting, knowing where to attack your attacker's body for maximum physical and psychological effect. You already learned about your attacker's most vulnerable targets in Part 1 of Level 3. The second meaning describes controlling the area around you and leveraging the environment to your advantage.

Location

If you have any control over where an encounter occurs, look for the most advantageous place to make your stand, such as high ground. High ground can be any area of elevated terrain, like up a flight of stairs. Being in an elevated position puts your attacker at your kicking level while limiting his ability to strike you. Walls, corners, doorways, and other obstacles each offer their own unique set of advantages and disadvantages. For example, a wall can be a detriment when it limits your mobility, but it can be advantageous if it offers you concealment, cover, or a solid base against which you can push. Strive to quickly identify and leverage the potential advantages of any given location while simultaneously mitigating the potential disadvantages.

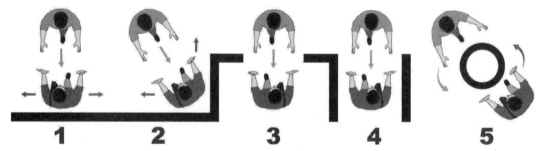

Environmental Factors: Common architectural features you might encounter include 1) walls, 2) interior corners, 3) doorways, 4) narrow hallways, 5) or obstacles.

Walls

Since walls are such an integral part of almost any building, they are very common architectural features. Generally speaking, interior walls are of far lighter construction than exterior walls, which are made stronger to endure the elements. All walls have some advantages and disadvantages that should be considered for self-defense.

Advantages: You have lateral mobility, so an escape to the sides is an option. Before escaping, you could let the attacker rush in, then duck away and to the side to smash him against the wall, preferably face-first, by simply borrowing his own forward momentum.

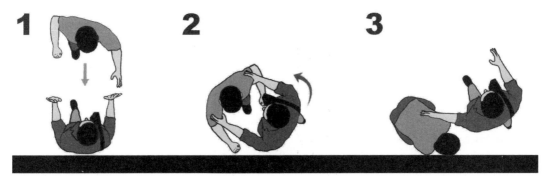

Wall Slam: 1) An attacker rushes in with a punch. 2) Use lateral movement to escape to the side. 3) As you duck sideways, use his own momentum to smash him against the wall, giving you an opportunity to escape.

Disadvantages: With your back to the wall, you can get pinned, limiting your mobility and ability to defend yourself.

Corners

Like walls, corners can be inside or outside. However, unlike walls, "inside or outside corners" describes the intersection of the walls. Think of it this way: you can get trapped in an interior corner, and you can hit your head on an exterior corner. Our discussion here will be concerning interior corners.

Advantages: You have a strong brace against which you can root and press off, preferably with your legs. Brace one foot against the corner and kick out.

Disadvantages: Your mobility is greatly limited in this scenario. The angle of escape is half of what it was in the previous scenario, when you were up against a flat wall.

Doorways

Any entrance to an area, room, or building can be considered a doorway. Some have doors and some do not. In most circumstances, it is beneficial to close an open door between you and your attacker to create an obstacle and maintain distance.

Advantages: An open doorway makes a good choke point. There is only one way for the assailant to get at you, and that's directly through the "fatal funnel"[1] created by the doorway. This makes it easier to defend yourself by limiting a would-be attacker's mobility and target availability. If possible, block his ability to get through the doorway and escape in the opposite direction. Look for short sections of wall on either side of the doorway that you can use

1. A fatal funnel is a law enforcement term for a doorway that allows someone to be seen easily but that makes it hard to get out of when being shot at or having other projectiles hurled at you.

to your advantage. If you can conceal yourself behind one, you can smash the assailant against the far wall when he rushes in

Disadvantages: Tight quarters restrict your mobility. You don't want to get trapped somewhere with no avenue for escape.

Hallways

Hallways are narrow spaces that have their own unique set of logistical attributes.

Advantages: A narrow corridor can be a mobility limiter but also serves as a centerline concentrator. If your assailant doesn't know how to occupy and hold the center and you do, you have a lot of advantage here. Since you don't have much room to either side, use linear techniques like front kicks to fill the low line and tiger claw strikes to occupy and control the high line.

Disadvantages: Your assailant is not the only one whose mobility is limited by the narrow confines of the hallway. Yours is, too. Unless you can disable your opponent, perhaps by dropping his sensor grid with a quick strike to the eyes and ducking past him, you only have one avenue of escape.

Obstacles

You can create an obstacle by maneuvering to place something between you and your assailant, such as a table, planter, chair, or even a slick spot on the floor.

Advantages: Obstacles can offer cover and concealment. If that object is high, such as a floor-to-ceiling column, then your attacker can't see around it. If the object is low, like a table in a restaurant, then he can't see your feet, allowing you to set up for a quick low-line attack or an escape that doesn't telegraph. This scenario allows for a lot of movement laterally and backward. If the object is low enough, it can allow mobility across it as well.

Disadvantages: Your attacker is on equal ground: the advantages mentioned above are also the same advantages your attacker could leverage against you. The key would be to maximize your advantages and minimize his by controlling the ground game through superior footwork, or, if possible, by shoving that object into your attacker to do some damage and cut down his mobility.

Part 3: Right Technique

By applying the scientific method, one can determine which techniques are most dependable, demonstrating the highest degree of repeatable results. Unlike heroes on television and in movies who consistently knock out villains with a single blow, you cannot depend on disabling or even discouraging an attacker with a single strike. Therefore, you should plan to attack in combinations of multiple techniques that flow smoothly into each other. Since every shot needs to elicit maximum effect, targeting is crucial. Strikes need to be chosen for maximum effect and reliability.

Necessity Is the Mother of Invention

In 2016, a gentleman with an interesting problem contacted me. His wife and daughter were both visually impaired, and given their vulnerable condition, he was very concerned that they learn to defend themselves. Since I had written a book on staff fighting, he was hoping I could give him some advice on how to effectively utilize the long white cane, a tool commonly utilized by people with impaired vision, in self-defense.

He sent me an assortment of canes, and I began testing with my advanced rank students. We took turns playing the role of attacker and blindfolded defender. After running through countless scenarios over the next couple of weeks, we discovered some interesting facts. First, the cane was almost useless as a preemptive tool. Attackers were consistently able to maneuver past it before a threat warranting its use could be perceived.

Two of my students working through scenarios to help develop a self-defense program for the visually impaired. Note the blindfold the victim is wearing. The gear her attacker is wearing was necessary since the victim was encouraged to react realistically, including striking with the cane.

What was needed was a quick combination of super techniques, capable of inflicting significant damage even against a larger and stronger attacker. Furthermore, the defense had to be performed one handed since the victim's other hand had to retain a hold on the cane. And of course the techniques needed to be consistently effective even when blindfolded. What I was looking for was some sort of Grand Unified Theory for Self-defense, and after several weeks of testing, I found what I was looking for. I call the result of that study and experimentation the Tiger Claw Set of Self-Defense.

The Tiger Claw Set

The Tiger Claw Set is an easily learned combination of four strikes that individually have a high probability of success in a wide variety of situations. The overall strategy is to neutralize your attacker's fighting ability by attacking several critical body systems in rapid succession. It is designed to finish your attacker in the fewest possible moves while leaving few openings, in either time or space, for him begin to mount a defense. Having a combination that is functional in a wide range of situations minimizes your choice reaction time, allowing you to respond faster and more effectively.

The combination systematically attacks four key bodily systems: visual, circulatory, respiratory, and nervous in quick succession. Since the high stress of a self-defense situation can cause you to lose much of your fine motor control, each movement is a large, gross motor action that attacks a relatively large, vulnerable target area. These techniques are then linked in such a way that they not only flow naturally into one another but also build on the success (or failure) of the previous technique.

The standard combination has only four moves: tiger claw, chop, knee, and elbow. Each has been carefully chosen for maximum effectivity. The principle behind the Tiger Claw Set is simple: drop your attacker's primary sensor system at the earliest opportunity before striking other various vulnerable targets until you can escape to safety.

The first attack, the tiger claw, is a linear strike that targets the attacker's eyes. The visual system provides the brain with 80 percent of external stimuli, so impairing his vision will prevent him from mounting a strong defense. The combination of your five fingers and his two eyes gives you ten chances to score with a single strike, giving this technique a very high chance of success. A solid hit will often immediately inflict a great deal of pain as well as deprive your attacker of his major source of sensory input, making it momentarily difficult for him to continue attacking you or defending himself effectively. This shocking surprise attack has a good chance of discouraging all but the most determined attackers. If your initial strike fails to find its target, readjust and vigorously repeat the technique. Even if your attacker sees your attack coming and flinches away, he has exposed his neck for your second strike.

Since you've already made contact with the attacker's head, you should have a pretty good idea where his neck is, whether you have managed to effectively strike him in the eye or not. The second technique, a short, sharp chop to the side of the neck, is delivered a fraction of a second after the eye strike. The neck is vulnerable to a classic "karate chop," striking with the outside edge of your open hand. A sharp strike to the carotid artery located on the side of the neck can cause lightheadedness and has a good chance of triggering an involuntary vagal response, stunning or even knocking out your attacker.

Once your chop lands, don't pull it back. Rather, use it to control the attacker by grabbing his collar or hooking the back of his neck. This allows you to pull the attacker into your third attack, a knee strike to the solar plexus targeting his respiratory system, with the goal of "knocking the wind out of him," taking away his ability to breathe.

As he doubles up in response, either from the impact of your knee against his body or merely from his flinch response to avoid being hit, he is now open for the final strike, a downward elbow to the thoracic spine delivered just between the shoulder blades (see Part 1 of Level 3 for the location of the thoracic spine). This attack on his nervous system results in weakness of the extremities and is aimed at driving your attacker to the ground.

If the attacker remains on his feet, a strong lateral push will propel him away from you, creating valuable distance between you and your attacker. It may even send him crashing to the ground.

The entire Tiger Claw combination should only take a few seconds to execute completely. With practice, you can deliver all four moves in less than three seconds.

If at any time your Tiger Claw Set fails you, just start again at the beginning. Your attacker will not know that you are performing the same combination of techniques, and you may have better luck on your second try!

If a man can't see, he can't fight.
If a man can't breathe, he can't fight.
If a man can't stand, he can't fight.
—The Quick Silver Method
Karate Kid III

Defending Against Strikes

The Tiger Claw Set provides you with effective defenses against the most common striking attacks. Begin by assuming a strong, stable neutral guard. This leaves your attacker with only a limited number of biomechanical ways in which he can attempt to strike you. He can either punch inside or outside your guard. Similarly, he can hit you high, targeting your head, or low, targeting your abdomen.

As you learned in Level 3, a wide, arcing punch is commonly referred to as a hook punch or haymaker. Since your arms are up in the neutral guard, covering your flanks, you should be fairly well protected from these attacks already. Intercept and stop them with an inner block. A straight punch is called a jab if it is thrown with the front hand and a cross if it thrown with the rear hand. Attacks to the inside are parried from the outside. Those attacks that are launched between your hands are referred to as inside your guard.

Aggressive punches come in fast and strong. In order to mount an effective defense, you will need to correctly anticipate the attack by staying alert for the threat indicators that will telegraph your attacker's intentions. Knowing what he is going to throw and when will aid you in selecting an effective response capable of countering his attack while minimizing its damage to you. When possible, block and counter simultaneously.

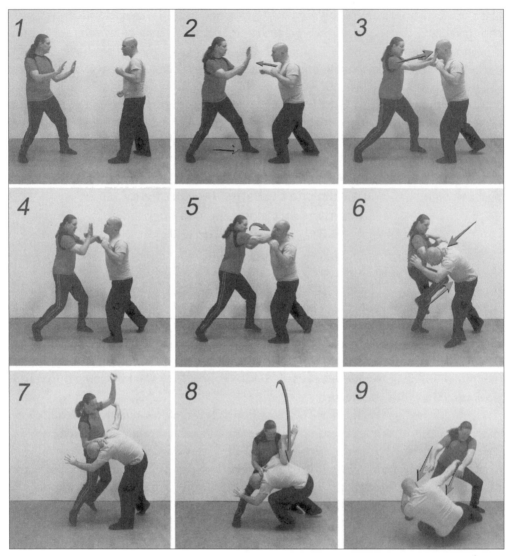

Wide Punch (Hook or Haymaker): 1) When threatened by an aggressor, adopt a neutral guard, and use footwork to maintain a safe distance while watching for attack indicators as you attempt to de-escalate the situation. 2) The aggressor attacks with a wide arcing right punch. Step in and block his punch with a left inside block. 3) Counter with a simultaneous right tiger claw strike to the attacker's eyes, inflicting pain and depriving him of his sight. 4) Check or grasp his right arm with your left hand as you chamber for a right inside chop. 5) Deliver a short, sharp chop to the side of his neck to stun or even knock out your attacker. 6) Without withdrawing your hand after the chop, hook behind his neck, pulling him into a knee strike. 7) Keep your attacker unbalanced by pulling down and forward against the back of his neck as you raise your left arm in preparation for a downward elbow strike. 8) Drop your weight as you drive the point of your elbow downward into his exposed back, aiming for his thoracic spine. 9) Push your stunned attacker sideways, knocking him to the ground as you run in the opposite direction.

Self-Defense Story: Master of the Face Block

As an undergrad, I did a brief stint on the Gettysburg boxing team. I didn't particularly enjoy boxing, but I saw it as a great way to expand my martial arts knowledge. I certainly found what I was seeking. The knowledge cost me blood, sweat, and tears, and it took me years to come to understand all the lessons I learned in those few months. Here is one of those lessons.

Loch Haven University, December 1990. It was my first, and last, dance in the squared circle. Since I was already a black belt with several years of martial arts training and did well boxing my teammates in sparring practice, Coach decided to put me up against a slightly more experienced boxer. I think we both found out the hard way that a little bit of extra knowledge can go a long way.

Round One: the bell rings, and we move out of our corners. We meet in the center of the ring and circle each other a bit. He held his hands pretty far apart in front of him, and his head seemed wide open. So I threw a sharp jab at his chin. I was more confused than hurt when I realized that, rather than hit my attacker, *I* got hit in return! I shook it off, and there he was again, right in front of me with his hands wide. So I tried again and got punched again, right in the mouth. I didn't even see it coming. This was unlike anything I had encountered sparring anyone in our club.

I spent much of the rest of that first round blocking with my face. Every time I jabbed, it seemed I was taking damage. After the bell rang, I went back to my corner, spit my mouthpiece into the bucket, and was a little surprised at how bloody it was. Coach gave me some advice, and come the second round, my attacker couldn't get me with that little trick anymore. I had learned some excellent lessons and, as I mentioned, it took me years to realize the importance of some of them.

Post-encounter Analysis: The stance my attacker adopted was a variation on the neutral guard, and the technique he used to turn the inside of my lips into shredded hamburger was an outside parry with a simultaneous return jab. Simple, but effective. He probably hit me with it a dozen times, and I still didn't figure out his trick. All I knew was that his big, stupid face right was in front of me, yet I was having a heck of a time hitting it. The more frustrated I got, the easier it was for him to control me and dominate the round.

Since then, I have analyzed that fight over and over to wring out of it as many lessons as I could. One of the best was realizing the potential effectiveness of the neutral guard and outside parry and how to use it in self-defense. I made sure to study it and make it part of my arsenal. In fact, you can see it in the first three moves of the following series. My thinking is that, if I fell for it, then others probably will too. Of course, like all the techniques presented in this book, you have to train it properly, the same way you grow a plant from a seed, but if you do, I can assure you that it can be *highly* effective.

Straight Punch (Jab or Cross): 1) Keep your guard up and maintain a safe distance from the threat. 2) When he strikes, parry his straight punch across your centerline, using the hand that is on the same side as the attacker's punch. 3) Counterattack with a simultaneous tiger claw strike to his eyes. 4) Quickly withdraw your hand to chamber for a chop. 5) Deliver a short, sharp inner chop to the side of his neck. 6) Hook behind his neck and pull him into an upward knee strike. 7) Continue to pull him down and forward as you chamber for a downward elbow strike. 8) Land in a wide stance, dropping your weight into a downward elbow strike to the attacker's back.

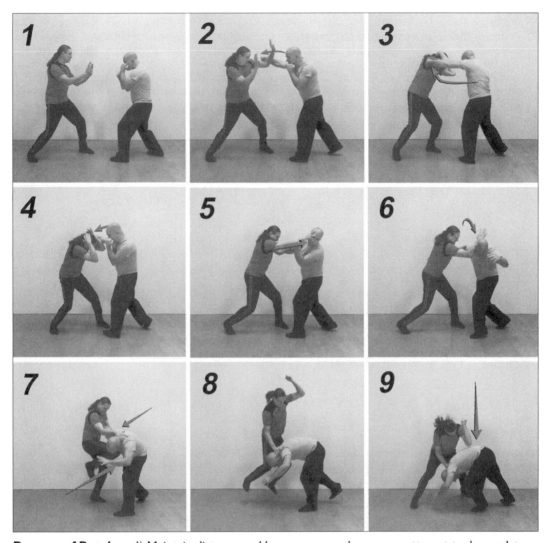

Barrage of Punches: 1) Maintain distance and keep your guard up as you attempt to de-escalate the situation. 2) The aggressor attacks with a savage barrage of punches, beginning with a right hook, which you block. 3) The attacker swiftly launches a second attack, so you assume a full defensive cover to protect yourself. 4) Keep your eyes open and peek through your arms to determine where his next attack is aimed so you can mount an effective defense and determine the right time to strike back. Don't wait too long! 5) Take the fight to your attacker. Explode out of your defensive position with a tiger claw strike to the eyes to drop his visual sensors, which supply the vast majority of external stimuli to the brain. 6) Follow up with an inner chop to the side of the neck, attacking his circulatory system, stunning or possibly even knocking him out. 7) Attack his respiratory system by pulling the attacker into a knee kick, targeting his diaphragm. 8) Continue to apply downward pressure against the back of his neck as you load up for a finishing blow. 9) Deliver a downward elbow strike to the attacker's back, driving him to the ground. Push him away and run.

Baiting

If you feel like a physical confrontation against a single unarmed attacker is inevitable, forcing him to initiate and throw the first punch not only gives you a tactical advantage but also a legal one. While this might sound antithetical at first, drawing a punch actually allows you to better control the dynamics of the fight because the attack comes on your terms, when and how you are expecting it. Begin by inciting your attacker into taking a swing at you, then be ready for it when it comes.

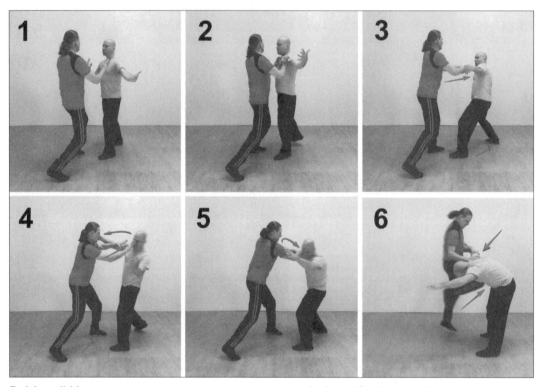

Baiting: 1) Your aggressor is posturing, attempting to make himself as large and intimidating as possible by puffing out his chest and spreading his arms wide. Keep your guard up as you attempt to de-escalate the situation. 2) When he presses in too close, use your neutral guard to check his arms and keep him away. 3) Use your lead hand to push hard against the aggressor's right shoulder to create space and elicit a response. Expect him to respond by immediately throwing a right punch at your head. 4) Use your left arm to block his punch as you tiger claw his eyes with your right hand. 5) Immediately follow up with a chop to his neck. With luck this will stun him by tripping his vagal response. 6) Hook your attacker behind his neck and pull him into a knee strike to the solar plexus. Finish with a downward elbow strike to his exposed back before running away.

Upper Cut

An uppercut is a low-level attack aimed at your abdomen when you are standing, and at your face when you are doubled over. Since it is a wide, arcing punch, you can think of it as a vertical hook punch. Defend against the uppercut by dropping your same-side forearm down and across your attacker's forearm. Block the path of his punch with the bony outer edge of your forearm. Counterattack with a tiger claw strike to the attacker's eyes with your opposite hand. Continue with the Tiger Claw Set by following up with a chop to his carotid, hooking behind his neck and pulling him into a knee strike. Then finish by driving him to the ground with a downward elbow strike.

Low Inside Block: Defense against an uppercut.

Defending Against Grabs

When grabbed by an attacker, you need to react quickly, reclaiming the initiative and never relinquishing it. Stay on the attack until you either have a good opportunity to escape, or the attacker has been subdued and no longer poses any threat to you.

The attacker's weakness lies in his strategy. For whatever reason, he is attempting to grab you rather than immediately striking or punching. This necessarily occupies one or both of his hands. He most likely expects you to try to break his grip in order to escape. Your strength lies in your unpredictability. Suddenly and decisively launch a surprise counterattack. Place secondary emphasis on releasing the hand that is grabbing you. Instead, use it as a point of control to counterattack and drop your attacker's vision. If he grabs your wrist, you not only know where that hand is, but as long as he retains a grip on you, you also have some control over where his hand goes. Pull your hand downward, dragging his hand low as you tiger strike his eyes with your free hand. This strategy allows you to regain the initiative in the fewest possible moves.

Same-Side Grab: 1) Attacker's right hand grasps your left wrist. 2) Immediately strike to the attacker's eyes with your free hand, using the arm that is being grabbed to pull him into your strike. 3) The strike to his eyes should drive his head backward, exposing his neck. Without withdrawing your right hand very far, deliver an inner chop to the right side of the attacker's neck. 4) Maintain contact with your attacker, hooking behind his neck with your chopping hand and pulling him into a right knee strike, doubling him over. 5) Deliver a powerful downward elbow strike to his spine, landing in a low, wide stance. 6) If your attacker is still on his feet, push him over sideways before running away.

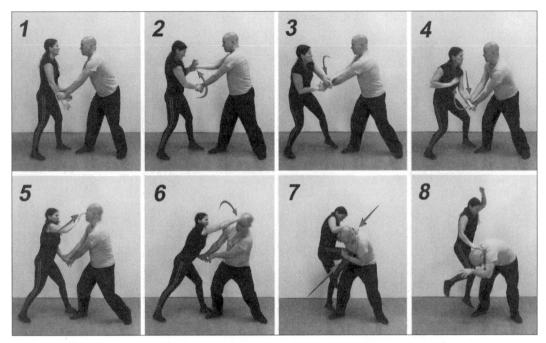

Both Wrists Grabbed in Front: 1) An aggressor has grasped both your wrists. 2) Pull one hand up as you push one hand down. 3) Suddenly reverse the motions, slamming the attacker's wrists together. 4) Pull your bottom hand out of his grasp. 5) Counterattack with a tiger claw strike to the attacker's eyes with your free hand. 6) Follow up with a chop to his neck. 7) Hook behind his neck and pull him into a knee strike. 8) Continue applying downward pressure upon his neck as you finish with a downward elbow strike.

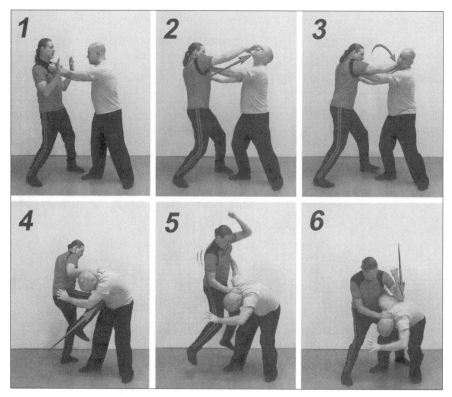

Choke or Lapel Grab: 1) The aggressor has grabbed your shirt. 2) Grasp the attacker's right wrist with your left hand as you counterattack with a tiger claw strike to the attacker's eyes with your opposite hand. 3) Follow up with a chop to his carotid artery on the side of his neck. 4) Hook behind his neck and pull him into a knee strike. 5) Continue pulling down on his neck as you hop in the air. 6) Drive him to the ground with a downward elbow strike.

Defend Your Throat: 1) If the attacker attempts to choke you, 2) guard your throat by tucking your chin tightly to your chest and shrugging your shoulders to your ears. Can you guess what technique comes next? You guessed it . . . tiger claw!

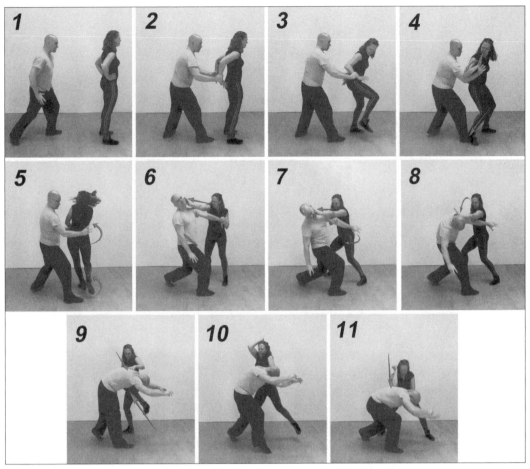

Both Wrists Are Grabbed from Behind: 1) An assailant sneaks up behind you. 2) He grabs your wrists from behind. 3) Glance behind you and target his lead foot. 4) Bring your elbow down on the top of his arm, levering your wrist out of his grip. 5) Turn sharply to your left, pivoting on your left foot. 6) Grasp his left hand as you deliver a tiger claw strike with your right hand. 7) Deliver a second tiger claw with your left hand, setting you up for a clean chop to the side of the neck. 8) Chop to his neck, with the intention of stunning or even knocking out your attacker. 9) Pull him into a knee strike to the solar plexus. 10) Continue applying downward pressure against the back of his neck with your left hand as you raise your right over your head. 11) Drive him to the ground with a downward elbow strike to the center of his back.

Bear Hug: 1) An attacker sneaks up from behind and grabs you about the waist. 2) Your arms are pinned at your sides. 3) Reach behind you and strike your assailant's groin with a chop or tiger claw. 4) After striking, grab whatever skin you can through his clothes before ripping strongly away from his body. 5) Now that his grip has loosened, turn into him, driving your elbow into his sternum. 6) As soon as he releases you, turn and tiger claw to his eyes. Knowing this reference point, finish with a chop into the side of his neck, knee strike, and downward elbow strike.

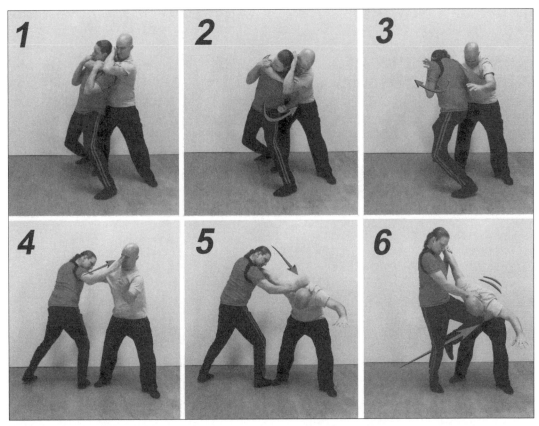

Rear Choke: 1) An attacker is attempting to choke you from behind. Prevent this by pulling down on his forearm with both arms. 2) Deliver a back elbow strike to his exposed ribs, repeating several times if needed. 3) Suddenly reverse motions, grabbing his arm and turning out. If you cannot move the arm, reach behind and strike the attacker's groin with a hammer fist, then try again. 4) Once you have broken his grip on your neck, continue turning and deliver a tiger claw strike to his eyes. 5) Follow up with a chop to his neck. 6) Hook behind his neck and pull him into a knee strike. If needed, drive him to the ground with a downward elbow strike.

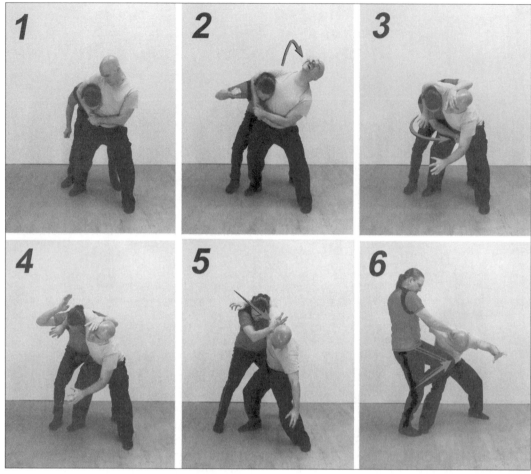

Side Headlock: 1) Your attacker has your head held tightly against the right side of his body with his right arm. 2) Reach over the attacker's right shoulder with your left hand and attack his eyes, pulling his head back and loosening the hold enough for you to escape. 3) Strike the attacker's groin with a hammer fist strike. 4) Continue pressing against his face as you quickly chamber for a chop. 5) Chop to his neck, targeting the carotid artery with the intent to trip his vagal response. 6) Hook behind his neck and pull him into a knee strike. This sets you up for a downward elbow strike finish.

Front Headlock: 1) Your attacker has your head locked against the side of his body with his arm. 2) Grab his body and pull him into a knee strike to the groin, momentarily weakening his grip on your head. 3) Suddenly reverse directions, pushing his body away as you pull your head out. 4) As soon as you have broken his grip on your neck, deliver a tiger claw strike to his eyes. 5) While his neck is exposed, deliver a quick, sharp chop to his neck. 6) Hook behind his neck and pull him into a knee strike to the solar plexus. 7) Continue to apply downward pressure against his neck as you jump to set up the elbow. 8) Drive him to the ground with a downward elbow strike.

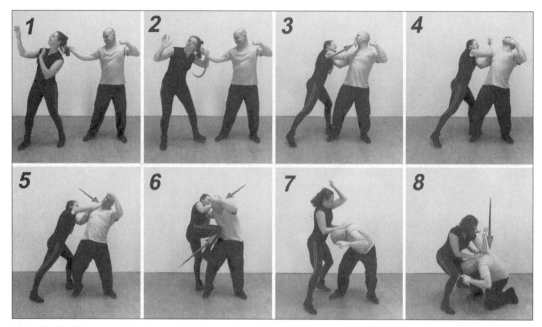

Hair Pull: 1) An attacker has grabbed you by the hair. This could just as easily be a collar grab. 2) With one hand, grab the attacker's hand that is grabbing your hair. 3) Turn and deliver a tiger strike to his face. In this case, the attacker is caught under the chin. 4) As he is recoiling from your first shot, load up for a chop. 5) Deliver a sharp chop to the side of his neck. 6) Grab the attacker behind his neck and pull him into a knee kick. 7) Continue applying downward pressure against his neck as you set up for your finishing strike. 8) Drive him to the ground with a downward elbow strike.

Hey, This All Looks the Same

By now you're probably thinking, "This is just the same thing over and over." Well, I am glad you noticed since this is purposeful and by design. Having the ability to apply a single combination of effective techniques against a wide variety of attacks cuts down on your decision-making time, allowing you to react as quickly and efficiently as possible. Each technique is designed to work regardless of whether your last strike landed or not. If your attacker turns his head to defend his eyes from your tiger claw, he opens his neck for your chop. Defending the neck in turn opens the lower abdomen to the knee strike. If the attacker defends against the knee by doubling over and blocking with his arms, he opens his back to your downward elbow strike, which maximizes your available striking power in a final attempt to take your attacker out of the fight long enough for you to escape.

What you *can't* do is memorize a different counter for every attack and expect them come out in a high-stress situation, at least not without years of training under your belt, and often not even then. Choosing from a long menu of possible counters only serves to lower your reaction time, essentially slowing you down. Furthermore, since each technique requires dedicated practice time to acquire, it is more beneficial to spend the majority of your time honing your skills in a few very versatile techniques.

> ## We are what we repeatedly do. Excellence then, is not an act, but a habit.
> ### —Aristotle

Reality Check!

As well thought out as this plan may be, there is still no guarantee that any of this will work. Self-defense is violent, shocking, and chaotic, so don't be afraid to vary or improvise on the basic combination. Use the strikes as reference points. For example, if you throw a roundhouse elbow, and it leads to an inner chop with the same hand, then you can jump into the Tiger Claw Set at that point. You also always have the option of repeating a technique. Anything worth hitting once is worth hitting twice. You can double up any strike if you feel it is to your advantage. If you hit a stumbling block, you can even start the whole set over. For example, if you knee your attacker only to have him stand up rather than doubling over, attack his eyes again with the tiger claw. Keep your wits about you enough to recognize what is working and what is not, and then modify your strategy and tactics accordingly.

Improvisation

The dynamics of any self-defense situation are fluid and constantly changing. Your first attempts at self-defense will not always be successful. But you must not give up! Understanding what to look for allows you to find another opportunity to take control of the situation. One second, you could be hit unawares, but if you fight through it, half a second later you recover enough to see your attacker winding up for a second shot. This observation instantly changes the dynamics of the situation. By reading his intentions, you have greatly improved your odds of successfully responding and defending yourself.

Of course, an attacker may grab and attack you in a wide variety of other ways than the ones described above. Therefore, it is important to practice against a wide variety of grabbing and striking attacks. If necessary, create new, effective combinations using the Tiger Claw Set as inspiration. Here is an example.

Improvisation: 1) You are faced with an aggressor, so you assume a neutral guard. 2) He suddenly grabs your neck in an attempt to choke you. Tuck your chin to protect your throat as you grab his arms to control him. 3) Deliver a short, sharp kick to the groin. 4) Pull your foot back in preparation for a second kick. 5) Attack his knee with a low stamping kick. 6) As you land, strike him in the head with a roundhouse elbow strike. 7) Immediately come back with a hammer fist strike to the nose. 8) The threat has momentarily been neutralized.

There are countless variations to the standard Tiger Claw Set combination. Circumstances will dictate the precise tactics you need to employ in any given situation, and any plans you make will undoubtedly change upon contact with the enemy. Luckily, technique transcends environment, meaning that your overall body mechanics will stay the same even when the scenario changes. The root skills you learn when building your arsenal (Level 3) will give you the necessary tools to create new, effective combinations, even on the fly. For example, instead of pulling your attacker into a knee strike to the abdomen, you might target his IT band (the iliotibial band runs along the outside of the leg from the hip to the knee), groin, or head because they present a better target at the moment. If your knee strike fails to double him over, finish him with a roundhouse elbow strike to his head instead of a downward elbow. Or you may choose to deliver a stamping kick to his knee in lieu of, or perhaps in addition to, your elbow strike. Don't allow yourself to be constrained by the rules, because there aren't any. When you get stuck, continue to rely on your strongest techniques, but think outside of the box and alter your strategy for applying them.

As soon as you sense you are no longer making progress, alter your tactics and redouble your efforts. If your hands are being held too tightly and you cannot get out, take advantage of the fact that your attacker is focused on holding onto your wrists and kick your attacker in the knee instead. You can then go back to working your hands free, hopefully with greater success.

Learning to use your creative imagination to express technical proficiency and emotional power is part of the *art* of self-defense. Everyone is different. You will have some techniques that feel more natural for you than others. Can you practice these other techniques? If they work, then yes. What if you punch instead of tiger claw? If that works, then it was the right technique! "But I would kick here." Cool, then do it! "But I would do this or this or this . . ." Awesome, *do it!* The Tiger Claw Set is a framework, not a rule set. Go with what you are comfortable with. Play to your strengths. If you have boxing experience, then punch. If you were a wrestler, then throw. If you were a track star, then *run!*

Make your training fun. Be creative. Customize it to fit you, your life, and your needs.

> Absorb what is useful, reject what is useless,
> add what is essentially your own.
> —Bruce Lee

Part 4: Right Perspective/Run

Right Perspective

Once engaged, don't stop until the threat stops, but once the threat stops, disengage.

After a physical altercation has begun, continue the necessary, reasonable use of force in self-defense until the threat is neutralized. Depending upon the situation, it may be difficult to determine when this point has been reached.

Defending your ego exposes you to needless risk. Even when self-defense is justified, you are still required to follow the law. Do not take it upon yourself to punish or teach your attacker a lesson. Your priority needs to be safety, not "justice." This means not causing any more damage than necessary to ensure your safety. Do not seek retribution. Once the threat has been neutralized, stop using force.

How do you know you have done enough damage to your attacker to safely leave the situation? The obvious clues are physical, such as holding the face in response to an eye poke or doubling over after a knee strike. You can also be reasonably sure that you have stunned your attacker when you hear him make an involuntary exhalation of air, usually accompanied by a sharp, audible noise. When you score a successful strike to his eyes, the sound is usually a higher pitched "ahh!" Contrarily, when you land a strike to the attacker's body, he makes a deeper "oof" sound. Either can be your signal that you have temporarily stunned your attacker and have an opportunity to run.

Run

We discussed avoidance in Level 2. Running is almost always a safer alternative to engagement in a physical altercation. Therefore, as soon as you safely can, remove yourself from the situation to avoid incurring potential harm through further violent confrontation. Escape to safety but do so as carefully as possible. Avoid letting high levels of adrenaline and a fragile emotional state cause you to make any poor decisions. Keep your head about you. Make a plan that ensures your safety and then execute it.

After an Encounter

The first thing you need to do after a self-defense encounter is assess any damage that may have been done to you. Check yourself thoroughly for injuries. Occasionally, victims do not even realize that they have been wounded as their adrenaline is high and masking pain. Always check yourself thoroughly.

Next, you need to report your encounter to authorities. Use your cell phone to take pictures of the location and your injuries. Record notes by typing or dictating the entire story as a text or e-mail and send it to yourself. Describe your assailant in as much detail as possible, noting distinguishing characteristics that cannot be changed such as race, height, build, eye color, tattoos, or pitch of voice. Note hair color and length, including facial hair, as these can be changed, but not easily. Clothing, on the other hand, *can* be changed easily and so provides the least amount of useful information. When it comes to attire, you want to observe those things that are least likely to change, so work from the bottom up. Note his shoes, pants, shirt, and hat in that order. If you had physical contact with the assailant, you may have a sample of his DNA under your nails, so do not wash your hands. If he was driving a vehicle, try to note his license plate number, as well as other details such as the color, make, and model of the car. Your goal is to be able to provide as much information about the subject and getaway vehicle as possible to have him identified and apprehended.

Don't let a negative experience take away your happiness and make you live in fear. It is only natural to experience stress or anxiety as a result of your encounter. Don't be embarrassed. Instead, be proactive. The best way to alleviate these symptoms is to seek professional assistance with a counselor, therapist, or support group.

Level-4 Activities

Visualize Scenarios

When you don't have a partner available, mentally rehearse how you might react in a given situation. What would you do if such and such person approached you? What weapons do you have at your disposal? How would you escape? Picture the details of the encounter to make the event as real as possible in your imagination.

Training with a Partner

Everyone needs to know what it feels like to be attacked by a bigger, stronger person. However, use caution when choosing your training partner. Many men, even boyfriends or husbands, will unfortunately feel threatened by you empowering yourself, even if it is to learn self-defense. Such a man may attempt to dominate you by attacking too fast or grabbing too tightly, thwarting your ability to practice your techniques in a misguided attempt to prove that your moves are ineffectual. His reaction overlooks several facts. First, the "for practice" context gives him an advantage because he knows what you are attempting to do, allowing him to counter your technique and make you think it will not work. In a reality-based situation, an attacker will not know what type of response he will get, giving your surprise counterattack a far greater chance of success. Another is that you cannot respond with full speed, full power, or bad intention with your training partner as you would in an actual self-defense situation. You can avoid this type of conflict with your training partner by practicing with someone who is studying self-defense with you, or a trusted friend who "gets it" and understands that repeated practice is needed to engrain techniques into muscle memory.

Remember to respect your partner and thank them for their cooperation. Practice your techniques in a slow, controlled manner until you are comfortable with the combinations. Work your way up to performing full-speed applications as you would in a true self-defense situation, but still be careful to use control and pull your techniques just short of striking. Use a heavy bag to practice striking hard and develop power.

Blocking Drill: Have your partner strike you from the left and right, inside and outside your guard, both high and low. Your job is to watch for any movements that telegraph your partner's intentions, allowing you to perform an effective inside block or outside parry. When first learning, have your partner begin softly and slowly, but steadily increase the amount of speed and force behind their strikes as your blocking skills increase.

Grabbing Drill: Like the blocking drill mentioned above, have your partner grab you in a variety of ways. Again, move slowly against light resistance until you get comfortable with each technique, only adding speed, power, and focus after you have become comfortable with all the parts of a given combination.

Optimal Learning Zone

You want to train as realistically as possible, yet at a rate conducive to learning. To maximize your growth, you want to train at a pace where you are successful between 50 and 80 percent of the time. Any easier, and you are not being adequately challenged. Any harder, and frustration begins to set in, hindering your growth.

The Goldilocks Rule

Comfort Zone (too easy): 80–100% success rate
Learning Zone (just right): 50–80% success rate
Danger Zone (too hard): Less than 50% success rate

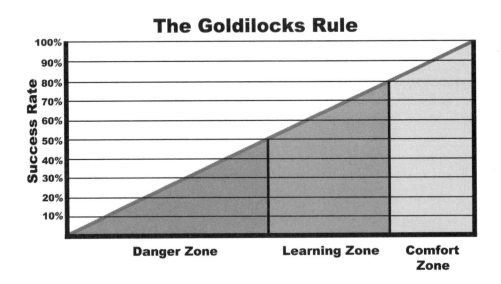

Learn to Take a Shot

You need to be able to fight through the pain and shock of getting hit. One of the most valuable lessons I learned during my short time boxing was that I could get hit in the face, hard, and still keep going. I recommend training as hard as you comfortably can while keeping it enjoyable so you will want to do it. Get some boxing gloves and headgear so you can practice with a greater degree of speed and power while still ensuring your safety and that of your training partner. You won't train if the cost is too high, whether in pain, emotional stress, or recovery time. That said, you need to learn what it feels like to get hit. When it happens, take it as a valuable lesson. Shake it off and keep fighting!

People who have experience fighting are more confident in their skills and stay cooler under stress. While inexperience makes a self-defense situation more chaotic, frightening, and confusing, fight experience gained in training is directly transferable to actual street encounters. The best, and perhaps only, way to get this valuable experience is to practice fighting on a regular or at least semi-regular basis.

If possible, get some formal training in a striking art such as boxing or karate, preferably one that does a good deal of sparring. You don't have to become an expert or get a black belt. You just need to learn the basics and take advantage of opportunities to practice. Training in proper body mechanics and then using them to fight other people will greatly advance your skills.

Stalk and Evade

Are you ready to take your training to the next level? Simulate self-defense situations with a trusted partner. Take turns playing the predator, stalking your prey throughout your day. The victim should practice awareness and avoidance skills to avoid a physical confrontation. When a physical confrontation becomes unavoidable, react with as much speed and power as you can while still remaining safely in control and not injuring your partner. Get as close to a real-world situation as you feel comfortable, but use some common sense (such as, don't attack your partner in public). Have fun, but don't get carried away. I don't want to read about you in the news!

LEVEL 5
Dirty Tricks

The only fair fight is a fight you win.
—Anonymous

Part One: When to Fight Dirty

Techniques like poking the eyes are often called "dirty tricks" because they are considered "unsporting." However, a violent assault is not a competition, and there are no rules restricting you (or your attacker) in a self-defense encounter. Since your assailant is not going to be playing by any rules, neither should you.

There are many things you can do to discourage someone who is stronger than you and trying to hurt you. While dirty tactics are legitimate methods of escaping an attacker, as stand-alone tactics, they are unreliable for ending a fight. A torn ear, lacerated nostril, or ruptured eyeball each have the capacity to end a fight; however, they can work against you by further enraging your attacker. An eye gouge might be appropriate if you're in a good position for it, but it might be more effective to box the attacker's ears or knee his groin. It's always a matter of circumstance, opportunity, positioning, and timing. Dirty tricks are just that: tricks to help you gain a quick advantage so you can transition to a stronger position.

Part Two: How to Fight Dirty

Pinching

Self-defense isn't always against someone who is trying to seriously hurt you. Perhaps an acquaintance is just inappropriately fooling around, not really attacking you. Where hitting would be inappropriate, pinching can be used as a relatively mild, yet surprisingly effective deterrent. Your target will most likely cease what they are doing and inadvertently flinch away, providing you with an avenue of escape.

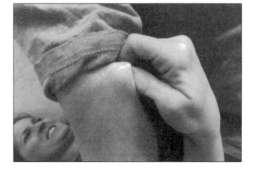

Growing up, we pinch playfully, catching the skin between the soft tips of the thumb and index finger. Much more effective is to make a fist, then grip the flesh tightly between your thumb and the edge of your forefinger, much as you would hold a key to unlock a door. Dig your thumbnail into the skin before twisting it sharply. Add to the pain by pulling the skin as you twist, ripping it away from the body. Try not to catch a lot of skin. The thinner the fold of skin you pinch, the more painful it can be.

Although you can pinch nearly any part of the body, the most effective targets are areas where the skin is the most sensitive. On the head, vulnerable targets include the ear lobes, nose, cheeks, and philtrum (the indentation between the nose and the top lip). On the torso, pinching is effectual against the insides and backs of the upper arms, the sides of the upper chest near the armpit, and the area around the nipples. On the lower body, pinch the inside of the thigh, from just above the knee all the way up to the groin. The male genitals are especially vulnerable to pinching.

Unfortunately, the effectiveness of pinching decreases with the intensity of the situation. The adrenaline of a determined attacker, not to mention the possible influence of alcohol or other drugs, can numb your attacker to pain. Pinching is best when used early in an encounter as a preventive measure, a warning to show your seriousness before an uncomfortable situation has an opportunity to escalate.

Attacking the groin from underneath with a front snap kick.

Groin Shot

As we discussed under "Targeting" in Level 3, a groin strike has the potential to effectually take an attacker out of the fight.

At long range, attack your attacker's groin with the top of your foot using a front kick, smashing his testicles against his body. From the side, you can flick the groin with a roundhouse kick. At close range, attack the groin with an upward knee kick. With the hands, you can attack the groin with a snappy backhand strike, hitting with your fingers with a flicking motion. You can also hammer fist strike or tiger claw the groin. Both put you in position to follow up by grabbing and ripping the genitals. Once you initiate a strike to the groin, your attacker will often instinctually flinch away and move to defend low. While this might prevent you from hitting his groin, it will expose other vulnerable targets, such as his eyes.

Breaking the Fingers and Toes

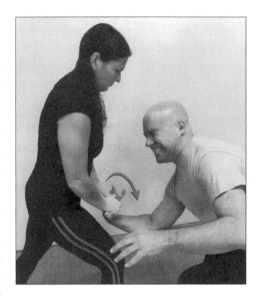

The fingers are the most frequently injured part of the hand. There are no muscles in the fingers. They consist of three bones called phalanges, connected by ligaments and powered by tendons. Fingers move by the contraction of forearm muscles that pull on the tendons attached to the finger bones. Bending the fingers and toes backward is an often unexpected, yet very effective attack. Sprained or broken fingers can be very painful and affect an assailant's ability to attack you further.

When grappling, if you should find yourself in a position to grab your attacker's toes, encompass one in your fist and make like you are trying to break it off. Bend it backward and twist violently as though you were trying to unscrew it. Bending and twisting fingers and toes will cause your attacker to change his position to relieve the pain. Think ahead and be prepared to immediately take advantage of this brief moment when it occurs.

Pulling the Hair and Ears

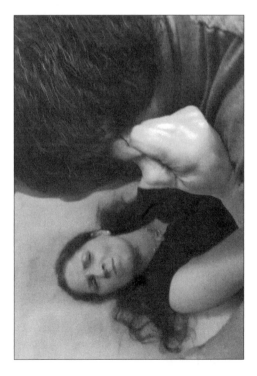

Since long hair makes a convenient handle for controlling and manipulating an attacker's head, grabbing and pulling the hair is a common tactic. Slip your fingers down to the scalp and grasp a handful of hair, then twist it and pull. This motion should have the effect of moving the attacker's head, and where the head goes, the body will follow!

Just reaching out to grab your attacker's hair, however, is a waste of motion. In a self-defense situation, every second and every movement count. Therefore, use the extension of your arm to launch a preliminary attack such as a palm heel strike to his nose or a tiger claw strike to his eyes. Then, without withdrawing your hand, grab the attacker's hair. Since he likely flinched away from your initial attack, you can then pull his head toward you with one hand while striking his nose or chin with your other. When performed with speed and power, this combination can be very effective.

You can also move an attacker's head by pulling on his ear(s). The outer ear is made up of flexible cartilage. Reach deeply into his ear with your thumb and pinch it between your thumb and the side of your index finger. Dig your thumbnail in deeply enough to break the skin to help provide you with a secure grip.

Head Butt

As a weapon, your head is better used for thinking than for hitting. However, when applied correctly, a head butt can be a lifesaving technique capable of seriously damaging an attacker and providing an opportunity to run away.

The head butt is a close quarters technique using the strongest parts of your skull, the forehead and back of your cranium, to strike your attacker. Tuck your chin to your chest, clench your teeth, and stiffen your neck muscles. Look through your eyebrows to aim, then drive your head toward the target. Maximize the power of your attack by getting your body weight behind the technique.

The most effective target for your head butt is your attacker's nose. A head butt to the nose shocks the brain through the external nasal nerve, a branch of the trigeminal nerve, resulting in excruciating pain. You can also target the temple or cheekbones to great effect. In grappling, a well-placed head butt to the solar plexus can help you get out of a desperate situation.

Head butts are so effective that they are illegal in all sports including MMA. The one exception is American football, where the players wear protective helmets, and even then, the effects of long-term concussive damage are a growing concern. Accidental head butts in sports such as soccer can easily result in a concussion for both parties involved, so you must take care not to accidentally stun yourself. When head butting, you also run the risk of cutting yourself and, since the head has a lot of blood vessels, this could result in serious bleeding that could hinder your performance, be that fighting or fleeing.

Head Butt: Attack from underneath the target to avoid bashing your foreheads together. Use your arms to pull him into your strike.

Biting

In 1997, boxer Mike Tyson infamously bit a chunk out of Evander Holyfield's ear during their world title bout. Tyson was disqualified from the match, but his action demonstrated how effective biting could be in a fight.

Bites are most effective against fleshy targets such as the hands, ears, nose, cheek, or neck. A human bite can exert up to two hundred pounds of force, which may seem like a lot, but it is not enough to bite through finger bones. Bite marks on the fingers are relatively common in assaults, but rarely lead to tissue loss, let alone complete amputation of a finger due to the considerable amount of force that would be required to sever the supporting bone (sorry, Gollum). The biggest risk from a human bite wound is actually infection. A third of all hand infections are the result of human bite wounds, so see a doctor about any bite that breaks your skin.

Boxing the Ears

Boxing the ears is the term given to a maneuver in which you strike both sides of an attacker's head simultaneously with your open hands. The ears contain a high concentration of nerves associated not only with hearing, but also balance.

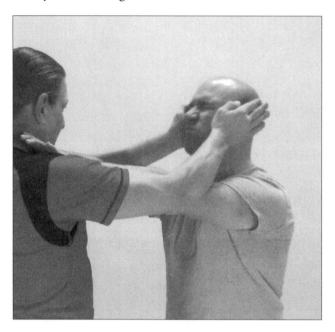

For maximum effect, cup your hands with your fingers held tightly together and your thumb pressed firmly against the side of your index finger. Strike your attacker simultaneously over both ears. When these clouts are delivered properly, air is forced into the ear canal. The sudden increase in air pressure shocks the delicate inner ear mechanisms, producing severe pain and dizziness. It may even rupture his eardrums.

Palm Strike to the Ear

The palm strike to the ear is a sneaky attack that you can use to catch your attacker by surprise. The physical effects on your opponent's body are similar to that described in the last section, "Boxing the Ears." Start by dropping your hands slightly and turning partially away. The attacker, sensing weakness, will likely advance right into your strike zone. Move fast and avoid telegraphing your strike by delivering it from wherever your hand happens to be. Begin the motion with a violent turn of your hips, followed by a whipping of your arm across the target. Swing as though you were going to clap his ear but strike with the heel of your hand just in front of his ear instead. You may still get the ear clap, but your primary emphasis should be on the palm strike. Keep your arm slightly bent to greatly increase the power of your strike and avoid hyperextending your elbow.

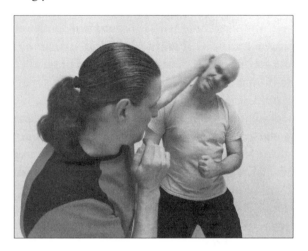

Grabbing Clothing

Your attacker's clothing can be used against him. Grabbing an attacker's clothing helps you to limit and control his movements. Pull your attacker's coat or shirt over his head to limit his visibility. If he is wearing a thin shirt, bunch up the material for a more substantial grip. Use your hold to push and pull your attacker, keeping him off-balance.

Self-Defense Story: Kickball Chaos

It was 1980 and I was a skinny ten-year-old kid in fifth grade. Many of us played kickball during recess after lunch. I was pitching when an argument broke out about a kid getting tagged out at second base. I got involved and told the kid at second that he was safe and to stay there. Then I turned around to get back to the game. I never even saw the second base-man coming at me. He hit me in the back at a full run with a flying sidekick, right out of a Saturday afternoon *Kung Fu Theater* flick. I was sent sprawling face first into the dirt. I remember lying there, looking around at all the kids looking back at me and feeling like I was going to cry. That's when the kid who kicked me started laughing, triggering something deep inside of me that made me get up, so I staggered to my feet. The kid dropped his hands, puffed up his chest, and challenged me. "What are you going to do about it?" he taunted.

I was not a cool kid. I was wimpy, scared, got picked on, and did *not* think of myself as a fighter. But I instinctually understood, or maybe I had learned, that elementary school was a dominance hierarchy, especially on the recess yard. There was a pecking order, and I knew that if I didn't stand up for myself then and there, these bullies were going see me as daily easy pickings. I remember thinking to myself, "What the heck, here goes nothing!" and I punched him square in the face. I don't know who was more surprised, him or me. He came back at me, and we exchanged some punches. Then I grabbed the hood of his jacket and pulled it down over his head. I held it there while I delivered some uppercuts to his face. The other kids broke it up after only a few punches, but not before I gave him a shiner and a bloody lip. He went to the nurse's office, while I had to stand against the wall for the last ten minutes of recess. After that, the bullies in my class pretty much left me alone.

Post-encounter Analysis: Don't overestimate your attacker or underestimate yourself. Sometimes you need to stand up for yourself, even when you are scared and lack confidence. Your attacker is human, and all humans are subject to pain and fear. Sometimes all he needs is a little taste of his own medicine. Granted, I was running on instinct when I pulled that kid's hood down over his eyes, but I took a long shot gamble on myself, and won. Granted, I used a "dirty trick," but it temporarily tipped the odds in my favor. Score one for the little guy!

Gouging

Gouging is the act of maliciously and violently pressing a finger into any orifice, but it is most often used to refer to pressing roughly into someone's eyes.

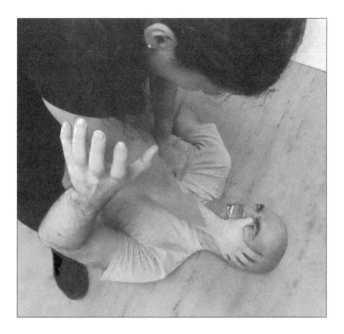

As we discussed with the tiger claw, a properly executed eye strike is one of the most effective of all self-defense moves. There are many ways to attack the eye, and they have varying levels of effectiveness. At one end of the spectrum there are flicks, wipes, rakes, and pokes. These are all relatively low-risk, high-payback techniques intended to stun and disorient. Gouging involves digging and grinding the thumb deep into the eye socket, with the intention of rupturing the globe of the eye.

Destroying someone's eye is very serious and requires legal justification, such as "disparity of force." This is when an aggressor who is savagely attacking you possesses such an obvious physical advantage, such as being significantly larger and stronger, that such extreme measures become rationally acceptable.

Still, the eye gouge is not an assured way to end a confrontation. Keep in mind that, if you can gouge his eyes, then he is close enough to gouge yours. Like all dirty tricks, the eye gouge is more of a means of distraction or getting your attacker to momentarily loosen his grip on you so that you can escape.

Fish Hooking

Fish hooking involves putting the finger or fingers of one or both hands into the mouth, nostril, or other orifice and maliciously pulling away from body. If you have ever blown up balloons too hard, you know how sensitive your cheeks are to outward pressure. However, use caution when inserting your fingers into an assailant's mouth so as not to get bitten. For best effect, insert your fishhook quickly, violently driving back toward the ear in a single motion, as if you were a fisherman setting a hook. When fish hooking the nostrils, pull upward toward the eyebrows.

Throat Strike

The throat, particularly the trachea or windpipe, is especially vulnerable to being struck. The trachea is constructed of strong but flexible rings known as tracheal cartilages that allow it to move and flex during breathing. However, this area can be hard to hit cleanly because the chin naturally protects it. Use a hair pull, eye gouge, or fishhook to drive the attacker's head back, exposing his throat for a strike. Target this soft tissue with the tip of your thumb by making a fist with your thumb extended and pressed up against the side of your index finger, then thrust forward. This will maximize the force of your strike by concentrating it into a small point. Any strike to the trachea will inflict pain and has the potential to impair breathing. You can also attack the throat from the front with a spear hand strike or punch and from the side with an open-handed chop.

If you damage your attacker's trachea, you run the risk of him asphyxiating and dying. Therefore, consider striking the throat as potentially lethal. If you were charged with a violent crime, a jury might assume you were intentionally trying to kill your attacker. Therefore, reserve strikes to the throat for life-and-death situations.

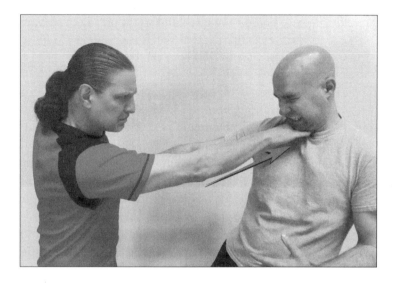

Spitting

Spitting entails forcibly ejecting saliva or some other substance from your mouth. The act of spitting into an assailant's eyes may cause him to inadvertently turn away, either out of revulsion or to protect his eyes, providing you with a short opportunity to strike or move. This is a close quarters tactic, with an average effective range of less than three feet.

My friend Chris suffered from arthritic hips (he's since had them replaced), so his side-arm became his primary means of defense. He developed several special techniques that would buy him extra time in a self-defense scenario. He wrote, "I also spent a couple of months chewing gum: I could ball it up behind my teeth and spit it up to ten feet away to hit a one-inch circle, the same size as an eyeball. These little things were not fatal techniques, just things that could buy me a few seconds to take over the initiative."

Throwing

Throwing objects can be an effective deterrent to keep an aggressor at bay while persuading him not to approach any closer. Anything you have on you or within your reach can be used as a projectile weapon. In a natural environment, gather a handful of dirt, sand, or leaves and throw them into his face. At close range, this can temporarily blind your attacker. Heavier object such as sticks and stones may break bones (get it?), or at least hit a lot harder than a handful of dirt. If you are wearing flip-flops or other footwear inappropriate for running, you might as well use them as improvised projectile weapons instead. Indoors or out, learn how to use the objects in your environment to your greatest advantage. With training, you will increasingly recognize how you might use these items to befuddle and distract your attacker.

Using a Jacket: 1) Hold the object in front of you as though you were going to use it as a shield. 2) Suddenly and unexpectedly throw it at the attacker's face, using the opportunity you have created to start running.

Water Bottle: Seeing that her attacker is armed with a weapon that gives him a long reach, the defender employs an attack with an even greater range, throwing a bottle directly at his face. She now has a split second to close the distance or run.

Foot Flicking

Flicking is like throwing, but you use your foot to propel an item at your attacker instead of your hands. You can flick any loose debris, such as dirt, sand, sticks, or leaves, from the ground toward you attacker's face to get him to flinch and turn away. In that brief moment, you need to move, either toward him, closing the gap, or away, running in the opposite direction.

Level-5 Activities

Dirty tricks can backfire on you. If they fail, they may only serve to further enrage an already aggressive attacker. Like anything else, these techniques require practice to perform

effectively under stress. The following is a list of ways to improve each of the skills presented in Level 5.

Pinching

Practice your pinching prowess on a firm pillow or cushion. You can also develop your grip strength by squeezing a tennis ball or pinching something heavy, such as a weight plate, and holding it vertically. Find a weight that is comfortable for you to hold for ten seconds, then gradually increase the weight and time to keep the activity challenging. Practice pinching a partner but do so carefully. Experiment gently on each other to discover what works best for you.

Groin Shot

Practice attacking the groin from underneath with the instep of your foot by kicking a pillow, cushion, hanging heavy bag, or commercially available striking pad. Point your toes and raise your foot in a straight line from the ground to the target, striking it from underneath. Maximize your power by leaning back slightly and tightening up your whole body at the moment of impact.

Front Snap Kick: Striking a pillow with the ball of the foot.

You can also smack the groin with an open hand. Have a friend hold a seat cushion or large pillow. Attack from underneath, smacking the cushion as though smashing the attacker's testicles against his body. You can even simulate the grab-and-tear follow up.

Fingers and Toes

The best way to learn how to break a finger or toe is to practice with a substitute. Go outside and find some dead sticks on the ground. Start with a thin stick, a little thicker than a pencil. Break it using your bare hands. Repeat, gradually working up to thicker sticks. If your hands are soft, you can wear light work gloves to protect them as they toughen up.

Pulling the Hair and Ears

Pulling the hair and ears requires a strong grip. One of the best ways to develop the type of grip strength required for pulling hair or ears is to do towel hangs. Drape a sturdy towel over a pull-up bar and grab one end in each hand. You could also use two smaller towels. Either way you set it up, hang from the towels. Start with ten seconds, gradually increasing the duration of your hang as your strength increases. When you get strong enough, you can start doing towel pull-ups.

Don't have a pull-up bar handy? No problem! Find a heavy door and drape one end of your towel over the top so that about six inches hang down on the other side. Now close the door, making sure it latches securely. Test the towel to make sure it will not slip, and check the door for structural integrity. When you are sure your set-up can hold your weight, plant your feet on the floor at the base of the door, grab your towel, lean back, and hang.

Head Butt

To get a feel for head butting, you can practice on an empty disposable plastic water bottle with thin plastic sides. Put the lid on it and then hold the bottle in your hand sideways. Start out moving slowly, learning how to align your head with your target before delivering the strike. Strike very lightly, only enough that you can feel what part of your head you are making

contact with. Gradually add speed to your technique; however, unlike your fists, feet, elbows, and knees, your head is not designed to absorb impacts, so don't practice butting things hard. The resulting impact may not be significant but can go a long way to developing your confidence in your head-butting technique.

It is not advised to hit anything harder than an empty water bottle. Repetitive head injuries can put you at risk for developing chronic traumatic encephalopathy (CTE). CTE and related head injuries can lead to short-term memory problems and difficulty in decision-making.

Biting

Known as "chewing foods," fruits and vegetables like apples, raw carrots, and celery not only clean your teeth but also strengthen your jaw muscles. Chewing on gum will also help to strengthen your bite. As an additional self-defense bonus, the American Dental Association says chewing sugarless gum for twenty minutes after meals can protect against tooth decay!

Boxing the Ears

To practice boxing the ears, cup your hands and clap them together. Try to make a popping sound. You should feel the compressed air being expelled through the hole left open just above your thumbs. When forced into an attacker's ear canal, this compressed air is capable of rupturing his eardrum.

Grabbing Clothing

You've already learned how to increase your grip strength in the sections on pinching and pulling the hair and ears. Now it's time to put that grip strength to work. Find a trusted friend who is willing to get yanked around a bit. Put on old clothes that you don't mind getting stretched out and torn. Take turns grabbing each other's clothing and using it to manipulate and throw your partner off balance. Take care not to give each other whiplash by yanking forward in such a way as to snap your partner's head back. Your partner can defend against this by tucking their chin to their chest in preparation for the pull.

Gouging

Hold a tennis ball in your hand. Place the tip of your thumb on the surface of the ball then drive your thumb hard toward the center, pushing a divot into the ball. Once you have strengthened your hands, you might want to try practicing with a grapefruit or orange (the bigger the better). Cradle the piece of fruit with your fingers as you drive your thumbs through the rind, sinking them deep into the center of the fruit. This is a messy exercise, so do it over a sink or outside.

Fish Hooking

You can practice fish hooking by simply slipping your thumb into any opening in your clothes as though you were slipping it into an assailant's cheek. You could use the waistband or pocket of your pants, the end of your sleeve, or the collar of your shirt. Once you have hooked your thumb inside, drive the material away from you, imagining it was an attacker's cheek. Take care not to rip your clothes!

Throat Strike

To practice the throat strike, you will need a substitute for the human neck. You could use a roll of bath tissue or paper towels. You can also fold and roll a towel into a cylindrical shape approximately the diameter of a large male's neck. Your hand should not be able to reach even halfway around. Practice attacking this substitute neck by poking it from the front with your fingertips (gently at first, don't hurt yourself) or gripping the sides with your fingers and pressing your thumbs deep into the material as far as you can.

Spitting

Learn to spit for distance and accuracy. Begin by gathering a large buildup of saliva in the front of your mouth. Lift the liquid with your tongue as you press your cheeks against your teeth. Inhale deeply through your nose and purse your lips. Rounded lips should help keep the projected saliva grouped in a tight wad. Arch your neck and snap your head forward as you exhale as quickly as possible, forcefully projecting the liquid from your mouth. Pick a small target within your range and let fly. It is best to practice spitting outside; however, keep in mind that spitting is inappropriate behavior in just about any culture. Therefore, it is best to practice this skill in private, even outside.

Throwing

You can improve your throwing accuracy by employing proper throwing mechanics.

Hold the object in your rear hand as you point your front shoulder toward your intended target. Step toward the target with your front foot and whip the object toward it in a straight line. For versatility, practice both overhand and underhand throwing.

Playing a game of catch is a great way to develop your mechanics, but this will not allow you to throw as aggressively as you would need to in order to be effective in a self-defense situation. Instead, hang a sheet or blanket over a clothesline. Mark a target on the middle of the fabric with a piece of tape. If it is an old sheet, you can draw or paint a person on it. Gather some common everyday objects such as an old coffee mug, book, hairbrush, stapler, or water bottle, and then practice trying to hit your target. Throw from a variety of ranges and angles. The idea is to get experience throwing a wide variety of objects with different sizes, shapes, and weights. Find a friend and make a game of it, keeping score by counting solid hits on the target.

Foot Flicking

To become a master of flicking things with your feet, all you need to do is think like a kid! When you are at the beach, practice flicking sand with your bare feet, scooping it with your toes then projecting it forward. While walking in the woods, flick sticks at trees with your feet. In the winter, use your boot to flick snow into the air ahead of you, about where you visualize an attacker's face would be. In the summer, learn to flick your flip-flop or sandal off your foot and send it flying toward a target. In fact, you can learn to flick any footwear out of which it is easy to slip your foot. As mentioned above, you can hang a sheet, mark out a target, and use it as a backdrop.

Takedowns

In defensive tactics it is not a matter of matching your strength
and power against the strength and power of your opponent but,
rather, the direction of all your strength and power toward
your opponent's weakness.
—FBI Training Manual

Understanding Takedowns

In a self-defense situation, an unexpected takedown can suddenly sway the odds in your favor. Takedowns involve throwing your attacker off balance and forcing him to the ground. Knowing how to take an attacker to the ground can help develop your confidence in your overall fighting ability in both stand-up and ground fighting.

The dynamics of any physical encounter are fluid and ever changing. Your strategy need be only to survive your attacker's assault at one range—say, striking range—long enough to transition into a different fighting range, such as grappling. This can rapidly change the dynamics of the encounter in your favor, allowing you to reclaim the initiative and control the action. Since your attacker is likely stronger than you, you must avoid any head-to-head testing of the same skill set at the same range. It's not wise to box a boxer or wrestle a wrestler. Changing tactics and ranges on your terms forces your attacker to reorient and adapt to you. You always want to be the one leading the dance.

All takedowns share this simple concept: disrupt your attacker's structure. When standing, we keep our heads over our shoulders, our shoulders over our hips, and our hips over our feet. To topple the tower, you need to disrupt this structure. Push his upper body far enough off his base or sweep his feet out from underneath him and he will fall down.

The first step in taking an attacker to the ground is to control his body by securely grabbing him. Then, use your whole body to pull or push him off balance. This is most easily accomplished by displacing the attacker's head. Where the head goes, the body follows, allowing you to move his center of mass off of its base. Your attacker must then either step to reestablish his base and regain his balance or fall to the ground. The more you understand about the science behind why your attacker falls to the ground, the better your takedowns will be.

You must wait until the right moment to attempt a takedown. If you move quickly and unexpectedly, your attacker may go down easily. It is much more difficult to try to throw an attacker who has his wits about him. If he is actively resisting, momentarily change tactics and stun him before trying again.

Part 1: The Clinch

Your attacker has grabbed you, or perhaps you have grabbed your attacker. Either way, you are now in some form of the clinch. Clinching is the act of tying up your attacker at close quarters, hugging him to smother his punches. Hook one hand behind his head and use your other hand to control his arm. When hooking from the inside, apply pressure with your forearm into his neck to create distance. You can also push his head downwards. Keep him off balance by leaning forward slightly and keeping him moving.

Two Ways to Clinch: 1) Hooking onto the outside of the neck and pulling in.
2) Hooking onto the inside of the neck and pushing out.

Striking in the Clinch

When in the clinch, remember that you can still strike with your arms, legs, and head. You can deliver hook punches and uppercuts with your fists and powerful strikes with your elbows. You can use your legs to knee the attacker in the legs, groin, or abdomen. Yet another option is to use your feet to kick his knees or stomp on his feet. Striking your attacker with sufficient force to a vulnerable area can stun him enough for you to execute a successful throw, dumping him to the ground.

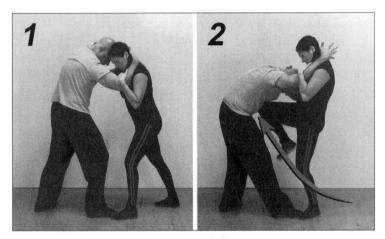

Attack Low: 1) Your attacker has grabbed you, leaving you no time or room to use your Tiger Claw Set. Grab him back to avoid getting tossed around, hugging him into the clinch. 2) Drive your knee into his solar plexus. You could also target his groin or the side of his thigh. Use a low strike to break his structure prior to a takedown.

Attack High: 1) From the clinch, prevent your attacker from punching you by pulling him close enough that you can press the side of your head against his. At the same time, control his arm by hooking inside the crook of his elbow. 2) Attack high by suddenly pulling your head back to create some space. 3) Sneak in a hook punch or two (after all, anything worth hitting once is worth hitting twice!). 4) Quickly pull your attacker back into the clinch, protecting yourself against counterpunches by pressing the side of your head against his. Once his attention has been drawn high, he should be easier to take down.

Unbalancing

Throwing an attacker who is in a stable stance is difficult. Rather than trying to take down an attacker who is standing strong, first compromise his structure before attempting a throw. To unbalance your attacker, imagine a line between his feet. Bisect this line with another line, perpendicular to the first, and you will know in which directions your attacker is weakest.

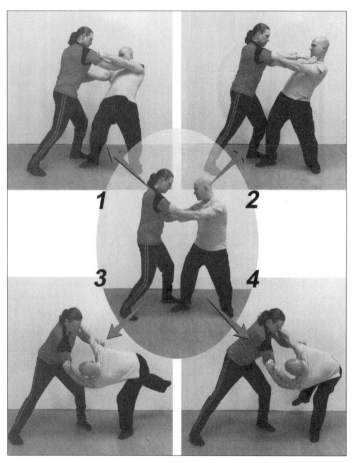

Unbalancing an Attacker: 1) Unbalance your attacker to the left by pulling down with your left hand and pushing up with your right. 2) Push your attacker backward with both hands to send him off balance to his rear. 3) Pull your attacker forward as you pull down with your right hand and push up with your left to pinwheel him forward. 4) Pinwheel your attacker to the side by pulling down with your right hand and pushing up with your left.

Part 2: Falling

In a self-defense encounter, you may find yourself on the receiving end of a takedown. Therefore, it is worth your time to learn how to fall in a way that minimizes your odds of getting hurt. Practice on a mat or other soft surface.

You can fall backward or to your sides. When falling, tuck your chin to your chest as you drop and interlace your fingers behind your head. At worst your elbow may hit and get bruised, but your head will still be protected. Exhale strongly to avoid having the wind knocked out of you. If you get stunned by the fall, curl into a ball and keep your head protected from kicks until you can recover.

Part 3: Throws

Some throws performed in combat arts, such as judo and wrestling, are incredible feats of physical prowess where one competitor sends his attacker soaring through the air. While impressive, throwing an attacker does not require that you literally pick him up and toss him. As we just discussed, all you really need to do is destabilize his posture by moving his upper body so it is no longer positioned over his hips. This will break his balance, allowing you to twist him off his base and dump him to the ground.

Basic Twisting Throw

The basic throw involves twisting your attacker to unbalance him, then turning your body to take him to the ground.

Any throw begins by unbalancing your attacker. Grasp him by the arms or shoulders, pulling him forward as you pull down with one hand and push up with the other, as though you were turning the wheel of a large truck. Complement this motion by turning your body, almost as though your imaginary truck were turning. Drop one foot back as you turn, pin-wheeling your attacker in that direction. The basic throw can be executed equally well to either side.

Basic Throw: 1) Begin from the clinch. 2) Drop your left foot back, pulling your attacker forward. Simultaneously pull down with your left hand and push up with your right. 3) Turn to your left, pinwheeling your attacker to your left. 4) Move into a dominant position to control your attacker, or, better yet, run!

Your attacker may attempt to regain his balance by taking a step. Reposition and try again. Keep him off balance by pulling him forward as you use your feet and legs to prevent him from stepping. This should make him trip and fall to the ground.

Self-Defense Encounter: The Bigger They Are, the Harder They Fall

For a few years, Live Steel Fight Academy met at my dojo on Monday nights. It was a Historical European Martial Arts (HEMA) program with a bunch of guys that liked to fight. While much of our practice was with weapons, we did some empty hand stuff as well.

One look at Big Vince and you knew why he was called that. At six foot six inches, he was by far the biggest guy in Live Steel Fight Academy. Big Vince wasn't just tall. He weighed in at over 280 pounds, a full hundred pounds more than me, and it wasn't just bulk. He often rode his bike about seven miles to class, fought for two hours, then rode home, so although he was big, he was also pretty fit.

One week we were messing around before class, fighting and grappling on the mats, when I matched up with Vince. I landed some controlled punches and kicks, but they probably wouldn't have stopped him even if they were real. He ultimately waded through my strikes, grabbed me, and threw me to the ground. He was immediately on top of me in side hold-down (you'll learn it in Level 7), flattening me beneath him. I lost several more times to Vince before I finally gave up, defeated morally as well as physically.

The next week, I tried again with similar results. He'd take my shots crossing the gap, get his big paws on me, and thirty seconds later it was over. Out of frustration, I started hitting him harder and harder until, after a nearly full-power sidekick that landed square on his ribs, he finally called me on it. "A little hard for a friendly match?" he asked.

"Sorry," I said with surprise, "you weren't reacting, so I didn't think you were feeling any of them!"

I remember he looked at me with big Teddy bear eyes and replied, "Dude, I bleed, too." I took heart in knowing that my giant wasn't invincible after all.

I spent the next week thinking hard about how to beat Big Vince. Short of a full-power strike to a vulnerable area like the neck, groin, or face, which wasn't appropriate in our friendly matches, my best shots weren't enough to stop him. I needed to drop him fast and already be in a dominant position when we hit the ground, because once he got on top I was finished. A possible solution suddenly came to me, and I eagerly awaited my next match with Big Vince.

We squared off, and I stayed out of range while throwing some long-distance shots. After a few hits, Vince was ready for a little payback. It was time to execute my plan. I stuck my head out a little too far, on purpose, and, sure enough, he jabbed at it. I faded back and he missed, but he jabbed again, only deeper this time. When he did, I parried his punch and leaped at him with everything I had. I was still in the air as I slipped my head past his lead shoulder and threw my free arm across his chest over his far shoulder. As I began my decent, I remember feeling him topple backward under me. It seemed like an unusually long drop, almost like it was in slow motion, and Big Vince landed hard, flat on his back, with a loud "oof!" I was already applying the headlock before we even hit the ground, so now I leaned all my weight on him and squeezed his neck as hard as I could (I had him in the same position as the photo on page 163). He turned to his side and pushed against me. Just when I thought he was going to slip out and get on top of me, he suddenly tapped out. I couldn't believe it. Vince was as surprised as I was, and, knowing how hard I had worked for it, shared in the joy of my success. After a long string of challenging defeats, I finally beat the giant!

Post-encounter Analysis: Fighting Big Vince gave me valuable insight into the difficulties of fighting an appreciably larger attacker. In the end, his biggest weakness was his stance. Using physics and an Aikido technique called *irimi nage*, or "entering throw," I attacked his structure, applying sudden pressure high on a line bisecting the line made by his feet. This drove him back over his heels and, since he had no time to step, he came crashing to the ground. When applied with good timing, the over-the-shoulder throw can be a very effective technique!

Over-the-Shoulder Throw

The over-the-shoulder throw depends on pushing the attacker's center backward over his base. Once you have driven him over his heels, his structure is compromised, and it becomes relatively easy to throw him to the ground.

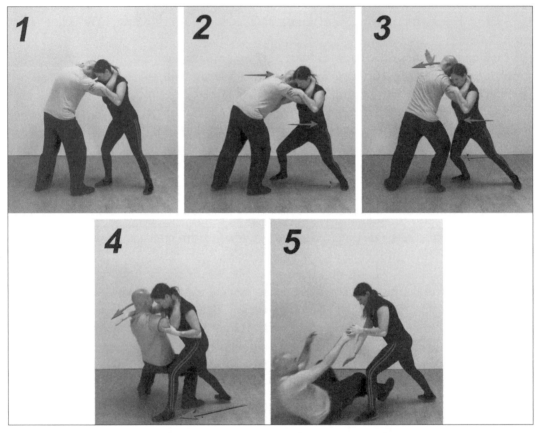

Over-the-Shoulder Throw: 1) Begin from the clinch. 2) Suddenly move back, giving your attacker a quick jerk forward. 3) As he resists your pull, suddenly switch directions and move with him, driving forward. As you do, slip your right hand over his left shoulder. 4) Step through with your outside leg as you simultaneously slide your arm across your attacker's chest and over his opposite shoulder as if it were a safety belt, lifting his chin and pushing it backward in the process. 5) Where his head goes, his body will follow. Break his balance by pushing him backward and then throwing him to the ground.

Rear Dump

There are several ways to take your attacker down. If one does not work, another might, so redouble your efforts with a different technique. The rear dump is similar to the over-the-shoulder throw in that you topple your attacker backward. In the rear throw you slip behind him before turning and throwing him over your leg.

Rear Dump: 1) An aggressor grabs you in a clinch. 2) Deliver a palm strike up the middle directly between his arms, catching him under the chin. 3) Move into position by quickly stepping your right foot around your attacker's left side, bringing your right hip behind his left hip. 4) Push the attacker backward as you land your right foot just past his left foot. 5) Turn your upper body as a single unit to your right, driving him backward. Your right thigh is pressed against his left thigh, preventing him from stepping and regaining his balance. 6) Dump your attacker to the ground.

Part 4: Foot Sweeps and Trips

Foot sweeps are ways to use your feet and legs to trip your attacker and make him fall to the ground. You can sweep or trip him with either foot. One is a big trip and one is a small trip. If you can swing your leg freely behind you, it is a big trip. If your tripping leg crosses your center, limiting your range of motion, it is called a small trip. Additionally, you can trip your attacker from outside his body, or inside by inserting your foot between his legs and catching his ankle. It is a simple concept but requires a good understanding of body mechanics to be effective. This understanding is best gained through training with a partner.

Big Outside Trip

The big outside trip is a heel-to-heel foot sweep. That means that your foot and your attacker's foot should meet at the Achilles tendon. The force of your leg against his foot needs to be enough to overcome the coefficient of friction between the sole of his foot and the floor. Friction is what is preventing his foot from sliding along the floor. The lower the value of coefficient of friction, the less force is required for sliding to occur. Therefore, reduce the amount of weight your attacker has resting on his front foot by pushing him backward while sweeping his foot upwards.

Big Outside Trip: 1) Begin from the clinch. Step your left foot to your left, unbalancing your attacker backward to his right. 2) Press the right side of your body against his right shoulder/neck as you kick your right foot outside your attacker's right leg. 3) On the return swing, bring the backs of your calves together. 4) Sweep his right foot out from under him. All these steps need to be performed in a single, fluid motion.

Small Outside Trip

The small outside trip works on the same principle as the big outside trip, only you use your opposite leg to perform the sweep. The small outside trip can be performed as a stand-alone takedown, but it also makes a good follow-up to a failed big outside trip. If your attacker steps out of your big trip, suddenly and unexpectedly sweep his foot a second time as soon as he goes to place it back on the ground.

Small Outside Trip: 1) The attacker has grabbed you. Pull him into the clinch. 2) Hook your left foot behind his right heel. 3) Perform a left foot sweep as you push him backward. 4) Continue your forward drive by landing in a long stance. 5) If needed, follow your attacker to the ground, keeping ahold of his shirt to control his arm. 6) Use your knees to keep him from turning toward you as you strike to his face.

Big Inside Trip

You can sweep inside as well as outside your attacker's stance. The big inside trip is a heel-to-heel foot sweep that is executed on the inside, between your attacker's legs. Sweeping on the inside has the added advantage of being able to knee your attacker in the groin as you set up for the sweep.

Big Inside Trip: 1) Begin from the clinch. 2) Slip your left foot between his legs, hooking his right leg from the inside. 3) Lift his leg high behind you as you drive your body forward. 4) Continue to drive your attacker backward as you step forward with your left foot. 5) Push your attacker backward until he falls to the ground. 6) As he falls, land with your hipbone against his groin as you simultaneously strike his eyes. This is an excellent segue into Level 7, ground fighting.

Small Inside Trip

The small inside trip is a foot sweep executed on the inside. Since there is no guarantee that any technique will be successful, always plan how to capitalize on the attacker's next position should your first technique fail. Like the small outside trip, the small inside trip is a good follow-up technique, this time to a failed big inside trip.

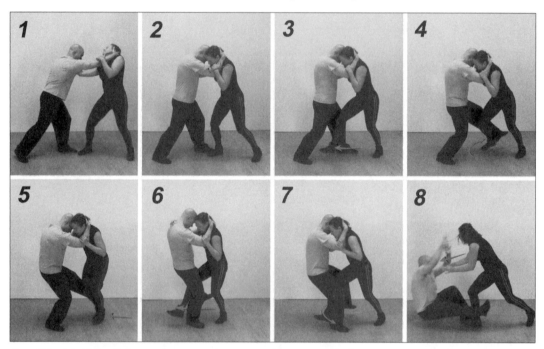

Small Inside Trip: 1) An aggressor reaches out and grabs you. 2) Rather than resist him, pull yourself tight into the clinch. 3) Insert your right foot between his legs, hooking his left heel from the inside. 4) Lift his foot as you drive your body forward. 5) He doesn't fall, so close the distance by sliding your back foot to your front. 6) Slip your right foot between his legs again, taking the opportunity to knee him in the groin as you do so. 7) This time, hook his right foot with your right to keep him from stepping back and regaining his balance. 8) Push him backward, sending him sprawling to the ground. Now would be a good time to run.

Reality Check!

The photos in this book are misleading. They make the moves look clean and easy to perform so you can see all the elements necessary to learn them properly. The truth is that a physical confrontation will be chaotic, intense, and sloppy. It may seem like you can't remember what to do, or that nothing you are doing is working. Expect this and *don't get frustrated*. Instead, identify a reference position that you are familiar with and work from there. This may be a full defensive cover to mitigate potential damage, a clinch to control your attacker, or a tiger claw strike to his eyes to go on the offensive and reclaim the initiative.

Level-6 Activities

Visualization

Imagine self-defense scenarios that end with you throwing or tripping your attacker. Close your eyes and visualize your surroundings in as much detail as you can. Then, visualize being attacked. Imagine in great detail how it feels to be grabbed or struck. How would you move in response? Picture stunning your attacker with a combination of strikes before unbalancing and dumping him to the ground, allowing you to quickly and safely exit the situation.

Shadow Practice

As an extension of the visualization exercise described above, move around in shadow practice, defending and counterattacking as if an actual attacker were attacking you. Practice in different places and different environments, both indoors and outdoors. Practice in a variety of spaces, from large spaces like a driveway and more confined spaces such as a hallway. Picture the places where an assailant may ambush you and work through the scenario, going through the physical motions while visualizing your attacker. End each scenario with a takedown, but remember that you want to avoid going to the ground yourself if at all possible, especially in situations involving multiple attackers.

Dummy Leg

Training equipment can help us practice our techniques with a physical object. Practice your foot sweeps and trips with a long-legged chair or barstool. Prepare the chair by padding the legs with foam pipe insulation, pool noodles, or old towels secured with rubber bands or tape. Another option is to simply hold a staff vertically in front of you, with one end planted firmly on the ground. You could pad the ends of your staff with foam pipe insulation. Use the chair or staff as a substitute for an attacker's leg to practice tripping from the inside and outside with both legs. Construct your own padded chair or padded staff using the blueprints in Appendix 4 at the end of this book.

Partner Work

The best way to learn how to perform takedowns is to practice with a partner. Begin by practicing the unbalancing drills, pushing and pulling to break your partner's balance. Since this is the first step in any takedown, take the time to practice it a lot. Once you are warmed up and ready to start taking falls, begin taking each other down using the basic twisting throw. Use a mat or thick carpet to cushion your falls. Work through each throw, moving slowly at first and gradually add speed and power to your takedowns, taking care not to injure your training partner, who should be simultaneously practicing how to fall correctly.

As above, practice in different environments, both indoors and outdoors. Have your partner ambush you and work through the scenario together. Remember not to accidentally injure your training partner.

Remember the Goldilocks Rule and strive for a 50- to 80-percent success rate.

LEVEL 7
Ground Fighting

Jiu-jitsu is for the protection of the individual, the older man, the weak, the child, the lady, and the young woman from being dominated and hurt by some bum because they don't have the physical attributes to defend themselves.
—Helio Gracie

Understanding Ground Fighting

Ground fighting can be scary and overwhelming, especially if you have limited experience with it. Don't be intimidated. Anyone can learn effective ground fighting skills. All it takes is practice. The techniques presented here are the very basics, but they will give you the tools you need for dealing with the most common situations.

Taking a fight to the ground can be a good way to neutralize an attacker. However, be very careful when and how you employ this strategy. Going to the ground limits your mobility and awareness of the area around you. This, combined with a preoccupied mind and vulnerable position, leaves you exposed to an attack by a second assailant. Therefore, avoid going to the ground in uncontrolled situations involving, or possibly involving, multiple attackers.

Part 1: Basics

Positioning on the Ground

You are on the ground, and your attacker is still on his feet. Don't turn away or go to all fours in an attempt to get to your feet. Doing so leaves you vulnerable to potentially devastating kicking attacks. Instead, keep your weapons facing your attacker. Roll to your back and move so that your feet are pointed toward your attacker. When your attacker moves to get around your feet, spin to reorient yourself, keeping your feet pointed toward your attacker so you can kick him. Target his knees, groin, and, if he bends over, his face. Keep away from him, or keep him away from you, until you have an opportunity to get back to your feet safely.

On the Ground: Keep your feet oriented toward your attacker. Then use your kicks to keep him at bay.

Getting Up

If you find yourself on the ground, you don't want to stay there! You are vulnerable on the ground, but you have to know how to get up safely. Leaning forward or rolling over to put your hands on the ground means bending over and exposing your head to attack. Instead, sit up. Keep one hand up to guard yourself as you get one knee under you. Continue to defend with your hands as you rise straight up to your feet. Avoid bending at the waist. Use your free arm to guard your upper body as you rise, ready to reengage or run.

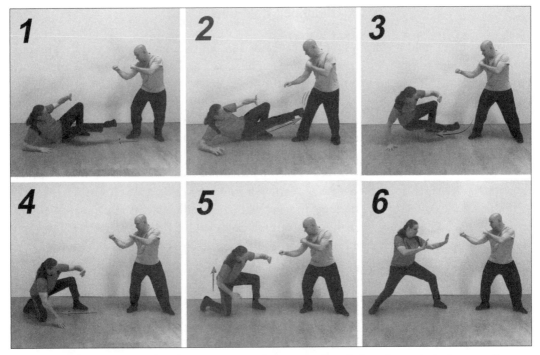

Getting Up: 1) Keep your feet between you and your attacker. As he advances, push yourself backward to maintain a safe distance. 2) If he comes within range, kick him in the knee. 3) Bounce off his knee and swing your kicking leg under you in one fluid motion, supporting your body on one hand and the opposite foot. 4) Keep your free hand in front to guard as you get one knee under you. 5) Continue to defend with your hands as you rise straight up to your feet. 6) As you rise to your feet, assume a neutral guard.

Part 2: Pins, Hold-Downs, and Locks

While you should usually avoid going to the ground, there may come a time when you fall, get knocked down, or need to hold down and control an attacker, as I did in my encounter with the burglar that I recounted in the introduction.

If you find yourself being taken to the ground, try to take your attacker with you. You don't want to be on the ground in front of a standing assailant. At the same time, you want to avoid being in the bottom position when on the ground. When your attacker is on top of you, he can use his weight to restrict your mobility, hindering your ability to defend yourself.

The first step to learning how to defend yourself on the ground is learning to identify the four basic positions you may encounter: headlock hold-down, mount, guard, and side hold-down. A working knowledge of these basic positions will allow you to escape, or even dominate and control, your attacker.

Headlock Hold-Down

The headlock hold-down is a simple yet effective pinning technique. Once you have become comfortable with this pin, you should be able to hold down and effectively immobilize a much larger attacker. It is best to begin applying the pin as soon as you have completed a throw, such as the big trip.

From the attacker's right side, wrap your right arm around his neck and grasp your left hand. Your right leg should be straight out to the front with your left leg bent behind you. Lower your hips and upper body, keeping your right buttock on the floor as you roll your weight back to apply pressure on your attacker's chest, making it difficult for him to breathe. Drive your head into your attacker's temple as you squeeze hard with your arms to compress his neck.

When done correctly, an unarmed attacker will have a difficult time escaping. The problem with this hold is that you cannot see your attacker's hands. If he were to draw a weapon, he could employ it to great effect before you could counter and control him.

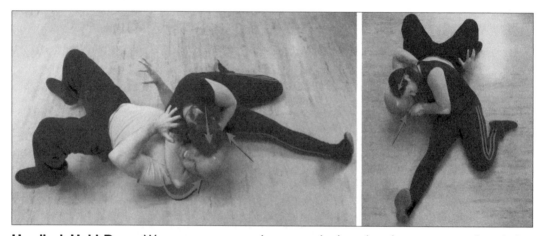

Headlock Hold-Down: Wrap your arm around your attacker's neck and squeeze to apply a choke. Increase the pressure by pressing your head into his temple.

Self-Defense Story: Kiss My Converse

When I was about fourteen, I was playing a nighttime game of Capture the Flag with a bunch of other boys my age. A disagreement broke out about something silly like someone getting tagged, and a few of us were gathered around in the dark arguing about it when things got heated between one of my friends on the other team and myself. He was holding a flashlight in my face, so I couldn't really see him, but something I said pushed him over the edge and, without warning, he attacked me. He dropped the flashlight slightly as he stepped one foot back, then launched himself into a jump front snap kick aimed directly at my face. In short, he sucker-kicked me!

I wish I could take credit for what happened next, but it was a lucky accident. I saw the telegraph (his flashlight beam dropped a bit as he set up his feet), so when he launched the kick I instinctually flinched backward, closed my eyes, and brought my hands up to try to block my face. A tenth of a second later, I opened my eyes to find that I had his size-eleven sneaker in my hands, with his foot still in it! I threw his foot sideways, spinning him around so his back was facing me. In the process, he clocked me in the side of the head with his flashlight, but since he was standing on one leg and off balance, his blow didn't have much effect. By the time his foot hit the ground, I had my arm wrapped around his neck from the rear. I immediately hip tossed him, and we both hit the ground. I kept ahold of his neck and squeezed as hard as I could until he gave up. Soon, we were friends again and went back to playing, no harm done.

Post-encounter Analysis: My friend had been studying taekwondo for several years and had a good jump kick. I, on the other hand, had no formal training. It was just dumb luck that I caught his kick. I wasn't even looking! Anyway, I kept thinking what would have happened if he hadn't dropped that flashlight beam as he set up his kick. He could have caught me right under the chin, very hard, which would have been incredibly bad for me. Soon after that incident, he stopped taking taekwondo. And I started.

Transitioning to Side Hold-Down

You have your attacker in a headlock hold-down, but he is struggling to free himself. Suddenly he manages to slip a hand in and begins to force your head back. Your position is no longer tenable, so it is time to preemptively transition to the side hold-down. If your attacker manages to get his hands on your face and begins to crank your head back, immediately transition to a side hold-down.

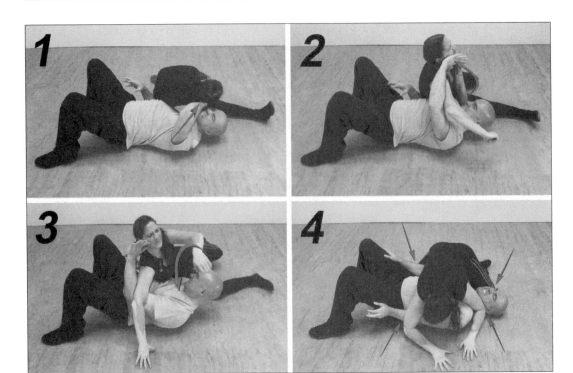

Headlock to Side Hold-Down: The side hold-down makes a good follow-up to a failed headlock hold-down. 1) Your attacker has managed to slip his hand between your heads. 2) He then presses your head up and backward. 3) Rather than resist his push, move with it, diving across his chest. Note how the defender is trapping her attacker's arms. 4) Transition to a side hold-down, squeezing your elbows to your knees.

Side Hold-Down

The side hold-down is a strong pin position in which you lay perpendicularly across your attacker. Unlike the headlock hold-down, the side hold-down allows you to better monitor and control your attacker's hands. It also requires very little energy to maintain, making it preferable to the headlock hold-down if you needed to restrain someone until he calms down or help arrives.

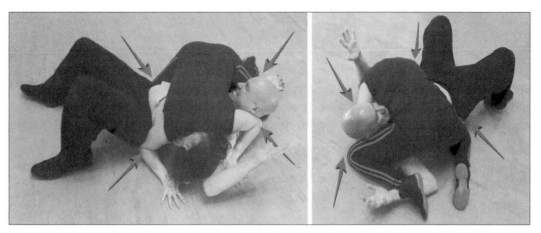

Side Hold-Down: From your attacker's right side, lean across him perpendicular to his body, pinning him down on his back. Anchor his four corners by pinning his head between your left elbow and knee and his waist with your right elbow and knee. From here, you can persuade him to stop resisting you by striking him in the head or ribs with your knees and elbows.

Dead Weight: Sink your body weight straight down onto your attacker, pinning him to the ground and making it hard for him to breathe. Note how the defender has used her shin to further control her attacker by pinning his arm to the ground.

Arm Lock

The side hold-down gives you an excellent opportunity to apply an arm lock. Arm locks can be used to attack your attacker's shoulder or elbow. The figure-four arm lock hyper-rotates the shoulder joint, while an arm bar hyperextends the elbow joint. Each is capable of tearing ligaments and tendons, and possibly dislocating the joint, but with practice each can also be used with a lower level of force to simply control and immobilize your attacker.

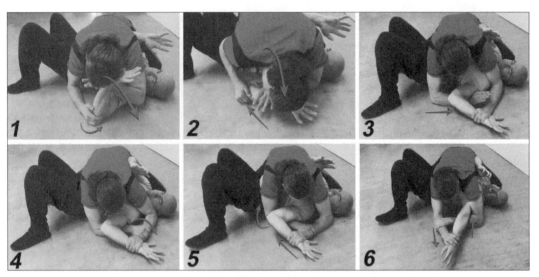

Arm Lock: 1) You have your attacker in a side hold-down. Base his elbow with one hand as you use your other hand to force his left arm backward. 2) Use your head and the weight of your body to help force the back of his hand to the ground. 3) Keep the back of his hand pressed to the floor as you slip your right hand under his left upper arm. 4) Grab your own left wrist with the fingers of your right hand on top. 5) Slide his elbow close to his body, bending his arm at a 90-degree angle, and then lift your right elbow, wrenching his elbow upward to apply torque to his shoulder. 6) If he straightens his arm, switch your hand placement, securing his wrist with your right hand and slipping your left arm under his elbow. Force his wrist down and elbow up. It's important to note that the purpose of the arm bar is not to break the arm, but to cause the hyperextension of the elbow joint.

Reality Check!

This is advanced material, which is why it appears in Level 7, not Level 4. These moves are far more difficult to employ than the relatively simple Tiger Claw Set. Therefore, expect that they will require more time, effort, and guidance to master. They are, however, the basics, and taking the time to learn them properly is the only way to gain proficiency in this particular skill set.

Mount Position

The mount is a dominant grappling position in which you straddle your attacker, using your body weight to pin him to the ground on his back. While keeping your feet tucked, widen your knees and sink your hips. This greatly improves your balance because it both broadens your base and lowers your center of gravity. It also puts far more pressure on your attacker beneath you.

In the high mount, you sit right over your attacker's sternum, with your knees forcing his arms up and away from his midsection. As a general rule, you should try to work your way toward a high mount because it offers you the most options for attack.

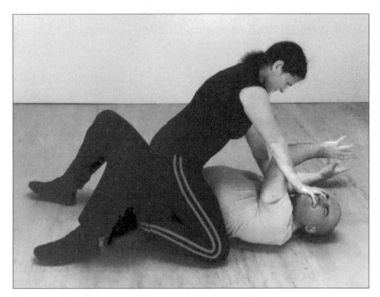

Mount Position: Pin your attacker by straddling his torso.

Guard Position

In the guard position, your back is on the ground with your legs wrapped around your attacker's waist, preventing him from standing up or moving away. The guard is considered an advantageous position because you can control your attacker with your legs. Oddly enough, it is a good position for rape prevention, as an assailant cannot get a victim's pants off when being held in this position.

The weakness of holding your attacker in the guard is that he will probably try to punch you in order to escape. To prevent this, grab his head and pull it tightly into your chest. Another option is to create distance using an extended guard. This is done by transitioning to a position with your knees in, on his chest, and your back arched, pushing him away. From there you can get your feet on his hips and walk your shoulders back. As soon as he is in position, deliver a stamping kick to his face or head.

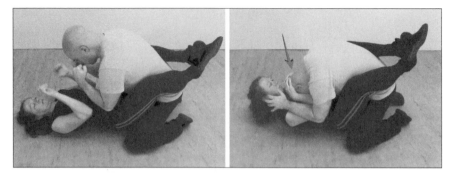

Guard Position: 1) Control your attacker by wrapping your legs tightly around his waist, locking your feet together behind him. 2) Limit his mobility further by grabbing his head and pulling it tightly to your chest.

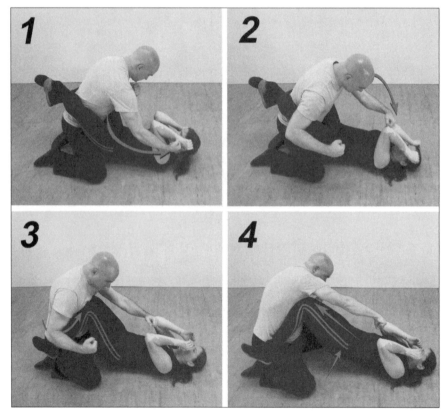

Extended Guard: 1) You have your attacker in the guard, but he starts punching you. Protect yourself by assuming a full defensive cover. 2) Peek between your hands to see his punches coming. Move your arms to make him hit your elbows. 3) Unlock your feet and slip your knees together. Turn your toes in and use your feet to control his hips. 4) Lift your hips and press the attacker away with your knees. His punches can no longer reach you.

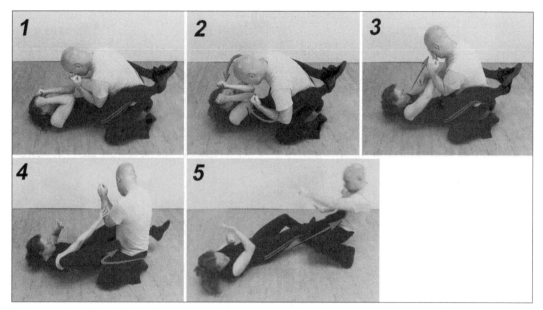

Drive to the Side: 1) You have your attacker in your guard, but you are unable to grab his head and pull it down to your chest. 2) He starts viciously punching you in the head. Assume a full defensive cover. Peek between your forearms, watching for the best time to strike. 3) Check his arms as you attack his eyes with a tiger claw strike. 4) Immediately drive to the side and put your foot against his hip. 5) Extend your leg to push him, or yourself, away. If he comes right back at you, kick him in the head. Keep your feet facing the attacker until you can get a knee under you and rise to your feet.

Part 3: Escaping

As important as hold-downs can be for you to know, they can also be used against you. Therefore, it is equally important that you know how to get out of an attacker's hold.

Escaping the Guard

Your attacker has you in his guard. Rather than struggle to get out of his hold, fall back on your striking skills. Avoid him grabbing your head and pulling you down and forward into his chest. Instead, sit up tall and strike his groin to counterattack. Press against his hips and push away to get back to your feet, taking care not to get kicked on the way out.

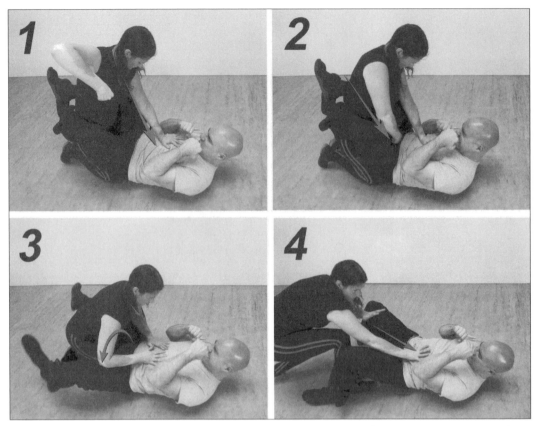

Escaping the Guard: 1) Your attacker has you trapped in his guard. Sit up tall, pressing against his solar plexus. 2) Punch his groin to loosen his hold on you. 3) Open his legs by driving the points of your elbows into the insides of his thighs, pressing them to the floor. 4) Push away to get back to your feet, taking care not to get kicked on the way out.

Escaping the Mount

Being trapped on the ground is a common yet extremely vulnerable and dangerous situation in self-defense, so it is worth your effort to learn what you need to do to escape. When an attacker has you pinned to the ground, he has the advantage of weight, leverage, and firepower. All of these escapes share the same principle: bump and drive to the side.

Against the Ground and Pound

Ground and pound means throwing someone to the ground, establishing a dominant, usually top position such as the mount, then raining down punches on them. This is a very dangerous position to be in. The secret to knowing how to defend yourself and roll your attacker off of you is a matter of understanding the physics behind disrupting his structure and unbalancing him.

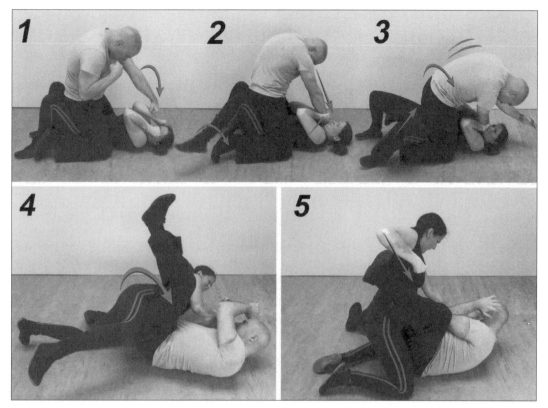

Escape the Ground and Pound: 1) Your attacker has knocked you to the ground, mounted you, and is viciously punching you in the head. Assume a full defensive cover. 2) Lock one foot over his ankle as you peek between your arms to watch for an opportunity to parry and catch a punch. 3) Hug your attacker's hand tightly in to the crook of your neck as you raise your hips and buck him forward. 4) Since he has no hand available to catch himself, he should roll off of you. 5) As soon as he does, roll with him, placing you in his guard. Sit up tall and counterattack by striking his groin. Press against his hips to pin him as you get back to your feet and run, taking care not to get kicked on the way out.

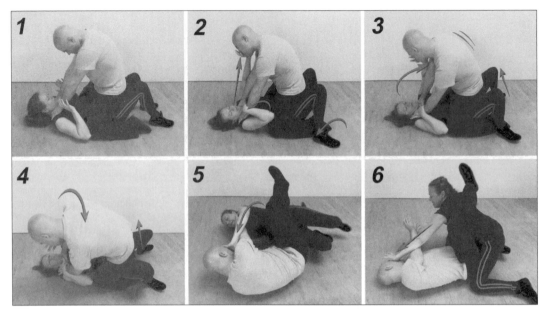

Against a Choke: 1) Your attacker has you in the mount and is choking you with both hands. Tuck your chin to protect your throat. 2) Since he can't see your lower body, begin by sneaking your same-side foot over his ankle on the side you plan to roll him in order to prevent him from moving his leg to catch his balance. Then hook his wrist with one hand as you simultaneously tiger claw his eyes with the other. 3) With the same-side arm and leg secured to prevent him from catching himself, use your legs to arch your back and lift your hips. 4) Drive him at a forward angle over his trapped arm. 5) Unable to catch himself, he should roll off of you. 6) Roll with him, placing you in his guard, but exposing his eyes and groin to counterattacks.

Against a Full Pin

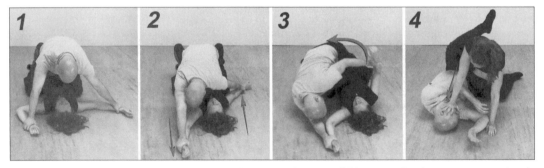

One-Up/One-Down: This is a quick escape that is worth trying. 1) Your attacker has you mounted and is pinning your hands. Since he can't see your lower body, begin by sneaking your foot over the attacker's leg on the side to which you plan to roll him in order to prevent him from posting with his leg. 2) Twist your body to help the hand slide up past your head on the side you are planning to roll, while your other hand is pulled down by your waist. 3) Immediately arch your back and drive your hips forward on an angle, driving his head toward the floor. Unable to catch himself, he should topple off to one side. 4) Roll with him, which will place you in his guard but also expose his face and groin to counterattacks.

If you try the one-up/one-down escape only to find that your hands are firmly pinned and won't slide, abandon this tactic and move on to step two, the "Snow Angel."

Snow Angel: 1) When the attacker has your hands firmly pinned, you will need to move his weight forward in order to move your hands. Shimmy down until his shoulders are directly over his hands. 2) Bridge your back and buck your hips up to drive his shoulders past his hands. At the same time, slide your hands down to your sides, as though making a snow angel. 3) When performed correctly, your attacker will not be able to stop his face from hitting the ground.

Fighting Dirty

There are no rules in self-defense, and grappling is the perfect time to use every dirty trick in your arsenal. However, make sure you are in a good position before employing any particular technique. For example, if you are trapped under an attacker's mount and you attempt to gouge his eyes, he is probably going to respond by punching you in the face. Rather, think multi-dimensionally, executing coordinated attacks from different angles. For example, grab an ear on one side and pull down hard while you drive the thumb of your other hand into his opposite eye. At the same time, hook his lower leg and arch your back, bucking him sideways.

Wall Pin

Being pinned to a wall is not unlike being pinned to the ground. The angle of the force has obviously changed, but this new angle of orientation allows you to use gravity to your advantage.

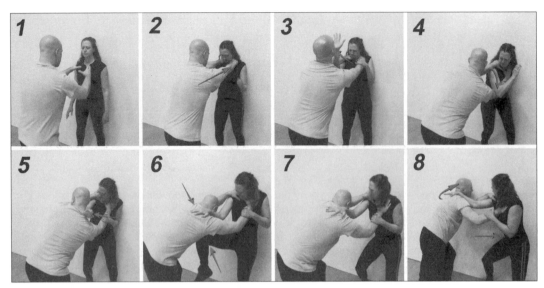

Elbow Release: 1) When enraged, an aggressor may instinctually attempt to choke you. 2) Your attacker has grabbed your neck and pinned you up against a wall. Tuck your chin and shrug your shoulders to protect your throat. 3) Reach one arm up and strike him under the chin with a palm heel strike. This move will act to straighten his arms, weakening them considerably. 4) Immediately slam your elbow downward sharply into the crook of his opposing arm, bending it. 5) Use that same arm to chop him in the side of the neck. 6) Use the momentum of your chop to pull him into a knee strike. 7) As you put your foot down, begin to slide sideways along the wall. 8) Slam your attacker face first into the wall.

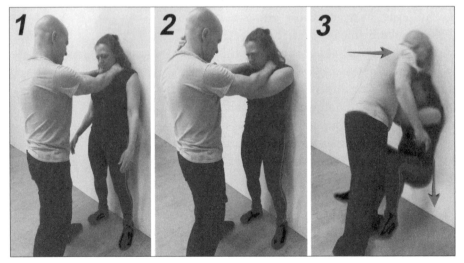

Grab and Drop: 1) An assailant has grabbed you by the neck. Tuck your chin and shrug your shoulders to protect your throat. 2) Grab the attacker's neck or shirt. 3) Kick your legs out from under you as you drop straight down, directly onto your bottom. As you slide down, your weight will drive his head into the wall, simultaneously stunning him and breaking your fall.

Level-7 Activities

Solo Practice

Perform a low fall, protecting your head, then move around on your back as you practice kicking an imaginary attacker. Get up using the proper method, getting one knee under you and guarding your head as you rise to your feet. Work up to ten repetitions on each side. This is a great whole-body workout, complete with built-in cardio work.

Partner Work

Practice the different hold-downs and escapes with a partner. Move slowly and methodically, working through each one until you understand the technique and can perform all the movements smoothly. That way, when you begin to apply speed and power to your technique, you will do so correctly, not wasting your energy in a brute force match-up.

Drill 1: Spinners

Lie on your back and have your partner stand over you. Your partner's job is to get around your legs and pin you to the ground. Your job is to use your hands and feet to defend yourself. Spin around on your back, keeping your feet oriented toward your attacker. When your partner comes within range, kick to his knees and, if he leans in, his head. Take care not to injure your partner by kicking too hard. Get up using the proper method, getting one knee under you and guarding your head as you rise to your feet. Switch roles and repeat.

Drill 2: Snakes and Blankets

This game is an excellent introduction to grappling and ground fighting. You should do this drill on a mat. One partner is the "snake" and lies down on their back while the other, the "blanket," lies perpendicularly across them, pinning the snake with a side hold-down. The snake then tries to escape from under the blanket. The blanket can move around and should be heavy but can't grab with the hands. If the snake escapes, he or she wins, and the roles are reversed. To discourage giving up your back (a bad habit in grappling), if the blanket can get into a "piggyback" position on the snake's back, blanket wins. Practice this drill with different partners.

Drill 3: Wrestle

Begin on your knees, facing your partner who is also kneeling. Grab, push, and pull to break your partner's balance. Attempt to dominate your partner by attaining a top-control position.

Start slowly, with minimal resistance. Gradually increase the intensity of your training by adding speed and power to your practice. As always, keep in mind that practice is just that. It is not an actual fight. Therefore, take care not to injure your training partner.

Grappling

Ground fighting is an art unto itself. Take your self-defense skills to the next level by studying a few months of grappling. You don't need to become an expert, but it helps to know how to handle yourself on the ground. Look for a judo, jiu-jitsu, or wrestling club and observe a class. They vary from inexpensive clubs at your local YMCA to high-end commercial schools that require long-term contracts, which, in my opinion, should be approached with caution. Don't be fooled by appearances. Sometimes the best instructors are the most low-key. If you like what you see, give it a try and stay a while. If not, then quit. The experiences you will gain rolling with different people in a class are invaluable. It will not only make you more comfortable ground fighting, but it will also give you valuable insight into your actual self-defense abilities.

Recommended Reading

If you've made it this far in your training, you would benefit from reading Rory Miller's book *Training for Sudden Violence: 72 Practical Drills*.[1] In it, he offers many activities that complement the teachings in this book and could only serve to expand your skills and understanding.

---

1. Rory Miller, *Training for Sudden Violence: 72 Practical Drills* (Wolfeboro, NH: YMAA Publication Center, 2016).

LEVEL 8
Weapons

The final weapon is the brain, all else is supplemental.
—John Steinbeck

Weapons are power multipliers and therefore potential game changers. A weapon in your hand can tip the balance of a self-defense encounter in your favor. Unfortunately, weapons can also be used against you. Worse yet, an attacker can take *your* weapon and use it against you! For both reasons, it is important to include weapons in your training.

Part 1: Improvised Weapons

Weapons can be found all around you. Start with the items you carry on your person. What do you have in your pockets? What items are in your immediate vicinity? How can you use these things to defend yourself?

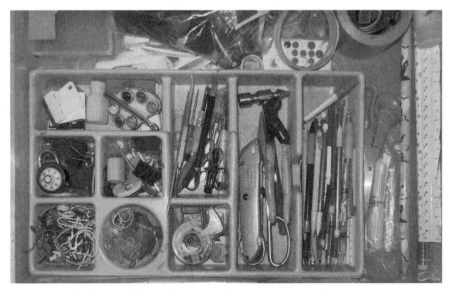

Contents of a Typical Junk Drawer: How many potential improvised weapons can you identify? What would your top three choices be?

Improvised weapons generally fall into four categories: close-range weapons, medium-range weapons, long-range weapons, and projectile weapons.

Close-range weapons, such as a knife or screwdriver, are typically short, thereby limiting their effective range. This doesn't make the weapon any less dangerous. In fact, it can make the weapon more difficult to defend against than a longer weapon.

Medium-range weapons vary from a foot long, such as a hammer, to about four feet long, such as a walking cane. While medium-length weapons give you a definite reach advantage, you are usually still within striking range of an unarmed attacker.

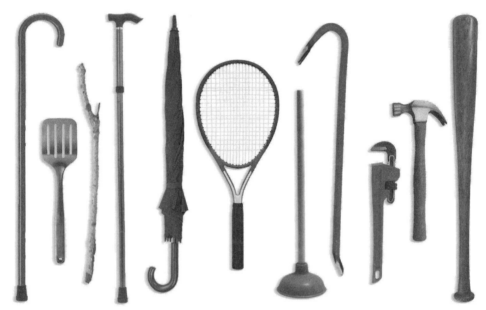

A small example of the wide variety of medium-range improvised weapons you might encounter in your everyday environment. Keep in mind that every one of these could also be used as a projectile weapon.

Long-range weapons include anything that is about as tall as you are or taller, such as a hockey stick, curtain rod, or coat rack. Long weapons allow you to strike an adversary while remaining outside of his effective unarmed striking range.

Projectile weapons are those that can be used at a distance. Anything you can throw effectively can be used as a weapon, such as a coffee mug, stapler, or remote control. The range and effectiveness of such weapons is limited only by the weight of the object and your individual throwing ability. Commercial products such as cleaning spray, hairspray, or insecticides can be propelled via a pressurized can or spray bottle. A fire extinguisher can be used to spray an attacker, obstructing his vision.

Weapons are force multipliers, but zero times anything is still zero. You must have some basic skills to wield them effectively. Use the object to augment your existing skill sets. Everything you have already learned still applies. Don't become so preoccupied with employing a weapon that you forget you can still strike with your free hand or kick with your feet.

Keys

One of the most common ideas people think of when it comes to self-defense is to take your keys and place them between your fingers in an attempt to turn you into an economy model Wolverine. Unfortunately, this does not work as well as you might think. In reality, striking with your keys between your fingers tends dig the serrated metal edges into the soft inner surfaces between your fingers, injuring you, the user, as much as your attacker, nullifying any benefit this technique might offer.

A far superior way to hold your key is the same way you hold it when you are unlocking your car, pinched between your thumb and forefinger. The key is anchored by your key ring and to the other keys being held tightly in the palm of your hand, forming a handle of sorts. This is not unlike a standard knife grip, so think of your key as a very small knife. Use it to swipe across your attacker's face or hands. A laceration of the forehead will not only cause pain, it can result in blood dripping into the eyes, hampering your attacker's vision and marking him for easy identification. A stab or swipe across the eyes could potentially blind your attacker, permanently. You can also stab

into other sensitive areas of your attacker's anatomy, such as his neck or ribcage. It is worth repeating that your key is just a tool, a small part of the overall equation. Don't prioritize it over your other weapons, such as stamping kicks. Instead, use it to augment your existing skills.

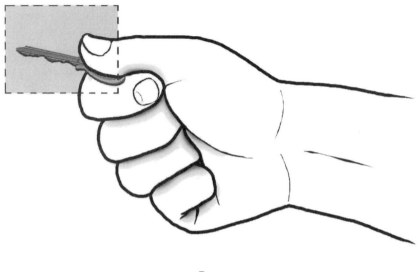

Pen

Anything with a pointy tip can be used as an effective tool for self-defense. One of the most common and easily implemented yet often overlooked improvised weapon is the pen. Pens are allowed even in areas that have tight security prohibiting the carrying of weapons of any kind. They are easily accessible, carried, hidden, deployed, and employed. Although any pen would work in pinch, tactical pens are available that are constructed of sturdy materials and specially made with self-defense in mind. If you want a budget alternative to tactical pens, check out the Zebra 301 and 701 lines. They're stainless steel, pretty solidly built, available in pencil, ballpoint, or gel, and are readily available in common stores such as Staples and Target.

Hold the pen in your fist with the tip facing downward, using your thumb to reinforce the back of the pen. Any attack that could be made with a hammer fist can be augmented to great effect with a pen.

Parrying an attacker's punches with a pen in your hand turns your defense into an effective offense. Hopefully, your attacker will learn his lesson after you catch him once. You can create a defensive screen by weaving it in the air in front of you using a basic figure-eight pattern, but break your rhythm by incorporating erratic timing, making it difficult for the attacker to accurately predict your movements.

In addition to stabbing strikes, you can make raking strikes that go side to side, holding the pen perpendicularly to the target. Imagine how effective it would be to rake a pen across an attacker's face or neck! A pen can also aid you in clinch work. Pressing into the neck with a pen, especially at the base of the skull, *will* cause your attacker to move in response to the pressure.

Belt

A belt with a heavy buckle can allow you to keep some distance between you and your attacker. Besides swinging it, you can use a belt for deflecting, trapping, choking, tripping, and throwing. Practice removing your belt and quickly wrapping it around your forearm as a deflective gauntlet against a knife attack. Create a defensive shield in front of you by swinging the belt in a figure-eight pattern. If your attacker grabs the belt, immediately change tack by closing on him and attacking with your free hand with a tiger claw to the eyes.

Flashlight

A flashlight can help you identify threats early and avoid them. Simply shining a light on a predator can be enough to discourage an attack. Larger flashlights can be used as clubs, but smaller, tactical flashlights can also be used to great effect. A tactical flashlight is one that has been specially designed primarily for military and law enforcement applications. They are typically smaller, brighter, and more durable than traditional flashlights. Most can be taken into places where weapons are banned, such as movie theaters or airplanes. Some are equipped with specialized ends that are toothed to focus the power of your strike for maximum effect.

Holding a flashlight low by your hip does not put you in a good position to strike an attacker. Rather, carry your flashlight in a reverse grip, so the illuminated end extends from the pinky side of your hand. Hold your hand high by your ear. This hold puts you in a good position to strike quickly in a tactic known as "flash, bash, and dash." Shine your light directly into the threat's eyes to disorient him. A defensive flashlight with four hundred lumens is enough to cause momentary blindness and disorientation, giving you enough time to attack or escape. If you choose to attack, strike his face as though forcefully stamping his forehead with a giant rubber stamp. While the threat is temporarily blinded, use low kicks to the groin or knees to impede his ability to pursue you, then run away.

Fire Extinguisher

A fire extinguisher can be a useful improvised weapon to fight bad guys as well as fires. It can be used to spray an attacker from a distance, obstructing his vision. While fire

extinguisher powder is nontoxic, it is not entirely safe. They often contain chemicals such as sodium bicarbonate (baking soda) and monoammonium phosphate that can cause mild irritation to the nose, throat, and lungs, resulting in symptoms like shortness of breath and coughing when inhaled in large enough quantities.

At long range a fire extinguisher can also make an effective projectile weapon, even if empty. At close range, the metal canister itself could be used to inflict blunt force trauma on your assailant.

Knife

Make no mistake about it, a knife is a deadly weapon, but, unfortunately, it is most effectively employed as an offensive weapon used by an attacker. Knives make surprisingly *unreliable* tools for self-defense. Unless you manage to inflict a grievous wound to a vital area, a cut is likely to have little effect against an adrenaline-fueled attacker other than to further enrage him. A knife's primary value may be as a deterrent before a physical altercation begins. Wearing a large knife on your hip when hiking may discourage an attack based solely on the perceived threat, not on your actual skill with the weapon.

In the United States, the only general restriction on knives is their intended use, not the physical properties of the blade itself. As far as the federal government is concerned, carrying a knife to use primarily as a weapon, in either attack *or* defense, is illegal. This distinction makes it technically illegal to carry a blade in a location where it's not required as a tool with an immediate utilitarian purpose. It also complicates carrying a knife into any situation where it's not clearly needed.

Knives that generally *are* legal to carry include multi-tools, utility knives, and pocketknives with blades shorter than 2.5 inches. Other knife laws can vary widely from state to state. These include laws restricting the types of knives you are allowed to own or carry. Many states have ownership laws outlawing certain types of knives. These include but are not limited to: automatic spring-loaded knives, centrifugal knives that can be opened with a flick of the wrist, gravity knives that drop open, push daggers with the handle placed perpendicular to the main cutting edge, belt buckle knives, ballistic knives capable of shooting a detachable blade a short distance, and concealed blades shorter than 30 cm (about a foot) disguised as everyday objects such as combs, pens, lipstick, necklaces, or credit cards.

Every state has its own laws stating what types of knives can be carried and whether they can be concealed or must be carried openly. These laws can include any knife within reach or in a vehicle. Some states regard any accessible knife found in your vehicle as a concealed weapon.

For example, in Tennessee, it is illegal to carry "any implement for the infliction of serious bodily injury or death, which has no common lawful purpose." That said, as of the writing of this book in 2021, it is legal in the same state to own, carry, or conceal just about any type of knife of any blade length, including switch blades, throwing stars, daggers, dirks, swords, sword canes, machetes, stilettos, butterfly knives, and ballistic knives. Cross the state line into North Carolina, and the knife laws become very strict. Except for small pocketknives, carrying, possessing, or selling all other types of knives is unlawful.

Learn the knife law where you live. Unless your state has a preemption clause (stating that federal law preempts state law, even when the laws conflict), local jurisdictions may have their own knife laws as well. Preemption nullifies knife laws made by municipalities in favor of state legislation, allowing you to travel from town to town without having to worry about learning and abiding by local knife laws. When in doubt, it makes sense to avoid unnecessarily carrying knives of any kind, if only to avoid litigation.

Self-Defense Story: The Shake Down

My grandfather, Alfonso Organtini, came to America from Italy in 1920, at just twenty years old. He did not speak any English, but he managed to get a job as a coal miner in western Pennsylvania. One day, a man told Alfonso that he needed to give up part of his paycheck every week as "protection money." Alfonso refused to pay and left out the back door of the building. The bad guy followed him outside where he knocked Alfonso to the ground. The extortionist straddled my grandfather and proceeded to choke him with both hands as he forcefully repeated his demands. Somehow, Alfonso managed to reach into the front pocket of his pants and fumble out a small folding penknife about three inches long. Alfonso needed two hands to open it, but with all his focus on his victim's neck, the assailant did not notice the small blade before Alfonso managed to stab him in the abdomen. My grandfather had created the opportunity to escape his attacker, and he ran away.

Post-encounter Analysis: The man's wounds were not immediately fatal. He was found unconscious in the snow behind the building and apparently died sometime later. Alfonso was arrested and kept in jail while the police investigated the case. After three days, my grandfather was exonerated and released. I only know this story from my grandmother. My grandfather was not proud of his actions and refused to ever speak about the incident.

Cane/Walking Stick

A cane or walking stick is legal to carry so long as it is used as a medical aid to help you balance. The minute you start viewing it as a weapon, even for self-defense, it could be classed as an offensive weapon.

A cane is normally carried in the hand, making it quicker to bring into action than a weapon that has to be drawn. Just having the cane can act as a deterrent. Even unfriendly dogs will not readily attack a person who brandishes a cane.

While doing research for this book, my good friend Chris Hall wrote to me, "When I still had arthritic hips [he's since had them operated on] and had to walk with a cane, there was no running for me: I had to stand and fight or do nothing at all. How do I do it best? Well, I spent time every day poking things at knee level with that cane. Hard. I poked high, at imaginary eyes and throats, too. It was a daily refinement of the tactics I'd need to deploy under the strategy of limiting an attacker's mobility or dropping his sensor grid to degrade his capability."

Part 2: Defending Against Weapons

As with most things in life, weapons are a two-way street. An armed attacker poses a far greater threat to you than an unarmed attacker. The weapon could be within his reach, on his person, in his hand, or maybe even in *your* hand should he take whatever you happen to be holding. Often, an attacker with a weapon will try to conceal its presence until he is ready to use it. Look for him hiding one or both hands behind his back or keeping them otherwise out of sight.

If your attacker has a weapon, it is safest to avoid engaging at all. Retreat without giving your attacker an opportunity to hit you. If you attempt to disarm an armed assailant, the odds are that you will be hit at least once while attempting to take control of his weapon. Due to this high risk of bodily harm, your first course of action should be avoidance. Assuming you can't retreat, you may have to face an armed threat with nothing but your bare hands. While the odds may be against you, don't despair. You can still succeed through good timing, sure footwork, and a warrior mindset.

Self-Defense Story: Taking the Beltway

In December of 2017, I received this message from one of my black-belt students, Sensei Nick Lolli, who had moved away from Pennsylvania several years prior:

Dear Master Joe,

 I'd just like to tell you about a situation when everything came together. I was walking home from some bars in Greenville, SC, tonight when I saw a man aggressively swinging a belt at two other men in the middle of the street. These two cab drivers had their hands up and clearly wanted no part of the altercation, so I decided to distract the man with the belt by engaging him and talking him down. I told him that he'd won the fight and that it was all over, and after a few minutes he walked over to me on the sidewalk and shook my hand. Despite this, all of a sudden he swung his belt at my head. I suppose it's due to years of being swung at by you and everyone else, but I was able to duck the belt and quickly close the gap to take him down with an osoto gari. I was able to pin him down, despite his kicks and punches, with the help of my friend who jumped on his legs after I took him down. I held him down until the police came. I'd like to thank you for not only making sure I didn't get hit tonight, but also that I had the courage to help the two men who were clearly frightened by the man who was very obviously violent and drunk.

 Post-encounter Analysis: When confronted by any attacker with a weapon, your first course of action should be to flee the scene. Nick, however, had years of training and made a judgment call. Luckily, everything turned out okay, but things could have gone differently. Disarming any armed assailant is a difficult and dangerous task. Success requires perfect timing, precise technique, and perhaps a little bit of luck.

 That said, this situation went by the book . . . *this* book! Nick saw a potentially dangerous situation (Level 1) and, after assessing the potential threat in relation to his proven skill sets, decided to intervene. At first, he employed passive tactics by verbally deescalating the situation, but he never dropped his guard (Level 2). By perceiving the threat indicators, he was able to anticipate and evade his attacker's attack (Level 3), tying him up in the clinch before executing a foot sweep takedown (*osoto gari* is just the Japanese name for the big outside trip you learned in Level 6). He then held the antagonist down using a headlock holddown (Level 7) until authorities arrived. Very good, Nick. You were a great student who paid attention and learned his lessons well. I'm very proud of you!

Luck is what happens when preparation meets opportunity.
—Seneca

Unarmed Defense Against Medium-Range Weapons

Shorter weapons tend to be faster than long weapons and hence are more difficult to defend against. Understanding the elements of an attack, such as ranges and zones, will help you increase your odds of success.

Range

An attacker's weapon will determine his effective striking range. Close-range weapons, those less than a foot in length, do not significantly extend the attacker's reach. Medium-range weapons are those between one and three feet long, while long-range weapons are considerably longer.

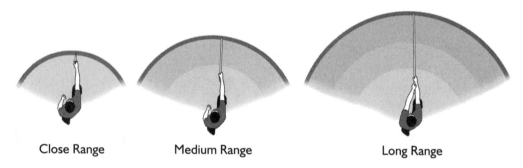

Close Range   Medium Range   Long Range

Because your attacker is armed and you are not, he has the obvious advantage. Therefore, to maximize your chances of success, you'll need to avoid getting hit until you can escape or gain control of his weapon. To accomplish the latter, hover just outside of your attacker's effective striking range, taking care to monitor his position and stay ready to maintain distance if he tries to close in on you.

The attacker's weakness lies in his strategy, which is usually to incapacitate you with a few hard hits. Read his movements and be prepared to act the moment you see him move to chamber for a strike. Better yet, draw a strike by feinting a quick motion as though you were moving to enter, but suddenly pause. Your attacker's reaction to your feint may be that he begins to strike, but quickly senses that you do not actually intend to enter and checks his attack. This moment will often be followed by a very brief instant of relaxation, which is a good time to quickly cross the gap. Explode forward while the attacker is still in the process of mentally and physically resetting. If you miss this opportunity to enter early and he gets off a swing, lean just out of range to avoid his strike before entering and neutralizing the attacker.

Zones

A strike can be dissected into three main parts: the initial phase when the swing is gaining momentum, called the acceleration zone; the area of focused concentration called the strike zone; and the deceleration zone, when the weapon starts slowing down. Needless to say, you do not want to get caught in the impact zone. The best opportunities to intercept an attacker's weapon are in the acceleration zone, entering early before the attacker's strike has gained sufficient power, or the deceleration zone whereby you avoid his initial strike and enter after the strike has passed by. Either way, you'll have to close the gap to get close enough to neutralize the attacker.

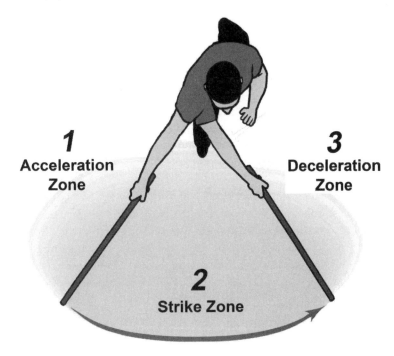

1
Acceleration Zone

3
Deceleration Zone

2
Strike Zone

The Three Parts of a Swing: 1) The Acceleration Zone, when the weapon is gaining momentum. 2) The Strike Zone, where the weapon is most dangerous. 3) The Deceleration Zone, when the weapon starts losing force and momentum.

Arming Yourself

When faced with an armed attacker, quickly scan your environment for improvised weapons, which means anything you can use to defend yourself. Keep in mind that defensive value is different than offensive potential. Items that make poor offensive weapons may still make good defensive tools. On the street, this may be a jacket, purse, shopping bag, or backpack. In a residence you might use a cushion, pillow, or blanket. In a bar or restaurant, it could be a chair or table. Look for anything that you might be able to use as a shield or projectile to disrupt your attacker's attack.

Long versus Short: Use a long object, such as a broom, to fend off an assailant armed with a shorter weapon, in this case a bat.

Making a Shield

Just about anything you can put between you and an armed attacker will help to lessen the impact of his blows. You can use a coat, backpack, or other object as a shield to block an attacker's weapon.

Make a Shield: 1) Wrap your jacket around your arm and use it to block the attacker's weapon. 2) Simultaneously step in and strike to his eyes. He will have a hard time hitting you if he can't see you.

Evasion and Counterattacking

Make your attacker miss his intended target and you can catch him in the vulnerable deceleration zone before he can strike again. The most common method is to draw a strike by exposing a target to your attacker, then leaning your body backward just out of range of the strike. As soon as the weapon goes by, step into close range to check his weapon hand and simultaneously strike his eyes with a tiger claw. Grasp the attacker's weapon and strike his arm to dislodge it from his grasp. Immediately follow up with various counterattacks, including those using the attacker's weapon.

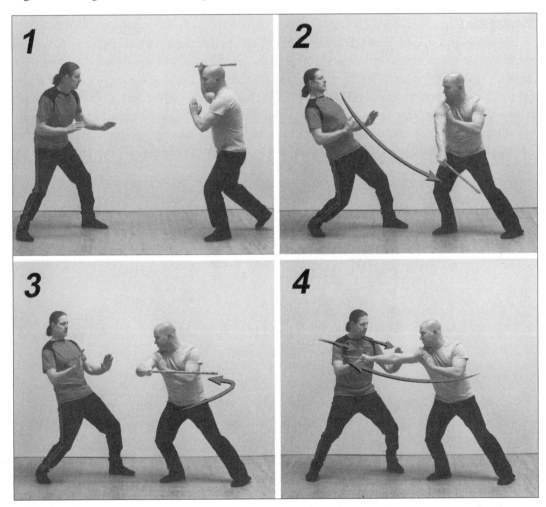

Fade Back: 1) Begin by hovering at the edge of your attacker's range, then expose your head to draw a strike. 2) When the attacker swings, lean your body backward just out of range of his attack. 3) The attacker returns with a horizontal backhand strike. 5) Stop the attacker's weapon arm, jamming him at the wrist and elbow. Grasp the attacker's stick and deliver a hard palm strike to the back of his arm to dislodge the weapon from his grasp.

The Gap

Getting close enough to counter the weapon is one of the most dangerous, and difficult, phases of defending against an armed attacker. There is a good chance the attacker will get off a swing on you as you attempt to cross the gap, so you'll need to cover your advance. Naturally, you'll want to avoid getting hit at all. However, if you can't avoid getting hit, avoid getting hit hard. If you can't avoid getting hit hard, at least avoid getting hit hard in the head. With this logic in mind, here are some strategies and tactics that will help you try to make the best of a bad situation.

Bridging the Gap

To block and disarm a strike while it is still in the acceleration zone, you will have to watch for the moment that the attacker begins to chamber his weapon for a strike and then suddenly close the gap, entering into close range. Since your limbs and torso can suffer damage without completely compromising your effectiveness, they are less critical than your head, which of course contains your brain. One good shot to your head can take you completely out of the fight. Therefore, the most important part of your anatomy to protect as you cross the gap is your head. The two safest ways to bridge the gap are the Arrow and the Cover.

Two Ways to Bridge the Gap: The shaded areas represent the most likely impact zones for a habitual right-handed strike. 1) In the Arrow, block your head with your left forearm. A painful strike to your left arm should not be enough to take you out of the fight. Even a debilitating strike to your left arm still leaves you with your dominant hand and arm intact. 2) The Cover protects your head with your shoulder and offside hand. The tactic is designed to absorb the impact of any strike not on the arm but on the broad surface of the latissimus dorsi muscle that runs along the upper edge of your back. It may hurt like heck, but it is unlikely to take you out of the fight.

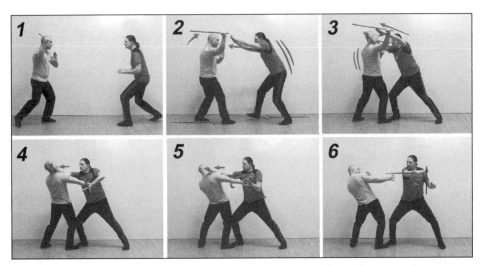

The Arrow: The arrow is a technique in which you shoot yourself quickly across the gap to minimize your odds of being struck. 1) Stand just out of range, baiting the attacker with your head. 2) The attacker takes the bait and steps through to close the gap and strike you. At the same time, extend your arms in front of you as you duck your head and rush forward. 3) Angle slightly into his weapon arm. Your left forearm strikes his arm and checks the weapon as you drive your right forearm into the side of his neck. 4) Maintain pressure on his neck as you snake your rear hand around the attacker's weapon arm. 5) Deliver a chop to his neck as you dislodge the weapon from his grasp. 6) You now have the attacker's weapon.

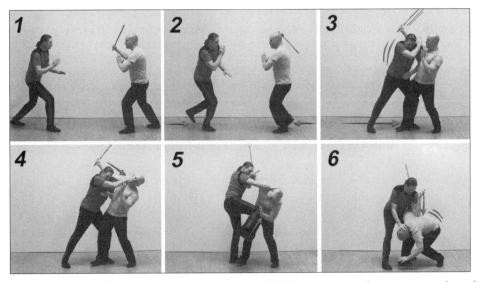

Cover and Charge: 1) Begin in mirror image stances. 2) When your assailant moves to close the gap, step in, presenting the left side of your body to the stick and protecting your head with your right hand in case you get hit crossing the gap. 3) Slam your shoulder into your attacker. 4) Immediately deliver an inner chop to the neck. 5) Hook his neck and pull him into a knee strike to the abdomen. 6) Continue applying pressure to the back of his neck as you drive a downward elbow strike into his thoracic spine.

Throwing

Crossing the gap is safer when your attacker cannot see you. You can throw an object at the attacker's face, immediately following in behind it or running away before your attacker can clear his line of vision. A benefit of throwing an object is that you can use this tactic at a distance, before the aggressor gets in range to attack you.

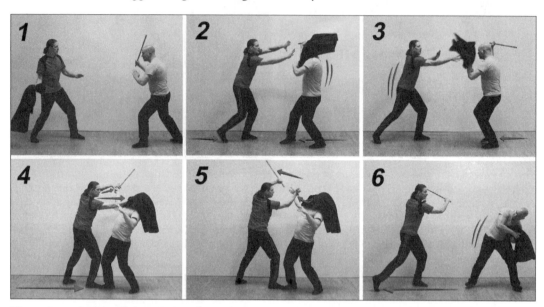

Throwing a Jacket: 1) An attacker threatens you with a weapon. Keep out of his striking range as you take off your jacket. Watch your attacker's movements, waiting for the right time to throw it. 2) As he closes to attack, throw your jacket or other object directly into his face. 3) Immediately follow in behind the projectile, taking advantage of his temporary blindness. 4) Step in and check his weapon hand as you deliver a right chop to his neck. 5) Slide your hand down and grasp the weapon, then strike his arm to dislodge it from his grasp. 6) Back out to establish distance while covering your retreat.

Unarmed Defense Against Long-Range Weapons

Long weapons include long-handled tools such as a broom, shovel, or hockey stick. Oddly enough, the longer the weapon, the easier it can be to disarm the wielder.

Since a right-to-left downward diagonal strike is an instinctual method of attack, there is a very good chance that you can draw a right high strike by leaving your head slightly exposed. Watch closely so you can correctly read and anticipate the attacker's attack. When he pulls back in preparation to swing, follow his weapon back, swiftly stepping into the acceleration zone to check his weapon before it gains forward momentum. This forward motion puts you in a position to disarm and disable your attacker.

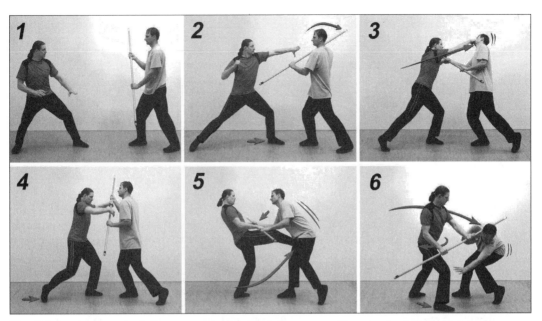

The Direct Approach: 1) Face your attacker in a left stance, rolling your lead shoulder inward to protect your major vital areas. Drop your hands, giving the illusion of an easy target. 2) He will feel the need to pull back his weapon in order to strike you. As he does, follow his weapon back, swiftly stepping into the acceleration zone to check his weapon before it gains forward momentum. If he strikes, take the impact on your left forearm. 3) Grasp the staff and smother the strike as you deliver a right cross. 4) Step forward, grabbing his weapon with both hands to control it. 5) Pull him into a strong rear leg kick, striking upward into the groin with the instep of your foot. 6) Take his weapon and strike him with it.

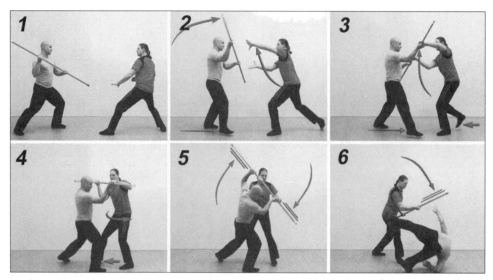

The Yielding Way: 1) Adopt a left lead against your armed attacker. This protects you somewhat from right-sided strikes coming in from your left. All of your senses must be on high alert, your body relaxed but ready to explode forward. 2) As you sense your attacker preparing to attack, step through, closing the gap as you raise your left hand to protect your head and intercept his weapon. 3) Grasp the weapon as you complete your step, but do not attempt to stop its movement. 4) Instead, allow it to continue its motion as it falls increasingly under your control. 5) Step you rear foot behind as you continue to rotate the staff. 6) Pivot to your left just as your left foot comes to rest, using your body weight to direct him to the ground.

Knife Defense

Any encounter with a knife-wielding attacker is about as serious and life threatening as a self-defense situation gets. Knife attacks are extremely fast and violent. Assailants rarely brandish the weapon, instead keeping it concealed until the moment of attack. Studies have shown that over 70 percent of knife attacks are ambushes, launched within three feet of the victim. In these attacks, the assailant typically leads with his free hand in order to grab and control his victim as he stabs repetitively in a very aggressive wave of five to ten short, repetitive stabs delivered at slightly different angles. These attacks don't last long. The average time is twenty-three seconds, but 50 percent of attacks last fourteen seconds or less.

The following are basic principles for knife defense:

1. Keep your vital areas out of the reach of the knife.
2. Put something between you and the knife (such as distance, a jacket, or a chair).
3. Utilize speed and completely commit yourself to your counterattack.
4. Move to the attacker's side and control his knife hand.
5. Immobilizing the knife hand is preferable to parrying or blocking it.

Upward Stab

A right-handed upward stab to the abdomen is by far the most common attack with a knife. Ironically, moving into the attack can help to stop the stabbing by reducing the attacker's space and movement. You may still get stabbed or cut, but it is better to get stabbed once than multiple times, as you might if you backed away from the attack. Therefore, charge forward, closing the distance between you as quickly as possible.

If the attacker checks you with his lead hand, bring your right arm down and across his arm, clearing it from above. Gain control over the knife-wielding hand or arm by checking the attacker's lower arm with your left arm and his upper arm with your right. Maintain forward pressure to keep your attacker from pulling back to chamber for another stab. Each time he pulls back, press in and fill the gap. Snake your left hand clockwise under the attacker's elbow as you grasp his upper arm with your right hand, pulling him down and off balance. Follow up with various strikes to neutralize your attacker, disarming him at the earliest opportunity.

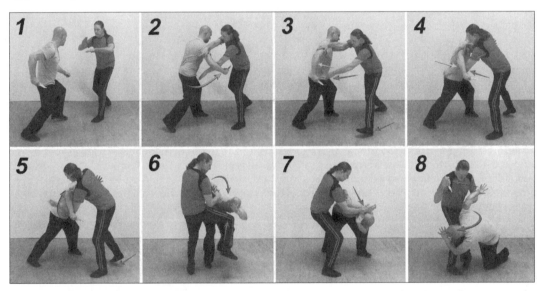

Upward Stab to the Abdomen: 1) The attacker is chambered for an upward stab. Position your arms to intercept and protect. 2) Charge forward, closing the distance between you as quickly as possible to intercept the assailant's attack. Block his strike with your left forearm as you check his upper arm with your right knife hand. 3) Control his shoulder with your right hand. As the attacker pulls back for another strike, follow him in to meet it in the acceleration zone. 4) Smother his next strike before he can make it. 5) Slip your left arm under the attacker's weapon arm, hooking the wrist of his knife hand in the crook of your elbow. 6) Pull down on his shoulder as you use the crook of your left elbow to crank up on his wrist, pulling him into a knee strike to the face. 7) Stun the opponent by chopping him in the side of the neck. 8) Reach across and strip the knife from his grip with your right hand as you pull him down, driving his face into your knee a second time.

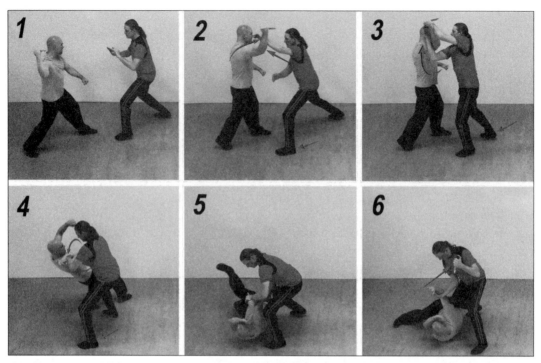

Overhead Downward Stab: 1) If the attacker is holding the knife in a reverse grip, anticipate a downward attack. 2) Watch for your assailant to pull the knife back in preparation for his attack, then lunge in, blocking the attacker's wrist with your left forearm. Intercept his attack as early as possible while it is still in the acceleration zone. 3) Bring your right hand under his upper arm to grasp your own left hand. Keeping the attacker's arm bent at a 90-degree angle, apply a figure-four arm lock. 4) Drop your left elbow straight down as you sink your hips, causing your attacker to drop backward to the ground. 5) Follow the attacker, keeping control of the weapon. 6) Strip the knife from his grasp as you pin his body with your knee.

Reality Check!

If you do see a knife, run! However, since you probably won't see the blade before the attack is launched, you probably won't be able to run away or avoid the assault. Your assailant's overwhelming aggression will leave you with very little time and space to react. You will likely be driven backward, preventing you from easily accessing the attacker's knife arm. Since you probably won't be able to stop his initial stab(s) yet alone draw a weapon (gun, Taser, pepper spray, etc.), you can expect to be cut or stabbed a number of times. If you are cut, do not stop and give in to the shock and surprise of the pain. Just because you have been stabbed does not mean you are dead. Mentally prepare yourself now for being cut. No matter how bad the damage may seem, assure yourself with the mantra, "Doctors are *amazing*, they can fix it!" in the hopes of staving off shock long enough for you to defend yourself and fight back. Keep your focus on neutralizing the threat before tending to your wounds. As soon as safely possible, apply pressure to stop the bleeding and seek medical attention.

Gun Defense

If an assailant brandishes a firearm, it is probably best to follow his directions so long as they only include giving up your valuables. If possible, do *not* let yourself be taken to a secondary location. Better to take your chances where you are.

Your best defense may just be to run. If the person wanted you dead, he would have already shot you. Get low and sprint away. As noted earlier, while running in a zigzag pattern might make you a harder target, it also leaves you exposed for a longer period of time and increases your odds of tripping and falling.

Disarming an attacker with a gun should only be attempted in the direst of situations when you feel like he is going to shoot you regardless of what you do. Even then, this is only an option when the weapon is within easy reach. If the weapon is a single-action pistol with the hammer already cocked, your chances of executing a successful disarm are greatly reduced. You have a better chance against a double-action firearm that requires more pressure on the trigger to cock the hammer back before firing, slowing his reaction time. In either scenario, the element of surprise and force of action are critical elements for success. To see some interesting results of pressure testing these techniques, I recommend a video on YouTube titled *Handgun Disarms—A Reality Check* by UF Pro. The participants wear protective gear and test handgun disarms with paintball guns to see what really works.

If you are shot, do not let yourself fall down or give in to the shock and surprise of the pain. Pain means you are still alive. Stay calm by assuring yourself that the human body is very resilient and that you will be okay. If you are in the midst of a disarm and are shot, don't stop fighting. Keep your focus on neutralizing the threat before tending to your wounds. If you are unable to continue resisting or flee the scene, seek concealment and cover. As soon as safely possible, apply pressure to stop any bleeding and seek medical attention.

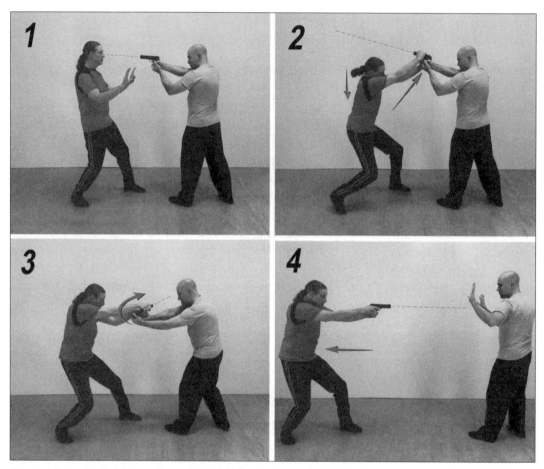

Frontal Attack: 1) An armed attacker is holding his gun in your face. Stand in the neutral guard to get your hands as close as possible to the weapon. 2) Watch for a moment when your attacker is distracted before suddenly dropping and twisting your body away from the line of fire. Simultaneously grab the barrel of the gun, directing it diagonally upward and away from you. 3) Violently turn your body, twisting the weapon toward your attacker. 4) Disarm him with a sudden yank back toward you. Be aware that his trigger finger may get caught in the trigger guard, hindering your attempt to take his weapon.

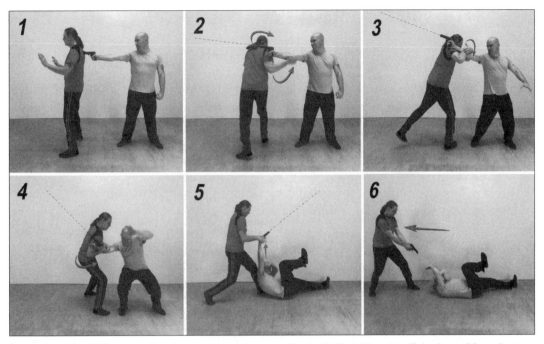

Rear Attack: 1) Your assailant has a gun stuck in your back. 2) Quickly spin off the line of fire, slipping your arm under the assailant's arm as you do so. 3) Secure his weapon arm with both hands, with his wrist anchored on your upper arm. 4) Hug the crook of his arm tightly to your chest, using your shoulder to control his weapon hand. Turn into the attacker to initiate a takedown. 5) Slide your hands down to the attacker's wrist, taking care to keep the barrel of the gun pointed away from you. 6) Strip the weapon from the attacker's grip and use it to cover your assailant as you retreat to a safe distance.

Reality Check!

"Didn't we just have one of these?" Yes, we did, and we need to have another. This may seem obvious, but you need to keep in mind that guns are *very* dangerous, and you are *not* Jason Bourne or John Wick. *Never* underestimate a threat with a firearm or overestimate your ability to successfully disarm him. If you do not execute the technique perfectly the first time, your odds of dying increase dramatically. Seriously contemplate these facts now so you can bring them to mind quickly in a self-defense situation before you commit to a rash attempt at disarming an attacker with a gun.

Level-8 Activities

Improvised Weapons Practice

Walk through various attack scenarios with a trusted training partner. Utilize improvised weapons that you acquire in your immediate environment. Practice slowly and with good control.

Padded Weapons Training

Build or buy an assortment of padded weapons. It helps to have trainers to mimic short, middle, and long-range weapons. Trainers are faux weapons that allow you to practice at more realistic speeds and with greater power. You can also add a padded helmet and padded gloves to increase the level of safety and allow you to train harder and more realistically, as well as more closely mimic what you might expect from an angry attacker with a weapon. Instructions for building your own padded weapon trainers can be found in Appendix 4 at the end of this book.

Recommended Reading

Self-Defense Against Knife Attacks: A Full Review is an excellent online article Patrice Bonnafoux. You can find it at: http://www.urbanfitandfearless.com/2016/09/self-defence-against-knife-attacks.html.

LEVEL 9
Multiple Attackers

Pessimists calculate the odds. Optimists believe they can overcome them.
—Ted Koppel

Defending yourself against a single aggressor is difficult enough but imagine being confronted by more than one attacker. When it comes to solving this problem, there is no simple solution. Your best weapons are your intellect and intuition. Use the following set of concepts and principles as guidelines for gaining control over the situation.

Part 1: Establishing Control

Surviving a mass attack requires that you gain at least some control over the situation. The three aspects of controlling any self-defense situation are to control yourself, control your area, and control your attackers.

Control Yourself

Don't panic. Stay calm and focused. Do everything you can to de-escalate the situation. This control includes leaving the area and if necessary running away. Attract attention. Get noticed by making a lot of noise. Draw attention to yourself by yelling, "*Help*! Call 911, I am being attacked! Use your cameras, get their faces!" These tactics may be enough to make your aggressors think twice and back down. Keep your head about you, reading the situation and reacting quickly without hesitation. Expect that you are going to get hit but resolve to endure and survive.

Control Your Area

Footwork wins fights! Control the area by combining good mobility with 360-degree spatial awareness. Keep your head on a swivel and don't let yourself be surrounded. The situation will be very fluid, dynamic, and ever changing, so you need to keep moving, constantly repositioning yourself in relation to your attackers. Keep moving to a new position where you are hard to reach. Look for locations that might restrict your attackers' access to you and help you defend or get away, such as a doorway, narrow hallway, or between two parked vehicles. However, be extremely careful not to get trapped.

Avoid uneven ground that may present a tripping hazard. Try to remain on an even surface such as a parking lot. Open spaces allow you to maneuver freely. Stay on your feet and avoid going to the ground. When you are on the ground, your mobility is limited, and you can't defend yourself well since your entire body, including your head, is now at kicking level.

Control Your Attackers

You can control your attackers by restricting their movement and ability to attack you. Focusing on one person can allow a gang of attackers to circle or surround you. Instead, keep your head on a swivel and keep moving to avoid being in the center of a circle or triangle.

Use your environment to your advantage. Move to place obstacles between you and your attackers. Putting your back against a wall may help prevent you from being circled but can also limit your mobility. Take great care not to get trapped or cornered. Maintain some space between you and the wall as a buffer to prevent being pinned against it. Use anything you can to arm yourself or use as a shield. Oddly enough, this may be one of your attackers. Maneuver to line up your attackers so they can only come at you one at a time.

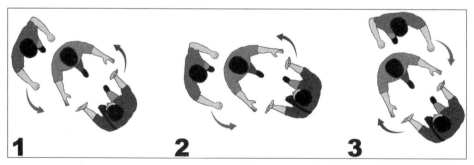

Use One Attacker as an Obstacle: 1) Keep your attackers lined up so only one can get to you at a time. 2) As the second attacker moves to his right to get to you, counter his movement by moving to your right. 3) When the second attacker changes directions, counter his movements with your own.

Line Up Your Attackers: 1) Three attackers are attempting to surround you. 2) Retreat backward and laterally to one side. 3) Continue to maneuver your attackers into a line or funnel shape so that only one can get to you at a time.

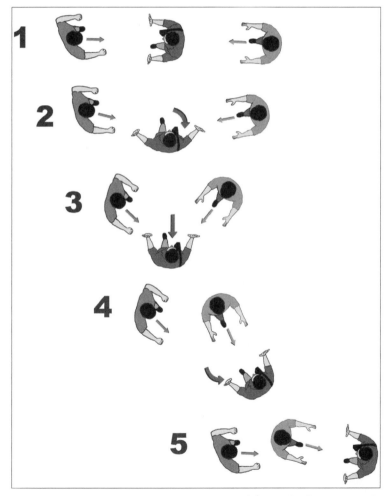

Squeeze Play: 1) It is common for one attacker to approach from the front as another comes up from behind. Since you can't see behind you, your back is extremely vulnerable. 2) Turn sideways to change your orientation to the attackers and alter the dynamics of the situation. 3) Retreat to draw them closer together as they pursue you. 4) Use lateral motion to maneuver one in front of the other. 5) Line them up so they can only come at you one at a time.

While your first strategy should be to find a way to exit, you may find that you have to go on the offense and attack before being able to escape. Which strategy you adopt depends on the totality of the circumstances. Your location, number of attackers, as well as your size and strength in relation to that of your assailants all factor into formulating and successfully employing a response that will ensure your safety and survival.

Part 2: Evading and Escaping

Evade with a purpose. Evasion alone is only a temporary remedy while escape can be the solution to your problem. Identify possible exit routes and then make for the closest one, provided it is not completely cut off. As you evade, don't turn your back on your attackers or turn to run as that is their cue to swarm you. Running will also expose your back to your attackers, reducing your ability to respond and defend yourself. Instead, move backward in a controlled fashion, keeping your eyes on your attackers and using your feet to sense and avoid any obstacles in your path. If you do trip and fall, spring back to your feet as quickly as possible, but defend yourself as you do so (see "Getting Up" in Level 7: Groundwork). You can't escape if you can't move.

Breaking Out

When surrounded, your first priority needs to be to get yourself out of the middle of the pack. Accelerate to a full sprint, slamming through your attackers. Moving closer to one attacker also works to move you farther away from others. Blast a path out with a series of rapid, violent palm strikes to the face. Don't get caught up on attacking a single attacker or the others will have an opportunity to close in behind you. It is vital that you stun one attacker quickly then shove him aside, preferably into the path of your other assailants.

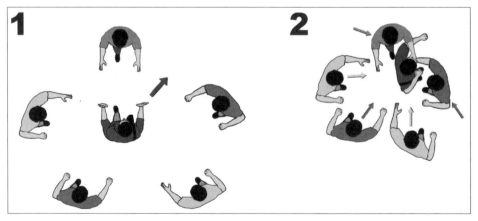

Trapped: 1) You find yourself surrounded by several attackers. You see a gap and try to slip through it. 2) Unfortunately, your attackers are expecting this tactic and are able to cut off your escape. You are now trapped as they swarm you.

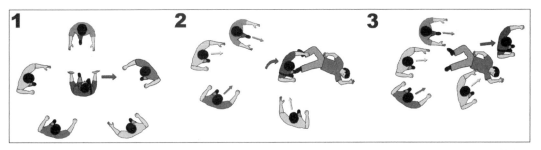

Break Out: 1) You are surrounded by several assailants. Choose a weak point and hit it hard. 2) In this case, breaking out to your right allows you to deliver a big left punch as you turn in that direction, catching an attacker by surprise and knocking him down. 3) Without hesitation, use your remaining momentum to carry you straight into a run. The others will give chase but moving toward one has carried you away from the others, giving you a slight head start and greater opportunity to escape.

Part 3: Going on the Attack

Attack is the secret of defense.
—Sun Tzu, The Art of War

In a gang attack, a self-defense mindset may no longer be sufficient for survival. The disparity of force presented by multiple attackers justifies immediately moving to a higher level of force. Go on the offense! He who hits first, hits twice (and he who hits twice will probably get in the third shot as well). If an alpha sticks his head out, don't hesitate to take it off with a palm strike to the ear (see Level 5: Dirty Tricks). In this scenario, the best defense is a good offense.

Of course, you must know how to strike effectively to successfully employ this strategy, but success is just as dependent on your attitude as your size. Hit fast, hit hard, then move. Don't over-engage, too much or too long. Stick and move, bouncing quickly from one attacker to another. Begin targeting your next threat *while* you are still in the act of hitting the one in front of you. Constantly moving and being unpredictable keeps your attackers disorganized, giving you an advantage while you seek an escape to safety.

Intensity

Exude confidence. Be aggressive. Use your battle cry to keep your attackers intimidated, making clear your resolve to go down swinging. Believe you are invincible, and attack fearlessly, without any hesitation or doubt. Shoot for controlled crazy. Hulk out. Attack relentlessly, destroying every attacker within reach. Employ straight punches and front kicks. Surprise them with your speed and the violence of your reaction. Make them sorry they messed with you!

Pack Mentality

The diffusion of responsibility in a group emboldens attackers into being more aggressive than they normally would. This dynamic unfortunately increases with the size of the group. Therefore, the greater the numbers you face, the higher the degree of violence you can expect.

The good news is that you don't have to fight them all. If you can knock down one or two, it may intimidate the rest. Alphas are leaders, and packs usually have only one. The alpha is often the closest or the loudest. Backing up the alpha, and ready to step into his place, is the beta, his number one. The rest are usually followers, omegas. Since predators are opportunistic hunters who don't want to get hurt, omegas will jump in quick when their side is winning but retreat just as readily when things start to look bad. When it comes to heart, they are usually cowards. If you can take out the alpha and the beta, the omegas will often flee. Knocking out the leader has the immediate effect of undermining the confidence of his followers.

Lining Them Up and Knocking Them Down

It's not easy to fight on multiple fronts against more than one person at the same time. Your two fists are no match against four fists, or six. Therefore, only fight one attacker at a time. Pick your closest target and attack.

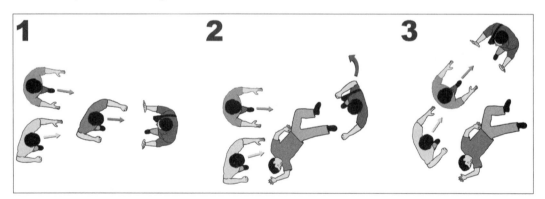

Create an Obstacle: 1) Use good footwork to line up your attackers. 2) When one comes in striking range, give him your best shot, hoping to knock him down and take him out of the fight. 2) This action momentarily creates an obstacle between you and the other attackers. 3) Maneuver to line up your remaining attackers.

Shield: 1) A stunned attacker can be used as a human shield. Grab his clothing and lock on, spinning him to face away from you. 2) As one attacker attempts to circle around, retreat and rotate your shield. The attacker sees he is blocked and switches directions to get around your human shield. 3) Swing your body to reposition your shield, keeping him between you and your attackers as you retreat.

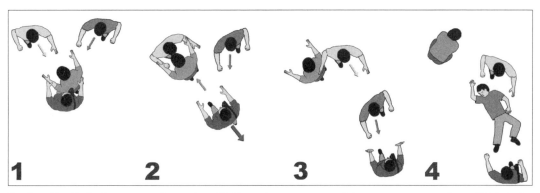

Projectile: 1) Grab a stunned attacker. 2) Shove him into one of the remaining attackers. With luck, their heads will bang together. 3) Back up, drawing your third attacker away from the other two as you wait for the right time to strike. 4) Knock out your attacker with a well-placed punch to the jaw. Use your downed attacker as an obstacle to impede the path of your remaining attacker.

Overwhelmed

The shock, stress, and anxiety of a mass attack are extreme. If you start taking damage, there is a good chance that you may get overwhelmed. Protect your vital areas by adopting a full defensive shell. Concentrate on protecting yourself with your arms and by moving, taking care to stay on your feet. Luckily, only three to four assailants can effectively strike you at once. There may be more, but they have to punch over and around each other to get to you. As soon as you can muster the strength and before you take too much damage, you must force yourself to explode out of your shell. Since you are probably bent over and already facing the ground, look for an attacker's foot and attack it by stomping on the arch as hard as you can. Then explode out, engaging the first target you see as ferociously as you can. Momentarily disregard the others as you strike to inflict as much damage as you can in one or two strikes, then pivot and unleash your fury on the next attacker within arm's reach. If there is no target within reach, use your first attacker, now stunned, as an obstacle by pushing him into the next closest attacker.

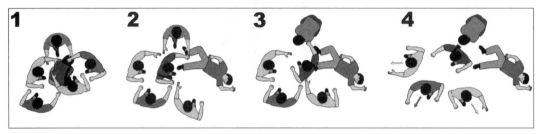

Explode: 1) You are being overwhelmed and have taken cover in a full defensive shell. 2) Suddenly give a fierce battle cry and burst out of your shell, temporarily disregarding all others to single out one attacker whom you attack with savage fury. 3) Immediately line up your next best shot and let fly. 4) With luck, your show of shocking violence and resolution to go down swinging will dishearten the others, causing them to flee.

Reality Check!

On May 17, 2021, Jose Campuzano, a BJJ (Brazilian jiu-jitsu) black belt and MMA coach, was leaving a bar in El Paso, Texas, when he came upon a fight already underway in the parking lot. Jose jumped in to help two other victims who were already getting beaten.

Despite Jose's excellent physical condition and extensive training, he was punched and kicked by the mob until he was unconscious and no longer breathing. Luckily, first responders on the scene were able to resuscitate and stabilize him enough to transport him to a nearby medical center where he was listed in critical condition.

No matter how well prepared you may be, no matter how good a fighter you are, multiple attacker situations pose a dire threat with a low chance of escaping unscathed.

Level-9 Activities

Self-Defense Sparring

Sparring is controlled free fighting, but this is not the type of sparring you see in karate, boxing, or taekwondo. This is self-defense sparring. Train with two to four partners. Have your attackers attempt to circle and trap you. Throughout the exercise, all parties are allowed to throw punches and kicks, but remember to engage wisely. Don't get suckered into a one-on-one fight. Self-defense is *not* about fighting; it's about protecting yourself and staying *safe*.

At first, move slowly until you learn how to move advantageously, lining up your attackers and evading their advances. As you gain confidence, have your partners speed up, but maintain a good degree of control so things don't escalate to the point where someone gets hurt. You can wear protective equipment to increase your safety margin. However, there should never be any guarantees. Your partners need to take shots and you need to take hits. This kind of training is critical for your brain to keep thinking and your body to keep moving, even when you are taking damage.

Train in different places, indoors and out. Practice on a sidewalk and in a stairwell. Practice in your driveway, in your car, and at your front door. Practice in your bedroom and bathroom. Each situation poses its own set of challenges. Identify advantages and make them work for you. Identify disadvantages and take action to avoid them. Always remember that this is self-defense-oriented sparring, not a competition match, so adjust your attacks accordingly. If your goal is to escape, practice avoiding confrontation and attacking strategically, meaning only when it is to your advantage. Think outside the box. Improvise and surprise your partners. Put your time in training this way because nothing is free. If you want to get good at self-defense, you have to practice and pay your dues!

Level-9

Activities

Acknowledgments

Special thanks go out to my talented and dependable production team: Andrea Hilborn, Madeline Rawley Crouse, Carol Riley, Robert Suiter, and Brian Lesyk; and, as always, to my wonderful wife, Kathy, and my two fantastic children, Cosmos and Kayla, for their continued support of all my crazy obsessions.

I would also like to thank Kirk Farber, Jan Nelson, and Chris Hall for their contributions to this project.

This book was influenced by the teachings of O Sensei Dong Ngo, founder of Cuong Nhu Martial Arts, and his son, Bao Ngo, creator of The Bao Way System of Self-defense.

Models: Joe Varady, Kathy Varady, Andrea Hilborn, Andy Gajewski, Robert Suiter, and Brian Lesyk

Photo Credits: Andrea Hilborn and Joe Varady

Cover Photo: Andrea Hilborn. The man with his back to the camera is Seth Clearwater.

Appendixes

There are many aspects of self-defense that did not fall neatly into the nine levels presented in the main body of this book yet are still important enough that they warranted inclusion. As with all the self-defense techniques in this book, practice what you would do in these different types of situations so you will be better prepared should you ever find yourself in similar dire straits.

Appendix 1: Dog Attack

You know the importance of learning to utilize appropriate defense strategies to protect yourself from other humans, but not all attackers walk on two legs. Dogs can attack, seemingly unprovoked, for many reasons. Victims are usually alone and defenseless. Children and the elderly are especially vulnerable to attack. Remember that your ultimate goal is to get yourself to safety as quickly as possible by not enraging the dog and getting hurt.

Strange Dog

You are out for a walk when a strange dog approaches you. Immediately shift into high alert. Don't be fooled by a wagging tail as this is a sign of excitement, not friendliness. If the dog is coming at you, don't take any chances. Shout firm commands such as, "GET AWAY," "NO," "STOP," or "BACK!" This isn't so much to assert dominance over the dog as it is to demonstrate to the animal that you are not prey. If the dog is yawning, it could be a sign of stress and should also be taken as a threat indicator. If the dog closes distance and directly threatens you, it is time to change tack.

Threatening Dog

Dogs are predators that will instinctually pursue their prey. Running will only serve to arouse this prey drive, causing the dog to chase you down. While a walking stick or cane may allow you to fend the dog off for a few seconds and pepper spray may act as a deterrent, these are not always reliable. Back away slowly in the nearest safe direction. Do not look directly at a dog that is barking and growling at you; the dog may take this as a challenge and act to defend itself. Do not attempt to talk to it, grab its collar, or otherwise touch it.

If you have any loose article of clothing around your body, such as a scarf or belt, slowly remove it and wrap it around your hand or forearm to protect it from a bite. If you have a backpack or purse, hold it between you and the dog. Seek to use your environment to your advantage. Back into a corner or against a wall so the dog cannot get behind you, or climb on something high, such as a car. Call using your phone call out loud for help and remain there until assistance arrives or the dog leaves.

Attacking Dog

When dogs attack, they commonly target certain places. Some dogs go after fingers, so keep your hands in fists to protect them. Hold your hands and arms tightly against your body to protect them. Smaller dogs concentrate their attacks on your calves and feet, so you may have some success defending yourself through kicking. Large dogs will most likely jump up to strike at your face and neck. If a dog jumps up at you, lift your knee high in front of you as you simultaneously cross your arms in front of you to protect your face, chest, and throat. However, against a larger dog, fighting may be worse than if you simply stop moving. Kicking a large dog will probably have little effect, as many dogs are far less sensitive to pain than humans, especially when excited.

If you are bitten, try to make it your shin or forearm. If the dog latches onto your arm or leg, resist the urge to get free by pulling away. This will only make the dog bite down harder and injure you more. If the dog refuses to let go, press the part of your body that is being bitten into the dog's mouth to prevent it tearing your skin.

Playing Dead

If you fall to the ground, roll into a tight ball or lay flat on your stomach. Clasp your hands tightly behind your neck. Squealing or crying out will only arouse the excitement of the attacking dog. Stay as calm as you can, remaining as quiet and still as possible until the dog leaves the area.

Appendix 2: Children

Part 1: Practical Advice

One of my students, Robert Suiter, has worked as a security guard for both retail business and elementary schools. Based on his experiences, he shared with me this advice for parents and their children:

How to Seek Help. I have helped find over fifty lost children in my career so far, and I can count on one hand how many times they approached me first. It's almost always a parent coming to me in a panic, or I am approaching a child who looks lost but is not seeking help. On one occasion I even found a child from our own dojo who knew who I was and was able to identify me by name yet didn't actually admit to me that he was lost until I challenged him directly on the location of his parents. The very next thing he said to me was, "Am I in trouble?" This is a question I've been asked many times when I locate lost children. Children are often convinced that getting lost will result in punishment, and this actually makes them more resistant to asking for help. This is why we need to get across to children the necessity of proactively finding someone to help them when they are in need.

Explain to children how to identify people they can safely approach to help them. Unfortunately, a lost child will rarely have the convenience of a security guard or policeman nearby, but virtually anywhere you'd have a serious risk of a child being lost in a crowd, there will be people working and willing to help. Everywhere you go, retail establishments have "lost children" policies in place designed to quickly reunite them with their families whether or not they have a dedicated security department.

Therefore, lost kids should seek out someone working nearby, preferably a woman with children, and tell her they are lost, as mothers and other female caregivers will often naturally take the lost child under their wing until they are safe. Teach kids to look for someone with a nametag or perhaps a shirt with the logo of the store. If the lost child can't quickly find a uniformed person, then advise them to seek out an adult woman with a child or children to ask for assistance.

How to Identify a Dangerous Stranger. Children are in the confusing and challenging position of being trained from infancy to obey adults and listen to them while simultaneously being told that some adults are bad and must be treated differently. While most children can reasonably identify the difference, they can run into problems, especially if they should have the misfortune of encountering a true child predator who knows how to effectively lure children.

It is extremely important to teach children that a stranger who wants to help them won't bribe them, offer them candy, ask if they want to see the puppy in their car, or offer to take them to a toy store. If a stranger is offering them something, they are *not safe*. If someone is offering to take them to security or the customer service desk, they can go with them, but they need to stay aware and be able to determine if the situation seems strange or abnormal. If so, then it's time to make a scene to bring attention to themselves. Assure them that someone is lying if that person tells the child that security, customer service, or their parents are in the parking lot, the bathroom, or any other isolated location. If anyone tries to take them somewhere they don't think is safe, it's time to make a scene. Assure your child that you *won't* be mad. In fact, he or she has your *permission* to do this, and you'll be *proud* of them for being courageous and standing up for themselves.

When and How to Make a Scene. Again, when a child thinks they're in danger, tell them to make a scene! Teach them how to pull away from the bad guy as they loudly declare that they don't know him, calling out to any other adults around them for help as they thrash, kick, and fight back. The unfortunate reality is that a child probably lacks the strength to stop a full-grown adult from carrying them, but they can make it so inconvenient that the abductor abandons the attempt or other adults get involved.

The key here is for the child to understand how to make a scene that will bring about the desired result. Children scream all the time, including in public, and it doesn't make people come running. I hear kids screaming every shift, and most people don't even look up. Key words and phrases, however, *do* trigger that reaction. "You're hurting me" is easily the most effective I've heard. When two children are roughhousing and one shouts that, a lot of people look up. I assume that "Help, stranger!" would also draw attention. The key is to be able to express that it's not a tantrum, it's real danger. "You're not my dad" is one I'm really not a fan of, because I've heard it a few times and it always meant, "I hate my stepfather" not "I'm being kidnapped," so it may not get the desired effect.

How to Describe the Stranger. Perhaps equally valuable to adults and children is learning how to get help quickly and accurately describe the perpetrator to others. Whether you have just escaped a dangerous situation, or maybe it's a child who just feels like something wasn't right about a certain adult, someone who can help needs to be told immediately and a description of the perpetrator needs to be given. This is also important if you are witnessing someone else in danger.

Bad people do not stop being bad just because their attempt to do harm was unsuccessful the first time. Time is the biggest factor in finding a suspect, so report the incident immediately. Take careful note of things that can't be changed quickly if a search were to be undertaken: skin color, tattoos or scars, hair color, pants, and shoes. It is possible to quickly change a hat, shirt, or jacket to avoid being identified, and in some extreme cases of kidnapping, abductors have changed the child's shirt as well. Yet very few people take the time or effort to change pants or shoes. Another important thing to note is the direction in which the perpetrator was last travelling.

A description such as "white male, short brown hair, wearing black shoes and gray pants—and he ran that way" is often enough for law enforcement to positively ID (and legally stop and detain) someone before he can hurt someone else. With practice, you can get that many details in just a few seconds. Have your children practice this skill in safe environments, such as when you are shopping with them. See how quickly they, and *you*, can identify traits about random people and describe them.

Part 2: Active Resistance

Anchor and Siren

Child abductors rely on speed and stealth to remain undetected. When grabbed, a child should do anything he or she can to slow down the abduction and draw attention to the situation. The child can use the tiger claw to attack an abductor's eyes or act as a human anchor by grabbing the attacker's leg, wrapping their hands and legs around it like clinging to a tree. All the while, the child should be yelling, "Help, Stranger! Kidnapper! He's trying to steal me! Somebody *help*!" Hopefully this will either draw the attention of nearby adults or cause the abductor to abandon his plans in lieu of escape.

The Anchor and Siren: This move slows the attacker while drawing attention to the situation, two things a child abductor does not want.

Recommended Reading

For more on how to teach your child personal safety, read *Spotting Danger Before It Spots Your Kids: Teaching Situational Awareness to Keep Children Safe* by Gary Quesenberry.[1] The book is full of good advice on how to teach children to spot abnormal behaviors and deal with confrontation, skills that will serve them well for the rest of their lives.

1. Gary Quesenberry, *Spotting Danger Before It Spots Your Kids: Teaching Situational Awareness to Keep Children Safe* (Wolfeboro, NH: YMAA Publication Center, 2021).

Appendix 3: Sexual Assault

Sexual assault is any type of sexual activity or contact that occurs without your consent and can vary from unwanted touching to rape. Unfortunately, rape is the fastest rising violent crime in America. Not only can it happen to anyone, regardless of gender, age, or sexual orientation, it can happen anywhere, from cars to schools. Nearly 85 percent of victims of sexual assault knew the person who raped or assaulted them. Luckily, you can take steps to substantially reduce your risks of being victimized while still enjoying an active and full social life.

Set Clear Boundaries

Sexual abuse often starts off as seemingly innocent fun only to unexpectedly escalate and spiral out of control. Trust your instincts. If someone starts to offend you or do things that make you uncomfortable, say so, firmly and early. Passivity can be interpreted as permission, so assert yourself. Make a clear statement such as, "I don't like it when you touch me like that. Don't do it again." If polite rebukes are ignored and your wishes are not being respected, remove yourself from the situation immediately. It's alright to lie or make excuses if it will help you get away. Err on the side of caution. If you feel you are being pressured into unwanted sex, you probably are. If there was a miscommunication and you misread someone's signals, you can always explain yourself later. Even if someone is intoxicated or high, it is not an excuse for him to commit sexual assault. You should never do anything that you are not comfortable doing. Under no conditions should you let anyone violate your boundaries. If someone is sexually pressuring you, do not hesitate to make a scene. Push him away. Directly and firmly yell, "No! Let me *go!*"

Parties

Avoid being alone at parties or in other social situations. Instead, go with a trusted friend or group of friends. Practice the buddy system by keeping in contact with your companions during the party. Keep an eye out for one another and don't leave any friend alone. If your instincts tell you something is wrong, trust your feelings and leave the situation immediately. Create a special code word or sentence you can use to alert your friend if you are being pressured or are in an awkward situation and need help.

Keep track of how much you are drinking. Know your limits and avoid becoming overly intoxicated. Open your own beverages and keep them close to you to avoid someone drugging your drink. If you think you may have been drugged, tell your friends and leave the party right away. Do not go anywhere alone at the location of the party, such as a bedroom or basement, or leave the party with anyone you do not know.

Responding Physically

Unfortunately, even the strongest communication with a perpetrator to leave you alone and not touch you is not always effective. If someone is assaulting you, you have the right to physically defend yourself. It is understandable that you may feel awkward responding forcefully, especially to someone you know, but it is not *your* fault if *he* forces you to do so. If you find yourself in a situation where you are being pressured into sexual activities against your will, make up things that might deter your abuser from continuing, such as, "I'm going to throw up," "I have my period," or "I have a venereal disease." Say anything to discourage your assailant from proceeding with his attack. If you only need to discourage someone, start with pokey elbows and pinching, but do not hesitate to use higher levels of force if and when the situation escalates.

Reporting a Rape

Sexual assault is *never* the victim's fault, regardless of the circumstances. If you are raped, immediately call the police. They can only arrest your assailant if they are made aware of the crime. Do not change clothes, take a bath or shower, eat, smoke, or chew gum. Physical evidence, including seminal fluids, hair, blood, and DNA recovered from your clothes or under your nails can be used as evidence in court to positively identify your assailant.

If you or someone you know is in an abusive relationship, know that you are not alone. There are people close by who are willing and able to help you. It is important to tell somebody you trust so they can support you in dealing with the shocking, scary, and horrible reality of your situation. Take the difficult step and get in touch with a local organization that can help. The feeling of empowerment that comes from telling someone and getting help will help you recover from the awful event. Victims who take action during and after the assault feel less helpless and recover better.

The USA's National Sexual Assault hotline is 1-800-656-4673. It's staffed 24-7 by trained volunteers who can help in both short-term, such as rape, and long-term abuse situations.

Appendix 4: Training Equipment

Special equipment can help you get the most out of your training. Often, this equipment is simple and easy to make. Here are some plans for some pieces of training equipment that are specially designed to help you develop and hone your self-defense skills.

Padded Chair

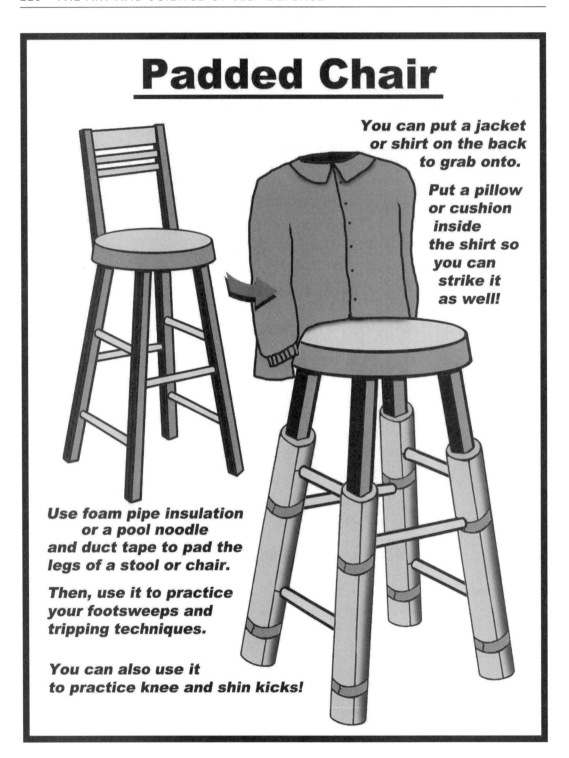

You can put a jacket or shirt on the back to grab onto.

Put a pillow or cushion inside the shirt so you can strike it as well!

Use foam pipe insulation or a pool noodle and duct tape to pad the legs of a stool or chair.

Then, use it to practice your footsweeps and tripping techniques.

You can also use it to practice knee and shin kicks!

Padded Staff

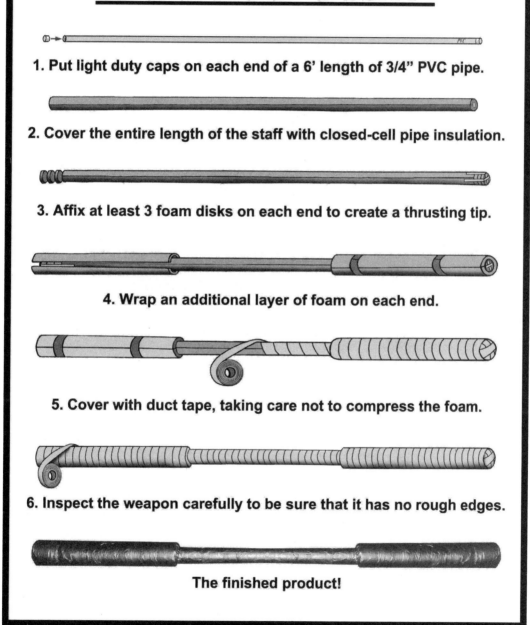

1. Put light duty caps on each end of a 6' length of 3/4" PVC pipe.

2. Cover the entire length of the staff with closed-cell pipe insulation.

3. Affix at least 3 foam disks on each end to create a thrusting tip.

4. Wrap an additional layer of foam on each end.

5. Cover with duct tape, taking care not to compress the foam.

6. Inspect the weapon carefully to be sure that it has no rough edges.

The finished product!

Padded Stick

1. Start with a length of 3/4" PVC pipe.

2. Cover the ends with electrical tape.

3. Cover the entire stick with 3/4" foam pipe insulation.

4. Cut and attach three foam disks to each end.

5. Wrap the entire stick in a smooth layer of duct tape.

6. The finished product!

You can used colored tape for a more professional result.

Always inspect your sticks carefully before each use.

Padded Knife

Begin with a quality, name brand foam sword.

Use a hacksaw to cut the blade into knife-sized pieces.

Tape the handle and you are ready to go!

You can also use the handle piece.

Use a hot glue gun to fashion a new tip.

About the Author

Joe Varady, M.Ed.
Head Instructor, Satori Dojo
Black Belt—7th Degree

Master Joe Varady began his formal martial arts training in 1986. Over the past three decades, he has cross-trained in Eastern martial arts, including karate, taekwondo, judo, wing chun, and eskrima, as well as various Western martial arts such as boxing, fencing, long sword, sword and shield, poleaxe, and various methods of armored fighting. In 2006, Joe became a certified Master Instructor in The Bao Way System of Self-Defense.

Joe currently shares his martial arts knowledge as the head instructor of two programs: traditional martial arts through Satori Dojo and eclectic weapons systems through Modern Gladiatorial Arts, both located in Phoenixville, Pennsylvania. He is also an active member of the Universal Systems of Martial Arts Organization, a fellowship that provides practitioners of different styles of martial arts with an open forum for sharing techniques and principles. He was inducted into the Philadelphia Historic Martial Arts Society Hall of Fame in July 2016.

Joe holds a master's degree in elementary education. He is the author of two books on fighting with weapons, *The Art and Science of Staff Fighting* and *The Art and Science of Stick Fighting* (YMAA 2016 and 2020). He considers this, his third book, *The Art and Science of Self-Defense: A Comprehensive Instructional Guide* to be his most important work to date.

BOOKS FROM YMAA

101 REFLECTIONS ON TAI CHI CHUAN
108 INSIGHTS INTO TAI CHI CHUAN
A WOMAN'S QIGONG GUIDE
ADVANCING IN TAE KWON DO
ANALYSIS OF SHAOLIN CHIN NA 2ND ED
ANCIENT CHINESE WEAPONS
ART AND SCIENCE OF STAFF FIGHTING
THE ART AND SCIENCE OF SELF-DEFENSE
ART AND SCIENCE OF STICK FIGHTING
ART OF HOJO UNDO
ARTHRITIS RELIEF, 3D ED.
BACK PAIN RELIEF, 2ND ED.
BAGUAZHANG, 2ND ED.
BRAIN FITNESS
CHIN NA IN GROUND FIGHTING
CHINESE FAST WRESTLING
CHINESE FITNESS
CHINESE TUI NA MASSAGE
COMPLETE MARTIAL ARTIST
COMPREHENSIVE APPLICATIONS OF SHAOLIN CHIN NA
CONFLICT COMMUNICATION
DAO DE JING: A QIGONG INTERPRETATION
DAO IN ACTION
DEFENSIVE TACTICS
DIRTY GROUND
DR. WU'S HEAD MASSAGE
ESSENCE OF SHAOLIN WHITE CRANE
EXPLORING TAI CHI
FACING VIOLENCE
FIGHT LIKE A PHYSICIST
THE FIGHTER'S BODY
FIGHTER'S FACT BOOK 1&2
FIGHTING ARTS
FIGHTING THE PAIN RESISTANT ATTACKER
FIRST DEFENSE
FORCE DECISIONS: A CITIZENS GUIDE
INSIDE TAI CHI
JUDO ADVANTAGE
JUJI GATAME ENCYCLOPEDIA
KARATE SCIENCE
KATA AND THE TRANSMISSION OF KNOWLEDGE
KRAV MAGA COMBATIVES
KRAV MAGA FUNDAMENTAL STRATEGIES
KRAV MAGA PROFESSIONAL TACTICS
KRAV MAGA WEAPON DEFENSES
LITTLE BLACK BOOK OF VIOLENCE
LIUHEBAFA FIVE CHARACTER SECRETS
MARTIAL ARTS OF VIETNAM
MARTIAL ARTS INSTRUCTION
MARTIAL WAY AND ITS VIRTUES
MEDITATIONS ON VIOLENCE
MERIDIAN QIGONG EXERCISES
MINDFUL EXERCISE
MIND INSIDE TAI CHI
MIND INSIDE YANG STYLE TAI CHI CHUAN
NATURAL HEALING WITH QIGONG
NORTHERN SHAOLIN SWORD, 2ND ED.
OKINAWA'S COMPLETE KARATE SYSTEM: ISSHIN RYU
PRINCIPLES OF TRADITIONAL CHINESE MEDICINE
PROTECTOR ETHIC
QIGONG FOR HEALTH & MARTIAL ARTS 2ND ED.
QIGONG FOR TREATING COMMON AILMENTS

QIGONG MASSAGE
QIGONG MEDITATION: EMBRYONIC BREATHING
QIGONG GRAND CIRCULATION
QIGONG MEDITATION: SMALL CIRCULATION
QIGONG, THE SECRET OF YOUTH: DA MO'S CLASSICS
REDEMPTION
ROOT OF CHINESE QIGONG, 2ND ED.
SAMBO ENCYCLOPEDIA
SCALING FORCE
SELF-DEFENSE FOR WOMEN
SHIN GI TAI: KARATE TRAINING
SIMPLE CHINESE MEDICINE
SIMPLE QIGONG EXERCISES FOR HEALTH, 3RD ED.
SIMPLIFIED TAI CHI CHUAN, 2ND ED.
SOLO TRAINING 1&2
SPOTTING DANGER BEFORE IT SPOTS YOU
SPOTTING DANGER BEFORE IT SPOTS YOUR KIDS
SPOTTING DANGER BEFORE IT SPOTS YOUR TEENS
SUMO FOR MIXED MARTIAL ARTS
SUNRISE TAI CHI
SURVIVING ARMED ASSAULTS
TAE KWON DO: THE KOREAN MARTIAL ART
TAEKWONDO BLACK BELT POOMSAE
TAEKWONDO: A PATH TO EXCELLENCE
TAEKWONDO: ANCIENT WISDOM
TAEKWONDO: DEFENSE AGAINST WEAPONS
TAEKWONDO: SPIRIT AND PRACTICE
TAI CHI BALL QIGONG: FOR HEALTH AND MARTIAL ARTS
THE TAI CHI BOOK
TAI CHI CHIN NA, 2ND ED.
TAI CHI CHUAN CLASSICAL YANG STYLE, 2ND ED.
TAI CHI CHUAN MARTIAL POWER, 3RD ED.
TAI CHI CONCEPTS AND EXPERIMENTS
TAI CHI CONNECTIONS
TAI CHI DYNAMICS
TAI CHI FOR DEPRESSION
TAI CHI IN 10 WEEKS
TAI CHI PUSH HANDS
TAI CHI QIGONG, 3RD ED.
TAI CHI SECRETS OF THE ANCIENT MASTERS
TAI CHI SECRETS OF THE WU & LI STYLES
TAI CHI SECRETS OF THE WU STYLE
TAI CHI SECRETS OF THE YANG STYLE
TAI CHI SWORD: CLASSICAL YANG STYLE, 2ND ED.
TAI CHI SWORD FOR BEGINNERS
TAI CHI WALKING
TAIJIQUAN THEORY OF DR. YANG, JWING-MING
FIGHTING ARTS
TRADITIONAL CHINESE HEALTH SECRETS
TRADITIONAL TAEKWONDO
TRAINING FOR SUDDEN VIOLENCE
TRIANGLE HOLD ENCYCLOPEDIA
TRUE WELLNESS SERIES (MIND, HEART, GUT)
WARRIOR'S MANIFESTO
WAY OF KATA
WAY OF SANCHIN KATA
WAY TO BLACK BELT
WESTERN HERBS FOR MARTIAL ARTISTS
WILD GOOSE QIGONG
WINNING FIGHTS
XINGYIQUAN

AND MANY MORE . . .

VIDEOS FROM YMAA

AND MANY MORE . . .

more products available from . . .

YMAA Publication Center, Inc. 楊氏東方文化出版中心

1-800-669-8892 • info@ymaa.com • www.ymaa.com